Ne

GREAT
EXPECTATIONS

New Casebooks

New Casebooks

GREAT EXPECTATIONS

CHARLES DICKENS

EDITED BY ROGER D. SELL

MACMILLAN

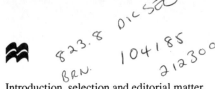

First published 1994 by
MACMILLAN PRESS LTD
Houndmills, Basingstoke, Hampshire RG21 6XS
and London
Companies and representatives
throughout the world

ISBN 0–333–54606–7 hardcover
ISBN 0–333–54607–5 paperback

A catalogue record for this book is available
from the British Library.

10   9   8   7   6   5   4   3   2
04   03   02   01   00   99   98   97   96

Printed in Hong Kong

Contents

Acknowledgements

The editor and publishers wish to thank the following for permission to use copyright material:

Peter Brooks, for excerpts from *Reading for the Plot: Design and Intention in Narrative* (1984). Copyright © 1984 by Peter Brooks, by permission of Oxford University Press and Alfred A. Knopf, Inc; Steven Connor, for an excerpt from *Charles Dickens* (1985), Blackwell Publishers Ltd, by permission of the author; A. L. French, for 'Beating and Cringing: *Great Expectations*', *Essays in Criticism*, 24 (1974), by permission of Essays in Criticism; Lucy Frost, for 'Taming to Improve: Dickens and the Women in *Great Expectations*', *Meridian*, 1 (1982), by permission of La Trobe University Press; Robin Gilmour, for excerpts from *The Idea of the Gentleman in the Victorian Novel* (1981), by permission of Routledge; Eiichi Hara, for excerpts from 'Stories Present and Absent in *Great Expectations*', *English Literary History*, 53 (1986), by permission of the Johns Hopkins University Press; Thomas Loe, for 'Gothic Plot in *Great Expectations*', *Dickens Quarterly*, 6 (1989), by permission of Dickens Quarterly; James Phelan, for 'Reading for the Character and Reading for the Progression: John Wemmick and *Great Expectations*', *Journal of Narrative Technique*, 19 (1989), by permission of the Journal of Narrative Technique; Linda Raphael, for 'A Re-vision of Miss Haversham: Her Expectations and Our Responses', *Studies in the Novel*, 21, Winter (1989). Copyright © 1989 by University of North Texas, by permission of Studies in the Novel; Jack Rawlins, for 'Great Expiations: Dickens and the Betrayal of the Child', *Studies in English Literature, 1500–1900*, 23 (1983), by permission of Studies in English Literature; Anny Sadrin, for excerpts from *Great Expectations* (1988), by permission of Routledge; Jeremy Tambling, for 'Prison-bound: Dickens and Foucault', *Essays in Criticism*, 36 (1986), by permission of Essays in Criticism.

Every effort has been made to trace all the copyright holders but if any have been inadvertently overlooked the publishers will be pleased to make the necessary arrangement at the first opportunity.

General Editors' Preface

The purpose of this series of New Casebooks is to reveal some of the ways in which contemporary criticism has changed our understanding of commonly studied texts and writers and, indeed, of the nature of criticism itself. Central to the series is a concern with modern critical theory and its effect on current approaches to the study of literature. Each New Casebook editor has been asked to select a sequence of essays which will introduce the reader to the new critical approaches to the text or texts being discussed in the volume and also illuminate the rich interchange between critical theory and critical practice that characterises so much current writing about literature.

In this focus on modern critical thinking New Casebooks aim not only to inform but also to stimulate, with volumes seeking to reflect both the controversy and the excitement of current criticism. Because much of this criticism is difficult and often employs an unfamiliar critical language, editors have been asked to give the reader as much help as they feel is appropriate, but without simplifying the essays or the issues they raise. Again, editors have been asked to supply a list of further reading which will enable readers to follow up issues raised by the essays in the volume.

The project of New Casebooks, then, is to bring together in an illuminating way those critics who best illustrate the ways in which contemporary criticism has established new methods of analysing texts and who have reinvigorated the important debate about how we 'read' literature. The hope is, of course, that New Casebooks will not only open up this debate to a wider audience, but will also encourage students to extend their own ideas, and think afresh about their responses to the texts they are studying.

John Peck and Martin Coyle
University of Wales, Cardiff

Introduction

ROGER D. SELL

THE FIRST HUNDRED YEARS

In October 1860 Dickens was hoping that the 'case' of *Great Expectations* would prove satisfactory.[1] Many readers, including his friend and future biographer John Forster, were complaining that his recent novels had become too serious and gloomy. Dickens, though he always gave his audience something over and above what they wanted, was never insensitive to feedback. He now told Forster that his new novel had a 'grotesque tragi-comic conception' and an 'exceedingly droll' opening: it 'put a child and a good-natured foolish man in relations that seem to me very funny'.

Another worry at the time was the fate of his weekly magazine, *All the Year Round*, sales of which had slumped drastically in response to its serialisation of Charles Lever's novel, *A Day's Ride, a Life's Romance*. Dickens had originally thought of publishing *Great Expectations* according to his customary pattern, as a long novel in twenty free-standing monthly parts (the last two parts issued simultaneously). Now he changed tack. The novel would be much shorter than usual and come out in *All the Year Round* in weekly instalments, demoting *A Day's Ride* from the front page.

He succeeded well enough on both counts. Sales of the magazine picked up nicely, and many readers found *Great Expectations* amusing. In 1874 Forster's *Life* even claimed that 'Dickens's humour, not less than his creative power, was at its best in this book'.[2] But not all the early critics saw the novel as a return to vintage quality, and most fellow writers were cool or simply silent. As far as we can tell, towards the end of the nineteenth century *Great Expectations* belonged with *A Tale of Two Cities* among Dickens's least popular works.[3]

It so happens that *A Tale of Two Cities* was his only other novel to be serialised in weekly parts for *All the Year Round*. In both cases this circumstance of original publication, together with the subsequent book editions' relative thinness of spine, may have suggested something lightweight in the contents. Although some commentators praised *Great Expectations* for an exceptionally well put together plot,[4] others complained that the tight format, in preventing Dickens from rambling, deprived his imagination of air.[5] Perhaps, too, there was something odd or unsettling about the book's general mood. The 'grotesque tragi-comic conception' was never likely to provide quite the unadulterated mirth which Dickens had seemed to promise Forster.

Over a hundred years later, the 'case' of *Great Expectations* could hardly be more different. For one thing, the novel has become an international popular classic, and is holding its own within cultures where literacy exists side by side with a new orality and visuality. It has been translated into many different languages; it has often been simplified and abridged; and there have been radio and television serialisations, stage versions, film versions, cartoon versions, and tape recordings. As a result, its scenes and characters – Pip's meeting with the convict on the marshes, the ghastly Miss Havisham and her decaying bridal feast, Jaggers and his hand-washing – have lodged themselves in folk mythology everywhere. At the same time, the novel has also become a canonical text within the institutions of literary education and scholarship.[6] It is now studied in schools and universities all over the world, and is discussed in the fora provided by specialist conferences, learned journals and research networks.

The critical rehabilitation of the novel began at the very beginning of the twentieth century, with suggestive accounts by Algernon Swinburne, Andrew Lang and George Gissing.[7] Since then *Great Expectations* has been much praised for its characterisation, for its handling of the first-person narration, and for its general imaginative power. Even its liabilities in respect of length and mood have turned into assets. Mid-century scholars, influenced by New Criticism's concern with artistic form, linked the shortness of length to a remarkable effort of self-discipline. Here, they said, was an economical beauty of structure that was unusual by any standard.[8] As for the problematic mood, Modernist champions of difficulty in literature, and New Critical connoisseurs of ambiguity/ tension/paradox, were not to be put off by a little 'tragi-comic' oscillation, and right down to the present day the novel has been much praised for a treatment of the human condition that is both sobering and heartening. Among the existential, religious or moral 'themes' detected have been: vain longings; freedom, identity, love; Christian love, true fatherhood, redemption; the transference of guilt onto scapegoats; genuine relationships versus false ceremony; self-absorption versus self-abnegation; and moral maturity as a melancholy thinning of the blood.[9]

Other twentieth-century commentators, from the debunkers of Victorianism onwards, have pinpointed concerns that are less universal, treating the book as representative of a particular phase of English society. They have also tended to find its comedy far less salient than its darker sides, and in this they have not been alone. Even Forster, not completely persuaded by Dickens, had felt that the revised and official ending of *Great Expectations*, which is marginally more happy than the original ending, was less 'consistent with the drift, as well as natural working out, of the tale'.[10] In 1937 George Bernard Shaw, in his edition of the novel,[11] actually restored the less happy ending, and from the late 1940s onwards several other editors, though less radical than Shaw, have given it as an appendix.

Especially within the institutions of education and scholarship, the Dickens who was a 'very funny' popular entertainer and pillar of society steadily came to be seen as the least authentic Dickens of all, a tendency strengthened by biographical revelations. Forster's *Life* had already caused a minor sensation, by showing that young David Copperfield's experiences as a warehouse worker were based on a demeaning episode in Dickens's own childhood. But in the 1930s it finally began to be common knowledge that Dickens had kept the actress Nelly Ternan as his mistress, a secret which Forster and the few others privy to it had closely guarded. Ever since the middle years of the twentieth century, the more sombre later novels have risen in official esteem, not only because New Critics praised their artistry or thematics, but because psychoanalytical and sociological critics have spoken of their disturbing inwardness to some very Victorian duplicities. In this connection the emotional and fantasy life of Pip turns out to be a mine of bitter knowledge.

PSYCHOANALYTICAL APPROACHES

The tradition of probing psychoanalytical criticism goes back at least as far as 1872, when G. H. Lewes discussed Dickens's force as a writer in terms of hallucination.[12] But in the twentieth century, the single most important landmark was Edmund Wilson's essay of 1941, 'Dickens: the Two Scrooges'.[13] Wilson's implied model of the human psyche was broadly similar to that proposed by Carl Jung (1885–1961), who said that we have it within ourselves to be and to do so many different things that we find it difficult to achieve any sort of self-control or direction. In the end we usually cope by allowing just one main side of ourselves to be developed, and this becomes our official 'persona': the version of ourself which we hold up for inspection by other people. All our other spiritual potentialities are suppressed and become a mere 'shadow' to that official self. This is not the whole story, though, since the submerged energies of our shadow self are for ever bursting through into our dream life and creating various kinds of psychological disturbance.

According to Wilson, Dickens was hardly less than a Jekyll-and-Hyde. His public persona brought him success and respect within his society, but as a child he had been crushed by that society's cruel demands, and in his shadow life he remained secretly rebellious against it. He was always restlessly caught up in a manic-depressive cycle of boisterous social cheer and malevolently anti-social gloom, and was disturbingly fascinated by murder, a capital offence in the society. Wilson also found aspects of this pattern in the story of Pip, who passes 'through a whole psychological cycle'. In Pip, Dickens showed from the inside what it is like for one and the same person to be both of, and not of society. A similar opposition, between the professional and the private selves of Jaggers and Wemmick, was analysed in an influential article by Barbara Lecker on 'The Split Characters of Charles Dickens'.[14]

Jung suggested that our shadow self can also haunt us in our dealings with other people. If we find ourselves strongly disliking somebody, for instance, this may be because we are projecting onto that person some trait which we have tried to relegate to our own shadow side. In 1950 Dorothy Van Ghent began to trace similarly unexpected psychological tensions and complementarities in pairings of characters in *Great Expectations*. Suddenly Estella and Miss Havisham became virtually two aspects of a single character, and the same went for Joe and Orlick, and for Pip and Magwitch: 'the opposed extremes of spiritual possibility' actually belong on a 'spiritual continuum'.[15] Julian Moynaham took this kind of approach one stage further by linking it to a psychology of sado-masochistic power relations, so developing Wilson's point about the effects of cruelty experienced in childhood. Moynaham's suggestion was that Pip has self-projecting fantasies of revengeful domination over his tormentors.[16] Unconsciously, he endorses Orlick's attack on his sister, Drummle's brutalisation of Estella, and the real burning and hallucinated hanging of Miss Havisham. Sado-masochistic implications are further explored by A. L. French (in essay 1 below), who adds that Dickens instinctively thought of some people as simply born evil.[17]

The challenge of Jungian approaches to Dickens is that they tend to see him as less than fully self-aware, or perhaps even less than fully frank. The argument is that, as an eminent Victorian with a professed belief in moral ameliorability, Dickens was reluctant to recognise his own most unsettling insights into human nature. This line of thought has been extended by some feminist critics, in further explorations of the field of sado-masochism in Dickens. One of their main concerns has been with the images of women in literature, and it is to this that Lucy Frost (in essay 2 below) links her concern with author psychology. While praising Dickens's treatment of Mrs Joe, Estella and Miss Havisham for uncanny powers of perception, Frost also suggests that he was secretly afraid of what he saw in these 'strong' women. His secret impulse was to master and tame what he dimly apprehended as a threat to his own manhood.[18]

There has also been a line of Freudian critics of Dickens, who have been no less keen than the Jungians to lay bare hidden significances in his work. In doing so they often draw attention to interesting details and can sometimes be sensitive to larger patterns as well. But their concern to match the rich texture of Dickens's novels with the Freudian master narrative has sometimes been criticised as insensitive and reductive. Another complaint has been that they allow themselves to be carried away by their own imagination. Certainly they often disagree about the precise details of the Freudian insights Dickens's novels are supposed to substantiate.

In dealing with *Great Expectations*, Freudian critics have seen Magwitch as the cruel, castrating side of the father, Joe as the loving side. Desire is said to be interwoven with guilt on the classic Oedipal pattern, so giving rise to various displacements of desired objects.[19] In so far as Mrs Joe is a mother figure, great importance is sometimes attached to her apron as forbidding the young boy's desire,[20] and sexual implications are also found in Mrs Joe's death and in Pip's 'saving' of Miss Havisham, which Curt Hartog has even described as a kind of rape.[21] On the other hand, Pip is just as often said to be deficient in the phallic energy necessary for social success. That thrusting phallicism is sometimes located in Jaggers, in which case Pip's reluctance to emulate Jaggers becomes a central focus and Pip's own development is said to be arrested at, or to regress to, childish pre-Oedipal states. One critic says that Pip thinks of money as filth in a clearly anal manner,[22] while another hints that the novel's preoccupation with food and eaters stems from a widely representative oral fixation: Pip, Dickens and Victorian society in general did not recognise genital pleasures as openly as oral ones, and regarded the mouth as central to social and intellectual community – to eating, laughter, song, story, comedy.[23]

Although Freudian criticism is not generally as fashionable as it used to be, some of the recent Freudian interpretations of *Great Expectations* are especially interesting. Jack Rawlins (in essay 3 below) gives one of the best accounts of Pip's hesitant ego drive, which he sees as reflecting Dickens's own problems in keeping alive a child-like integrity of vision amidst the convenient hypocrisies of society.[24] For Anny Sadrin, Pip's development traces out an Oedipal pattern which runs through all of Dickens's work. In the leading role there is always what she describes as a Telemachus figure: a male orphan who has to redeem his father's death and return to his origins. So the 'true' ending of *Great Expectations* is Pip's return to the parental graves, and his story is about his mistakes in projecting his paternal ideal. Magwitch tries to become a father figure, insisting that Pip remain 'Pip' against his will, and there are other patrons as well. But finally Pip accepts himself as the son of a poor man long since dead and forgotten. All of which Sadrin expounds with great tact, fully recognising that there are other story-lines in the book as well.[25] Peter Brooks (in essay 4 below) also thinks of Pip as having to return to his true origins, though for Brooks the narrative terminus is the return of Magwitch. Like Sadrin, he is also concerned with more than one story line, but he subsumes them all under the Freudian theory of a conflict between Eros (desire) and Thanatos (the death wish).[26]

Both Freudian and Jungian commentators, then, argue or imply that Dickens was secretive about things which modern analysis can easily bring out into the open. This point is well taken, though in fairness to Dickens we should perhaps add that his indirectness of expression is in principle not dissimilar from some of our own behaviour. There are sensitive issues in all societies, and even today, if we want to secure somebody else's attention, we may have to avoid using the plainest words: as Aristotle remarked in defence of rhetoric, the truth may need to be 'helped' if it is to be understood and accepted. This is simply part of the pragmatics of communication. We tune our language to suit the communicative context, sometimes embracing, however reluctantly and temporarily, the values of our addressees. If Dickens now seems even more indirect than we ourselves, this is merely a trick of perspective resulting from the fact that notions of directness and indirectness of speech, like the criteria for *décolletage* and hemlines, change over time and from one culture to another. Dickens himself was perfectly conscious about this kind of thing, complaining bitterly about Mrs Grundy, and protesting that French writers enjoyed far greater freedom.[27] A number of recent studies are about how he dealt with the facts of life *in spite* of the Victorian 'Young Person' in his audience,[28] and Beth F. Herst has argued that not even his typical central heroes – the Nicholas Nicklebys – are the stuffed dummies they are usually taken for.[29]

So the best psychoanalysing criticism articulates significances which, at some level, Dickens and many earlier readers probably understood all too well. Perhaps its impact can even be traced in the work of critics who prefer to abstain from psychological terminology. In John Carey's book on Dickens, for instance, as in much of the finest literary criticism, the mileage still comes from an alertly intelligent use of a critical vocabulary with a long history behind it. Carey's key term is 'imagination', and he studies Dickens's imagination through a close analysis of what the novels' descriptions actually make us see, and of the language, especially the figurative language, they use to achieve this. Analysed in this way, *Great Expectations* is a novel which 'plays with fire'.[30] Yet in this observation Carey catches, not only the frequent fire metaphors and mentions of real fire, but also that underlying preoccupation with danger and violence which Wilson, Moynaham, French and Hartog approach so differently.

SOCIOLOGICAL APPROACHES

Another main line of Dickens criticism pays far more attention than psychoanalytical criticism to the society within, for, and about which Dickens was writing. George Orwell and Humphrey House were among the first of many critics to comment on Pip's love for

Estella as the aspirant gentleman's hankering after the superior lady,[31] since when *Great Expectations* has often been praised as a kind of snob's progress. In itself this would mean that the novel is potentially comic. But like psychoanalytical critics, sociological critics dwell on its darker sides and draw attention to some very unpleasant secrets. Pip's snobbishness is the cause of great personal misery and could only thrive in a society morbidly riddled with class. Many critics have followed Lionel Trilling in seeing the class system, and the great expectations it nourishes, as ultimately rooted in 'a sordid, hidden reality': 'The real thing is not the gentility of Pip's life but the hulks and the murder and the rats and decay in the cellarage of the novel.'[32] A frequently noticed irony is that even Estella turns out to be the child of that marginalised and criminalised reality.

Robin Gilmour points out that the Victorians distinguished at least five main types of gentleman: the 'gent' of the 1830s, i.e. a young man at the very bottom of the fashionable classes who wore flashy clothes to draw attention to himself; the more refined dandy; the traditional gentleman by birth; the self-made man; and the manly Victorian gentleman. Dickens himself, especially in his childhood and early adulthood, was obsessed by such discriminations, and his experience of factory work and of his wastrel father made him feel unjustly excluded from his rightful place in society. During his middle years he consolidated a reputation which concealed such early shame until the posthumous revelations in Forster's *Life*. Yet by the time of *Great Expectations* there was a part of him that no longer really cared about his own social standing. Gilmour argues that he had come out on the other side of the dream of gentility, considerably disillusioned about the culture in which it flourished, and conscious of a curious interrelationship between polite society and the underworld, between the socially central and the socially marginalised. Even in his own life, there was the continuing show of respectability after he had broken with his wife, and there was the secret liaison with an actress at a time when actresses were associated in the public mind with prostitutes.[33]

On a larger scale, the magnificent achievements of Victorian civilisation had their foundations in a very unedifying reality indeed. England was the first society in the world to become predominantly urban, and throughout the century people were pouring into the towns and cities at such a rate that disease, both literal and metaphorical, inevitably ensued. It was not until the middle years of the century that the principles of sanitation began to be understood, and even then the knowledge could not be translated fast enough into hygienic waterworks and efficient sewers. Millions of people lived in conditions of unspeakable squalor in which typhoid and cholera were endemic, as were every kind of exploitation, violence and inhumanity. This was part of the 'sordid, hidden reality' Trilling has in mind, not hidden from the poor themselves, needless to say, but not willingly viewed by most members of polite society.

Dickens himself was not squeamish, but his attitude towards cities, above all towards London, was certainly complicated. From one point of view London suited him very well just as it was, and his incessant street-wandering at all hours of the day and night could never give him enough of it. In all its filth, danger, energy, and prolific variety, it was simply the most vital stimulus to his imagination, so that in a novel such as *Bleak House* the slums and the fever become integral parts of the conception. Yet at the same time Dickens was one of the first to campaign for proper sanitation, actually using *Bleak House* to do so, and was tireless in his efforts to alleviate the condition of 'fallen women' and other unfortunates as well. London was in fact very far from perfect, and Dickens was for ever harking back to his more rural childhood, perhaps hoping he could somehow reinstate that earlier world when he took up residence at Gad's Hill in 1857. Certainly his own novels, despite the grim realism of some of their scenes from village life, helped to give the myth of the golden-age simplicity of the countryside a Victorian form, and in doing so fuelled a nostalgia that inspired many second- and third-generation city-dwellers to move out to the rapidly spreading suburbs.

On the whole, the sociological critics give Dickens far more credit than the psychoanalytical critics do for conscious control over what he is writing. He is usually said to be, by the time of *Great Expectations*, a supremely penetrating observer of the world in which he lives, with an unmatched ability to open the eyes of others. The story of Pip is often taken to deal with the dream of gentility and the myth of the unspoilt countryside, to show them for the foibles they are, and deliberately to contrast them with 'sordid, hidden reality'. That Dickens himself was, or had been, partly under their spell is usually seen as one source of his writing's power.

The links between squalor and genteel finery in Pip's story are well brought out by Gilmour (in essay 5 below). As for the country–city dichotomy, it is one of the plot's main axes. Pip first moves from the country to the city; then backwards and forwards between city and country; then resolutely back to the country; only to be disappointed at Biddy's unavailability for his idyll; and consequently moving right away from England; to return to London, very soberly, on the final page or so. The country boy is bowled over by the city. The tired urbanite dreams of the country. But although the urbanite's fantasies may be mere wish fulfilment, they are terribly strong, and Dickens himself is worried that urbanisation may involve the loss of something profoundly important. As John Lucas puts it, the rural blacksmith stands for a moral economy, for a quality of relationships in work, that may be becoming a thing of the past.[34] This raises the question of whether some sort of spiritual compromise is possible, which is where Wemmick is sometimes taken to have a special role. While Jungian critics have spoken of Wemmick as a character 'split' between professional persona and private shadow, F. W. Schwarzback relates Wemmick's oddity to social history, seeing him as the quintessential suburbanite, certainly split, but split between town and country, and delineated with all Dickens's conscious mastery of cultural notation.[35]

Murray Baumgarten brings many of the novel's social significances together in terms of a binarism between what he calls 'calligraphy' and 'code'. 'Calligraphy' is a matter of reading 'through' letters to see things and people as they are, and it is close to oral communication and to truthfulness. 'Code' is closer to print culture and to civilisation, social snobbery, economic effectiveness, the city. As Pip moves from 'calligraphy' to 'code' he despises Joe for not doing so; in such an interpretation, Joe's hopeless struggle to learn how to read is profoundly symbolic. According to Baumgarten, although Dickens himself essentially stays closer to 'calligraphy', the power of the book comes from a tension. Dickens himself had aspired to 'code' and is well able to suggest its lure, in what is after all a prodigious outpouring of highly skilful words to be printed.[36]

One way or another, Dickens criticism is always coming back to some such tension or paradox. Dickens was somehow absolutely part of Victorian society and absolutely *not* part of it. Edmund Wilson's epoch-making article first made the point by hinting at the persona and shadow of Jungian psychology. Sociological critics, for their part, highlight apparent tensions or even self-contradictions in the ideological sphere. This also brings us back to the pragmatics of communication, since Dickens was not writing in a vacuum. James M. Brown argues that although Dickens understood his society better than any other contemporary author, he was nevertheless writing to earn a living from a bourgeois audience, self-censoring his language and subject-matter accordingly.[37] Of course the gentlemanly ideal was the root of much evil, and Dickens showed this. But Dickens also reassured his readers, thousands of whom had aspirations to gentility, that a man could be a gentleman by virtue of qualities of feeling and sheer hard work. When sociological commentary has been interwoven with traditional character criticism, one of the main points has actually been that not even Pip, and not even Pip at his most snobbish, is really such a bad chap. Q. D. Leavis, who felt that Pip had been much maligned by psychoanalytical critics and other sociological critics alike, argued that his guilt feelings are merely the result of normal Victorian social conditioning, that his gentlemanly aspirations are an understandable response to the deadly dullness of life in the village, and that Victorians were in any case all in favour of upward social mobility.[38] Others have pointed out that, as a narrator, Pip is admirably honest and tactful, not the least bit self-pitying in describing the injuries he sustained while rescuing Miss Havisham, and reticent about his own generosity towards Herbert.[39]

STRUCTURALIST APPROACHES

Social and ideological issues are also of central concern to some, though not all, of the Dickens scholars influenced by structuralism. Structuralism is an intellectual movement which, in the English-speaking world, gained force in the 1970s, but whose main ideas ultimately go back to structuralist linguistics in the tradition stemming from Ferdinand de Saussure (1857–1913).

Structuralist linguists saw language as a system which makes possible the communication of messages by means of pre-arranged patterns of opposition. For instance, the principle of 'emic' differentiality distinguishes one meaning from another by contrasts of phon*eme* or morph*eme* (e.g. *bat* from *cat* or *look* from *looked*). In addition to this there are also pre-arranged agreements as to what particular meanings should be attached to particular words. In principle there is no reason why a canine quadruped should be called *dog*, and in languages other than English it is called *hund*, *chien*, *koira* and so on; to use structuralist terminology, the relationship between the two halves of the linguistic sign, the signified and the signifier, is unmotivated and arbitrary. But for the sake of mutual understanding within the linguistic community, agreement was long ago reached as to which signified would go with which signifier, and the signifying arrangements of different languages actually distribute the range of things to be signified in very different ways. Different languages split up the spectrum of colours differently; there are many more subtly distinguishing words for ice and snow in Eskimo language than in African languages; and the same kind of variation applies with abstract concepts as well. From all this some scholars drew the conclusion that human beings are linguistically determined: that our experiences, thoughts and feelings are ineluctably moulded by the pre-arranged structures and communal agreements of whatever language we happen to speak.

In due time a structuralist poetics and a structuralist narratology developed. By analogy with language, all the possible types of literary work which can be written, and all the possible stories which can be told, were seen as determined by pre-established systems of contrast and relationship between constituent elements. The French structural semanticist A. J. Greimas, for instance, argued that stories which on the surface seem entirely different from each other are actually informed by the same underlying structure of oppositions between different actors, each of them embodying a different function that is essential to any narrative whatever.[40] These oppositions of functions can be diagrammed as they occur in the story of Perceval's quest for the Holy Grail as follows:

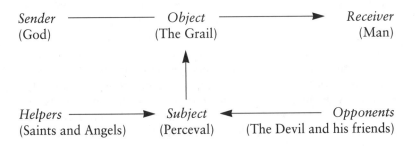

But this same 'actantial model' applies for other narratives as well, and Anny Sadrin (in essay 10 below) shows how it can be used to explicate the plot of *Great Expectations* as seen from the viewpoint of different characters.[41]

Structuralist poetics and structuralist narratology are what is meant by literary structuralism in the strictest sense. The scholarly task is seen as a matter not so much of literary criticism as of disinterestedly objective science. The aim is merely to describe, classify and catalogue recurrent features and patterns on both the surface- and deep-structure level of texts.

But the structuralist way of thinking has also been extended to areas such as society, culture and ideology, and much structuralist literary scholarship comes closer to a kind of social, cultural and ideological critique. This critique tends to be radical, in that it develops the deterministic strand in structuralist thought, so challenging the common-sense assumption that human beings are free individuals. In this respect structuralist literary theory is not all that different from the economic or social determinisms of writers such as Marx or Dreiser, and Marx is actually an important background influence. The assumption about free human individuality is sometimes described as a liberal humanist deception characteristic of bourgeois ideology.

Loosely speaking, this argument against liberal humanism tends to shift the blame or responsibility for everything which happens from individual human beings to one of the larger all-embracing entities: language or society or bourgeois ideology. But this way of putting it still speaks as if human individuality has some sort of self-grounded reality, an idea which to many Marxist structuralists is quite unacceptable. According to them, language or society or ideology consists of pre-structured subject positions which are imposed on people willy-nilly, so that what seems to be a person's own identity or character is not really that at all, but a linguistic, social or ideological construct. This may go against common-sense ideas of what human beings are like, but Marxist structuralism really is in open disagreement with common sense. The aim is to de-centre common-sense and liberal humanist ideas of the self, in order to argue that selfhood is merely the product of larger forces.

To the extent that structuralist literary critics engage in detailed textual analysis, they are often mainly concerned to undermine the individual responsibility of literary authors for what they write, sometimes even rejecting the idea of authorship altogether. One of the slogans speaks of 'the death of the author', and what this means is that, just as a chair is made by a carpenter out of wood, so a literary work is a product made by a mere writer-worker out of language, society or ideology. A second critical concern is to challenge the traditional type of character criticism, which speaks of characters in novels as human individuals. Characters, too, are seen by Marxist structuralists as the formations of language, society or ideology.

One influential French thinker who was interested in the social construction of human subjects and the shaping power of language was Michel Foucault (1926–1984). Foucault's main idea was that the languages of science, or of what counts for science in a society, can help to maintain an ideological supremacy over the underprivileged people whom science brands as deviant. Foucault referred to these potentially sinister languages of science as discourses, and one discoursal nexus of knowledge and power which he analysed in detail had to do with crime and punishment.

At the end of the eighteenth century, new penal codes moved away from corporal punishment towards more 'civilised' methods. Prison inmates were now to be classified as delinquents and kept under constant observation and psychological pressure. An example of what Foucault described as a new moral technology was Jeremy Bentham's plan for a 'Panopticon': a prison for solitary confinement in which circular tiers of cells were open to supervisory inspection by invisible warders positioned in a central observation tower. According to Foucault, such schemes were closely linked with the rise of the social sciences, which were based on the same idea of the individual human mind as an observable, describable, analysable object, about which information could be fed into political and social technologies. Such knowledge could be implemented not only in prisons but in hospitals, mental asylums, schools and workhouses – according to Foucault, it is no accident that nineteenth-century prison architecture became the model for institutional buildings of other kinds as well. The aim of such projects, however, was not that the people under surveillance should be normalised and brought into line. On the contrary, their mentalities were merely to be plainly distinguished and separated off so that they could be easily spied upon and efficiently managed. This was why many sections of the population were criminalised for the first time, and why police patrolling was greatly increased.

Foucault's thought has had a marked influence on structuralist literary theory, whence it has passed into literary criticism. In an essay entitled 'Prison-Bound: Dickens and Foucault' (essay 6 below), Jeremy Tambling argues that *Great Expectations* is about subject formation by criminalisation. This is one reason, for Tambling, why the element of first-person-singular confessional narration is so important in the novel: delinquents have to pour out their souls into society's pre-structured moulds and so be rendered harmless.[42] Pam Morris is also influenced by Foucault and, like Tambling, sees Jaggers as the arch-observer and classifier of delinquents. She emphasises, too, that criminalisation had been reinforced by the evangelical doctrines of sin and damnation, but according to her the discoursal methods for regulating the poor underwent a subtle shift during the 1860s. Quoting extensively from the *Christian Observer*, the *Methodist Magazine*, *The Times* and the great Victorian reviews, she detects a new rhetoric which spoke of everybody as bound together by social chains, and of a prosperity that was open to all. It was implied that nobody need ever again be 'common', a suggestion which, analysed as a kind of corporate deception, makes the Victorian ideal of gentility look even more sinister than in Robin Gilmour's analysis (essay 5 below). In Morris's reading of *Great Expectations*, both criminalisation and the fantasy of riches are part of the system of social control: she sees considerable significance in the fact that when the poor starving Magwitch was forced into a criminalising association it was with Compeyson the forger.[43]

It is important to note that different critics embrace structuralist determinism to different degrees. Tambling and Morris argue that *Great Expectations* shows the discoursal formation of human subjects, but mainly of those human subjects referred to by traditional criticism as the novel's characters. These critics say or imply that Dickens himself was in a sense superior or immune to social formation, and was able to communicate his insights into the phenomenon. They de-centre the characters, then, but in effect do not de-centre Dickens as the author. Like most earlier sociological and ideological critics, they attribute to him extraordinary powers of perception and writerly control – they even suggest that he anticipated Foucault. As so often before, Dickens's own complicity in Victorian ways of thought is not denied, but it is felt to make his ideological critique all the more penetrating. This line of argument is markedly different from that of a number of other structuralist critics, who tend to see Dickens as an unconscious channel of ideological tendencies rather than as their diagnostician.

David Trotter, for example, says that Dickens is strongly under the influence of the Victorian discourse of economics, the key idea of which was circulation. The scientific backing for this was in Adam Smith's advocacy of *laissez faire*, the idea that goods and services should be traded without any restrictions, but other areas of life, and other discourses, became involved as well. According to Trotter, Dickens's own restless mobility sprang from his belief that people, air and information should all flow about freely. He lived in constant fear of any kind of stagnation, physical or spiritual, and his association with the 'Moral Police' was an attempt to bring about social reforms by dispelling concentrations of disease or ignorance, for instance by means of proper sanitation or circulating libraries. In his novels, prostitutes and secretive lawyers are among those who block things up, whereas the detective police and the science of physiognomy open things up by allowing meanings to circulate freely from signs. As far as *Great Expectations* is concerned, however, Trotter draws a blank, which in itself is instructive; like Pam Morris, Trotter suggests that in the 1860s ideological shifts were taking place. Although the novel sometimes sees guilt as a kind of stain in Dickens's usual manner, and although some of the language even tends to suggest that the Miss Havisham syndrome is in the nature of a morbid stoppage, the change at the end of the novel is not conceived in terms of better circulation. Trotter suggests that what happens has more to do with a revision of family relations. The disnatured, false families of the novel's opening chapters are replaced by authentic families.[44]

In a somewhat similar way Philip W. Martin relates Dickens to the constant evolution of medical discourse, particularly as relating to mental illness, a topic on which Foucault wrote a monumental study. Above all Martin is interested in the question of madness in women, and his claim is that Dickens actually regresses to patterns of thought far older than Victorianism. Since ancient times, madness in women had been put down to a moving of the uterus, and the best remedy was said to be pregnancy or, better still, regular sexual intercourse, since the fundamental cause was supposed to be the lack or loss of a man. Victorian doctors were gradually beginning to mention educational background and social roles as important factors, and treatment was beginning to move away from physical restraint towards positive environmental influences. Yet there was still a sense in which to be a single woman *was* to be ill, and Martin says that Mrs Joe, Miss Havisham and Molly are basically conceived according to the ancient stereotype of the sexually frustrated witch, an observation with which some feminist critics would agree.[45]

POSTSTRUCTURALIST APPROACHES

In other recent ideological commentary on Dickens, there is an even stronger sense than in Trotter and Martin that no society will ever have one single discourse only, whether of criminology, economics, medicine or anything else. Old and new discourses exist side by side, and so do discourses representing widely different interest groupings within society. This type of perception sometimes reflects the influence of the great Russian literary historian Mikhail Bakhtin (1895–1975), who especially emphasised that no society is ever homogeneous. A ruling class may maintain its ideological domin-ance, but there will always be manifold alternative interest group-ings, based on variables such as gender, race, profession, class, religion or region. This gives rise, not only to the 'heteroglossia' ('different-tonguedness') of different sociolects, but to a corres-ponding variety of ideological positions, each entailing different understandings of human life and its goals and possibilities.

Bakhtin was especially interested in 'polyvocal' literary works which allow different sociolects and ideological positions to jostle against each other and even challenge the dominant ideology. He praised such writing for a liberating 'dialogism' and 'carnivalistic' topsyturvidom. Above all he was interested in the novel, as the genre which pre-eminently played off one social voice against another, often by means of parody. Bakhtin himself made some seminal observations about Dickens,[46] and studies of various Dickens novels along Bakhtinian lines are now appearing fairly regularly.

In applying Bakhtin to *Great Expectations*, Eiichi Hara (in essay 7 below) is particularly critical of Peter Brooks's Freudian claim (in essay 4 below) that Pip eventually achieves a stable identity by discovering his truest origin in Magwitch. Hara is suspicious of the idea of legitimating origins and espouses a more de-centred view of the self. For him, the human psyche simply locates itself within a range of subject positions already available within society's language and ideology, none of which is more personal or genuine than any other. Pip does not have much control over what happens to him or over what he and others think he is. The various story-lines in which he gets caught up are not of his own making but represent stereotypes already existing in various reaches of the socio-ideological spectrum. As for the end of the novel, Hara describes it partly as a collapse into carnival, in which no single ideological narrative solution seems more valid than any other.[47]

With Hara's sense of many different discourses and meanings in simultaneous circulation, and of human subjectivities as for ever slipping and sliding between them, we have already entered the mental climate of poststructuralist thought. Like structuralists, poststructuralists are suspicious of common-sense ideas of human identity, but they carry their scepticism still further by challenging the widespread beliefs that there is a world, and that we can know and say things about it. This means that they sometimes find structuralist ideological critique too naïve, because it assumes that social reality exists in a fairly simple and straightforward way. The structuralists sometimes retort that the poststructuralists are the victims or perpetrators of a bourgeois ideological deception, according to which social reality and all its injustices do *not* exist.

These disagreements should not be overemphasised. Many structuralists have themselves mutated into poststructuralists, and in practice the main difference between the two schools is often one of degree: for poststructuralist critics, words such as 'self', 'author' and 'character' are to be used with even more caution than for structuralist critics. It is argued that the ideas associated with these (and any other) words are very much a linguistic product, and a concept such as 'theme' is said to be especially problematic as well. The point is, that to say there is a self or an author or a character, or say that a writer expresses a particular theme, is to make the two common-sense assumptions which poststructuralists challenge: that there is a world about which things can be said: and that one person can communicate a hard and fast meaning to another.

The first of these common-sense assumptions is what the influential French philosopher Jacques Derrida (b. 1930) has described as the fallacy of logocentrism, i.e. the belief in some legitimating reason or rationale outside of language: a world of nature, a presence which was 'there' before a single word was spoken, an origin to which language somehow refers back, a truth against which linguistic utterances can be checked for their accuracy or otherwise. According to Derrida, we live so entirely within the language we speak that our sense of reality is a purely linguistic construct. It bears no necessary relation to anything there might or might not be outside of language.

As for the common-sense assumption that determinate meanings are communicable, Derrida, Paul de Man and other so-called deconstructionists have said that this again underestimates the workings of language. These scholars take the ideas of emic differentiality and of the arbitrariness of the sign much further than structuralist linguists had done, arguing that words are for ever entering into new polarities with each other, and into new relationships with what is thought of as the world. According to them, this means that the process of semiosis proliferates endlessly, with new and opposite meanings constantly supplementing old ones, only to be themselves supplemented in their turn. So although language has immense power over us, it is so incredibly slippery that nothing can ever really be said.

Poststructuralist thinking in these matters is of a piece with certain new developments within psychoanalytical theory. The seminal figure here is the French psychoanalyst Jacques Lacan (1901–1981), who in point of fact has been attractive to scholars on both the main wings of literary theory. His preoccupation with the psyche as a social formation interests structuralists engaged in ideological critique, while his preoccupation with the instability of meanings has influenced poststructuralist deconstructionist critics.

Lacan is often described as a neo-Freudian. But although he certainly relies on central Freudian concepts, in particular the Oedipus complex, in some respects Lacanian literary theory and criticism turns out more like Jungian literary scholarship. One of the main differences between the Freudian critics and the Jungian critics has usually been that the Freudians, as Hara complains of Brooks, tend to speak as if people can find out who they really are, whereas for the Jungians human identity seems a bit more complex and flexible. For the Jungian critics, the conflict between persona and shadow is a more or less permanent indecisiveness. For the Freudian critics, the psyche may well explore different stances or story-lines, but there is the ultimate goal of a stabilising return to origins which will legitimate a true personal identity. Lacanian criticism undermines this certainty about human individuality. It unsettles or de-centres notions of the self in the way so characteristic of both the ideological and deconstructive wings of literary theory.

According to Lacan's developmental psychology, the very young child has no unified sense of self. Even though consciousness gradually attaches to certain sites of pleasure on its own and the mother's body, its experience is mostly a formless fluidity of drives and sensations. But then comes 'the mirror stage', which is the start of the 'Imaginary order'. Typically as a result of seeing itself in a mirror, the child perceives itself as a unity and tries to take full possession of this new self-image. It greedily attaches to it everything that is pleasant, and fiercely spurns everything unpleasant. The Imaginary experience, in other words, is of the self in direct contact with other things and people, straightforwardly able to like or dislike them, and to accept or reject. It is a phase of strong certainties and clear-cut emotions. Then, however, comes the stage of the 'Symbolic order', during which the growing child has to realise that it is a social being, and that society intervenes with its own way of shaping people and relationships. The male child, for instance, with his Imaginary desire for pleasurable unity with the mother and for the death of the rival father, comes up against the incest taboo and has to accept substitute relationships. Language, too, is a kind of social structuring, which is arbitrary and not at all easy to control, and which similarly means that human beings are not responsible for the directions in which their own subjectivities develop. Their responses have to be far more hesitant and complex than the black-and-white certainties of Imaginary hedonism, and the self comes to objectify itself as merely one among many signs in a semiotic system. A telling example of the way in which human identity is complicated by language is the pronoun 'I', since this word signifies not only the person now speaking, but a 'separate' person of whom something is now being said. Socialisation is in fact nothing less than a process of ever-increasing self-division, doubt, hesitation, indirection. At the same time, desire is endless, and endlessly unsatisfied, and can still be felt with Imaginary intensity. This is where the anguish comes in: although the Imaginary is more typically associated with childhood and the Symbolic with adulthood, throughout life the two orders are actually in problematic alternation with each other.

This instability is the focus of the critic Steven Connor in his Lacanian reading of *Great Expectations* (part of which appears as essay 8 below). Connor shows how objects and the words associated with them (e.g. 'leg-iron', 'file', 'hammer', 'gun') sometimes seem to allow an Imaginary pinning-down of their significance, only to become at other times the disconcertingly variable signs of the Symbolic. That is, things do not simply mean in a pleasurably fixed and straightforward way, with a one-to-one correspondence between each word and its 'thing'. Words are for ever taking on new meanings by association, in a kind of slippage. Here Connor's Lacanian analysis is to the same effect as a deconstructive reading of *Great Expectations* by Christopher Morris, who argues that Pip's preoccupations with names, with allusions to literature and legend, and with the way people read writing, all point to Pip's own basic lack of an autonomous self. There is always an alternative way of reading events, and Pip cannot be said to have matured into something specific or to have learnt anything definite either.[48] Similarly for Connor, on the emotional level Pip is never sure of himself. His instinctive Imaginary sympathy with Magwitch is in constant conflict with social responsibility and the law, which leads to a sense of guilt, experienced by Pip as an aspect of the Other – as something imposed by violence from without. By way of response, Pip often tries to force other people into conformity with his own Imaginary patterning – a new way, this, of describing the behaviour which earlier psychoanalytical critics described as sado-masochistic or revengeful. But not only did Magwitch and Miss Havisham create *him*. They in their turn were created by others – by the Other. It is as if not even our desires are our own, and Pip's vague sense of this gives him a nightmare feeling of lost identity. As it seems to him, he is always being cheated out of something rightly his, an anxiety which is intensified as a result of his structurally identical struggle with the Symbolic of money in capitalist society.[49]

THE EMPHASIS ON READERS PAST AND PRESENT

Steven Connor is a wonderfully lucid and suggestive critic, but the type of analysis in which he is engaging makes considerable demands on the reader, and it is hardly surprising that structuralist and poststructuralist literary theory in general, given its open challenge to common sense, has been controversial. The most impatient reaction has been to dismiss it as ivory tower nonsense, or as a kind of guerrilla warfare on the values and ways of argument which underpin western society. Even within the narrow confines of the academic world, there have been problems of communication, since literary scholars who specialise in particular authors and literary scholars who specialise in theory sometimes have little to do with each other. Both groupings have their own professional and institutional organisations, which tend to wall them off from each other, and when their paths do cross the discoursal disjunctions can be pretty sharp. Theorists would see red at the very title of Gwen Watkins's book, *Dickens in Search of Himself: Recurrent Themes and Characters in the Work of Charles Dickens* (London, 1987), and many scholars certainly have behaved as if the literary theory movement never happened. By the late 1980s literary theory was also suffering, unjustly, from a kind of guilt by association and a version of the genetic fallacy: the assumption that an idea must be mistaken if the person who holds it can be discredited. With the collapse of the Soviet bloc, the anti-bourgeois wing of theory found itself automatically suspect in the eyes of many people, and the revelations about Paul de Man's wartime association with the Nazis were equally disastrous for the deconstructionist wing.

But the change in mood is not just a cowardly switch from one new fashion to another, and the deeper intellectual reasons and educational consequences have been debated in books with titles such as *The End of Literary Theory*.[50] No serious and open-minded commentator denies that structuralist and poststructuralist theory has drawn attention to some very important issues, often for the first time. Many literary scholars are now prepared to accept that the formation of the human psyche is by no means an autonomous process, that the workings of language certainly do repay the closest possible attention, and that common-sense ideas are, at best, a very reductive kind of shorthand. On the other hand, even common sense can be partially rehabilitated, as a mind-set disposed towards necessary rapid response in particular situations. Common sense is certainly subject to arbitrary intellectual limitations, which a deconstructive critique does well to expose. But a deconstructive 'free play' of signifiers signifying nothing has obvious functional limitations in face of real-life exigences, and also for the purposes of real-time reading and interpretation. One is reminded here of the ancient distinction between the active life and the contemplative life, both of which play their part in a fully rounded human development. What sometimes happens when structuralist and poststructuralist theory influences the discussion of particular literary authors is that the contemplative impulse gets out of control, an overemphasis which at worst has even resulted in obscurantism and self-contradiction.

As far as structuralist thought is concerned, one difficulty has been that, as already noted, the account of human subjects as ideologically determined sometimes goes hand in hand with an admiration of Dickens or Foucault for the free-thinking independence of their ideological critique. All things considered, this apparent anomaly is not really so surprising. The conflict between doctrines of determinism and doctrines of freedom has had a very long history, and we have probably reached a stage when absolute forms of both types of doctrine are unacceptable. In effect many people partly believe in some form of determinism and partly believe in some degree of free will, holding the two beliefs in a state of mutual modification. Even those who acknowledge the shaping force of society can see that one of the objections to extreme structuralist determinism is that it is sometimes bolstered by the synchronicity of structuralist methodology: from Saussure onwards, structuralists typically studied the structure of a system as it exists in a particular moment of time artificially separated from the rest of history. As soon as a diachronic perspective is introduced, historical changes in systems become apparent, and in order to account for them the most elegant solution would perhaps be that they were initiated by some human agency, even if we can no longer think of human agency in a completely autonomous or unmediated form. Given these kinds of philosophical balancing act, common-sense ideas about human identity and freedom, albeit in a far less heady form than during the heyday of nineteenth-century liberalism, are likely to receive continuing support from laymen and philosophers alike, which in turn means that concepts such as 'self', 'author' and 'character' are likely to have a continuing, if strongly modified role in literary criticism.

As for poststructuralist thought, on the one hand Derrida said that a belief in the ascertainability of truth was a logocentric fallacy, and determinate meanings cannot be communicated, yet on the other hand he seemed to think that he himself had got things right, and that people would understand him. In point of fact he has even come to be treated as a fully authoritative author, whose own words are quoted and requoted. But once again, the apparent anomaly is not really surprising. The terms 'self', 'author' and 'character' are partially resistant, not only to extreme structuralist determinism, but to poststructuralist deconstruction, and the same applies to the term 'theme' as well.

Derrida, Paul de Man and Lacan certainly showed the power that language has over us, and they also traced its potential for an unsettling proliferation of meaning. Given the differentiality and arbitrariness of language, there is no reason in principle why the process of semiosis should not go on as indefinitely as the deconstructionists suggested. But like the structuralist linguists before them, deconstructionists made a sharp methodological distinction between language (*langue*) and language in use (*parole*), and were only interested in the former; they separated language from history and from the contexts in which it actually works. Several more recent developments in linguistics, and particularly the branch of study known as pragmatics, have shown that this gives a misleading impression of the nature of language. In any given context, given senders and receivers of linguistic utterances tend to bring with them a set of information, attitudes and processing habits which makes certain interpretations much more likely than others. Neither in our everyday lives nor in our reading of literature do we allow our onward progress to be much slowed down by uncertainty as to what things mean. There fairly soon comes a point at which we momentarily freeze semiosis in its tracks. Drawing on all our knowledge and all our powers of contextual inference, for the time being we resolve that things have some particular meaning or meanings, so that we can then move on to the next interpretative challenge.

Among the aids we bring to the interpretation of literature, common-sense ideas about self, author, character and theme can have an important place. Indeed these concepts are almost categories of thought in the same way that time and space are, which we apply to our manifold impressions in order to get them into some sort of shape. As American pragmatist philosophers from William James to Richard Rorty have argued, in practice people regard accounts of reality as true for as long as they seem to work. And these particular old-fashioned concepts apparently do still work, even if we now see that they can always be deconstructed, and even if we usually experience literary texts as surrounded by a suggestive aura of indeterminate connotation. The paradox is that there would be nothing to deconstruct, and there would be no spreading ripples of association, if there were not also something specific, something pre-constructed and for ever reconstructable. As we read, our mind pulses in fluent alternation between deconstructive diastole and reconstructive systole.[51]

By the early 1980s there was already some interest in what readers of Dickens really do when confronted with ideological and linguistic ambiguities of the kind highlighted by structuralist and poststructuralist critics. To some extent this line of inquiry was a natural extension of James M. Brown's work on Dickens's double-edged ideological relationship with his first readers, but it showed, too, the influence of the reception aesthetics of Wolfgang Iser and the affective stylistics of the early Stanley Fish.[52] One of the first extensive studies, clearly influenced by Fish's early work on 'the reader in *Paradise Lost*', was Susan R. Horton's book of 1981, *The Reader in the Dickens World: Style and Response* (London). Horton begins by noting the general impression readers have of Dickens's emphatic tone and solidly deliberate meanings. But the rest of her book is a subtle demonstration of how such certainties can become oddly destabilised. Perhaps in allusion to William Empson's influential *Seven Types of Ambiguity*, Horton distinguishes seven types of doubt that Dickens's readers somehow have to cope with: the plot says one thing but the rhetoric seems to say another; there are repetitions which reassure, but also those which unsettle; there can be a sudden increase of modal qualifiers such as 'perhaps', 'seems', 'appears'; there are sudden shifts in style and world-view; the plots and the omniscient author's rhetoric can tend towards calm reasonableness, while the imagery of description is violently bestial; Dickens's moralising speaks of justice being done where none is seen to be done; and sometimes Dickens himself withdraws out of earshot altogether. Horton offers a wealth of detailed examples from the entire Dickens oeuvre, and her analysis amply proves her main point: that readers, in making any sort of sense out of him, are performing extra-ordinarily complex and energetic operations in the face of rapidly shifting textual challenges.

A marked feature of some work on reader activity is that it regards the concept of character as a kind of pragmatic aid. James A. Davies is certainly not oblivious of the advances of structuralist and poststructuralist literary theory, and significantly speaks of the 'textual life' of characters. His point is not that human beings have the straightforwardly autonomous identity envisaged by liberal humanism, but that readers 'work' on Dickens's texts and use the notion of character heuristically. According to Davies, the character which the text prompts us to shape for Pip the narrator is that of a rather self-satisfied and careful middle-aged business man, which of course is very different from the unwise, rebellious and sometimes generous young man whose story he tells.[53] This is one aspect of the tension between the Imaginary and the Symbolic discussed by Connor, a tension giving rise to considerable difficulties for readers, whose pragmatic processing can therefore include a search for some even more fundamental personality pattern in Pip the narrator. John O. Jordan suggests that readers can feel their way towards four deep-seated needs on Pip's part: a need to express his gratitude to Joe, Biddy and Magwitch; a need to get revenge on Pumblechook, Mrs Joe, Miss Havisham and Magwitch; a need to wrestle with his deathless desire for Estella; and a need to justify himself. According to Jordan, all this means that Pip's language actually tells lies, and that towards the end he is considerably less ironical at his own expense. Instead, readers will now criticise him by comparison with the quiet dignity of Magwitch and the truth of *his* autobiography. Pip's guilt lends some of his descriptions psychic powers of insight, but his less noble motives also make his narration 'stage' things to suit his own argument. For the same reason, particular words, and especially the word 'forge' (associated with both Joe and Compeyson), become highly volatile in their range of meanings, something which readers can again link back to the narrator's character and motives. Like Davies, then, Jordan offers deconstructionist insights into semiotic drift and destabilisation, but is also attuned to the part played by notions of character in the real-time pragmatics of reading.[54]

What also happens is that a pragmatically constructed character can take on such a firm reality for readers that they start to make moral judgements and have feeling about it. This affective dimension of reader activity is explored by James Phelan (in essay 9 below), whose discussion of *Great Expectations* is reminiscent of the so-called Chicago critics of the 1950s, best represented by a famous essay of R. S. Crane's on 'The Plot of *Tom Jones*'. The Chicago critics were particularly concerned with how a novel arouses and structures readers' judgements, hopes and fears, and they saw this as largely a matter of readers responding to the novel's characters as they move through the successive situations arranged by the plot.[55] Phelan injects new life into this school of thought by challenging some of the developments in Freudian and structuralist narratology mentioned in earlier parts of this introduction. His argument is that such approaches make the process of reading a novel sound too abstract and cerebral.

But the pragmatic processing carried out by readers is not just a matter of working out what something means and how to feel about it. Those questions themselves are partly affected by readers' sense of how the text in hand relates to other uses of language elsewhere, including other literary texts. There has always been a branch of Dickens scholarship devoted to tracing literary sources, influences, references and allusions, and the list of parallels recently advanced for *Great Expectations* includes: the grotesque of German romantic novels; the *Bildungsroman* tradition; the picaresque tradition; the European novel of social change; the Gothic novel; the pantomime tradition; Gray's 'Elegy'; several different plays by Shakespeare; *The Faerie Queene*, *Dr Faustus*, *The Pilgrim's Progress*; and Carlyle.[56] But in other recent scholarship, the emphasis shifts from Dickens's borrowings as author to the ability of readers to recognise intertextual relationships as part of their effort to decide what kind of text they are reading. Anny Sadrin (in essay 10 below), for instance, argues that we place *Great Expectations* in the category of romantic irony.[57]

Now Sadrin, like Horton, Davies, Jordan and Phelan, is discussing problems in comprehension which have always confronted, and always will confront, any reader of Dickens's texts. Such an inquiry naturally leads to a consideration of particular lines of interpretation, particular connections, particular ways of filling in gaps, to which readers have always resorted, and always will resort in their efforts to make sense of him. If succeeding generations of readers are to go on perceiving a Dickens text as one and the same text, then there are very many aspects of its processing that will have to remain unchanged with the passing of time. This is the fundamental and perfectly justified assumption of the theories of reading developed by Iser and the early Fish.

It needs to be complemented, however, with another insight. The point is that, over time, new readers are also becoming ignorant of things known to a text's earlier readers, and are for ever bringing to bear their own ways of thought and evaluation. This has been clearly recognised in Fish's own later work on the particularity of reading communities, and in the hermeneutic philosophy of Hans-Georg Gadamer (b. 1900).[58] As Gadamer puts it, interpreters are always rooted in their own particular present, so that interpretation becomes a matter of their trying, as much as possible, to make their own horizon converge with the different horizon of the text they are reading. In Dickens criticism, too, there have long been signs of some such more complex and all-embracing theory of reading. There is an increasing recognition that different readers in different times and places bring different resources and needs to their pragmatic processing of Dickens, and therefore will never actually get exactly the same things out of him. And this is matched by a recognition that if different readers within different present-day cultures are still to read *Dickens*, and not to fabricate meanings entirely of their own, then they need to have some understanding of what Dickens expected his own first readers to bring with them to their reading.

There are already discussions of the intertextuality of *Great Expectations* which clearly accept that certain reading strategies are not universal but specific to particular times, cultures and readers. Harry Stone has documented the fairy tale elements in Dickens, suggesting among other things that early readers would have picked up from the portrayal of Orlick strong hints of the devil as seen in folk mythology. Stone's presupposition in writing his monumental study can only have been that readers today no longer respond to such allusions, so that their world-knowledge needs to be extended in this direction.[59] The same kind of presupposition underlies a very different study by Jerome Meckier. In tracing Dickens's relations with other novelists, Meckier adopts Harold Bloom's theory of the anxiety of influence, according to which writers have a kind of Oedipal envy of their successful predecessors or rivals and want to out-do them. Meckier argues that every Victorian novelist was trying to undermine the credentials of other novelists by copying their style of work and going one better. Dickens himself, because of his pre-eminence, was attacked in this way from all sides, but he gave as good as he got. 'Dickens replied to all of his rivals by redoing *them* as spiritedly as they had re-used his characters and situations to make their own statements and discredit his.'[60] Meckier still sees things very much from the author's end, then. But for his Bloomian vision of literary history to have any credibility, one must accept that Dickens's authorial success depended on his readers' ability to spot which novels and novelists were in competition with which. By the same token Meckier's own scholarship would be unnecessary, if readers today could still be relied on to see intertextual relationships between *Great Expectations* and, say, the mystery novels of Wilkie Collins.

Similar intertextual comparisons of genre are provided by Thomas Loe (in essay 11 below). Part of his conclusion is that in *Great Expectations* three different kinds of novel are interwoven:

the *Bildungsroman,* the novel of manners, and the Gothic mystery
novel. Loe concludes that this last, though sometimes under-
emphasised by literary critics, is really the most important, because
it includes the 'hidden' figure of Compeyson to whom everything in
both the Magwitch and Estella plots can be traced back.[61] Perhaps
it is even the plot which the novel's first readers, and later readers
still unfamiliar with the sophisticated critical tradition, would be
most likely to seize on as the thread to take them through the
novel's labyrinth. In effect, Loe's intertextual scholarship is helping
his own contemporaries 'understand and actively reconstruct [the
novel's] plots and their relative importance, just as life's patterns
must be understood and evaluated in the constant process of
reappraising our own versions of reality'.

The indistinguishability of our reading activities from our every-
day processes of pragmatic contextualisation and understanding
could hardly have been more clearly stated, and as the distance
between Dickens and current readers of Dickens increases, scholars
such as Loe are recognising that the critical task will have to be a
partly informative one, a responsibility which at the same time calls
for great tact. Narrow-minded historical purism is always out of
place in criticism, and the same applies to any other sort of
authoritarian or normative attitude as well. Dickens will continue to
be interesting only for as long as readers feel permitted and
encouraged to read him according to their own lights. On the other
hand, in order for that to be possible, in order to read a Dickens text
at all, we also need to 'read' its first readers and their reading of it.
Rightly and inevitably, our responses to a Dickens novel are typical
of the epoque in which we ourselves live, yet they are actually our
responses to a communal event which happened one and a half
centuries ago. For this reason criticism is steadily entering into a
renewed synergy with historical scholarship, a development which
historians have already to some extent anticipated.

Take, for instance, the type of work pioneered by John Butt and
Kathleen Tillotson in the 1950s.[62] This investigates Dickens's
letters, manuscripts and dealings with his publishers in order to
chart as exactly as possibly each novel's history of composition and
publication.[63] What Jerome J. McGann has done for the poetry of
Blake, Byron and Tennyson,[64] Edgar Rosenberg has now done for
Dickens: he has shown how closely the impact of a text could be
bound up with the bibliographical details of its material
appearance. In the Charles Dickens Edition of *Great Expectations,*

for instance, Dickens deliberately refrained from naming Magwitch, not only in the main body of the text but in the running headlines as well. For the most part Magwitch is simply 'he', and so much the more distanced and mysterious.[65] As for the novel's 'two' endings, Rosenberg's work for a new edition involved him in a thorough consideration of the interpretative pros and cons of both, and he examines other, less well known states of the ending as well, a discussion which immeasurably sharpens our sense of what the novel is and is not.[66] Recently this entire controversy has been set in a new light by Anny Sadrin, who, developing a remark of George Bernard Shaw's, points out that Dickens could well have changed the ending because he suddenly realised that the first one was too like the ending of Charles Lever's *A Day's Ride, a Life's Romance*, the rambling disaster which *Great Expectations* demoted from pride of place in *All the Year Round*. From here Sadrin goes on to make the at first startling, but then obvious suggestion that nobody would have made so much fuss about the ending if Dickens's alteration had not actually come to light. Both endings, in her view, are irrelevant to the book he has actually written: its governing principle is its romantic irony, and this left him unable finally to plump for either bliss or woe. Here Sadrin draws attention to yet another arresting historical fact: when Dickens prepared a text of the novel for his public readings, he left out the Estella plot altogether.[67]

Not much has been written about what happens in the mind of a reader who reads not only Dickens's novels but biographies of Dickens. But clearly there will be some sort of synergy between the two experiences, and it is potentially important. In point of fact biography is the most widely read branch of Dickens scholarship, and roughly speaking there has been one new life of Dickens for every new decade, the main exception being the 1980s and early 1990s, when literary biography in general was booming more than ever. Perhaps the most interesting Dickens biography of this period is Claire Tomalin's *The Invisible Woman: The Story of Nelly Ternan and Charles Dickens*, which belongs to a whole vogue of books on the 'invisible women' of history.[68] These works show how women's studies, by de-centring men, can tell us a lot about women and men alike. When such new knowledge about Dickens is part of what readers bring with them to their reading of a Dickens novel, this must greatly extend their heuristic notion of 'Dickens' and of 'Dickens's themes'. It must mean that they find things 'in the text' which would otherwise simply not have been there for them.

One of the points brought home by Tomalin, for instance, is the day-to-day reality of Dickens's double life. The man who, as a young newspaper reporter, had exploited the latest advances in public transport in order to achieve unprecedented scoops, in late middle age continued to master the timetables of trains and cross-channel ferries, so that he could be constantly in the public eye but constantly with Nelly in secret. The strain on his nerves was almost unbearable, since there was always the fear that the secret life would suddenly become public and ruin him. In 1865 that very nearly happened, when the Folkstone-to-Charing-Cross train on which he was returning from Paris with Nelly and her mother crashed at Staplehurst in Kent. Tomalin herself does not make the connection, but as Dickens ministered to wounded and dying passengers, a demonstration of loving kindness which was to be depicted by an almost hagiolotrous print of him in *The Penny Illustrated Paper*, and as he immediately afterwards whisked Nelly herself away to yet another hiding place, in which to recover from her injuries, he may have remembered Pip. Five years earlier, both the beginning and end of *Great Expectations* had described Pip as saving and covering up for Magwitch with a similar intensity of anxious guilt and hectic energy. That was very much one of the wavelengths on which Dickens himself lived, and Tomalin's biography must be helping thousands of readers tune in to its messages in the novels.

Yet *The Invisible Woman* does not offer a single sentence of literary criticism in the normal twentieth-century senses of that term. Nor is it at all unusual in this respect. True, there have always been scholars in whose work critical concerns and historical or biographical expertise have explicitly converged. This became especially clear in the previous section on sociological critics of *Great Expectations*, and it is this kind of double focus which is once again becoming more common. But many other scholars have tended to maintain a certain division of labour, presenting themselves either as historians or as critics, but not as both at once.

One of the traditional channels for historical and biographical information connected with Dickens has been *The Dickensian: A Magazine for Dickens Lovers*, published by the Dickens Fellowship since 1905. The characteristic aim has been to winkle out all there is to know about the sources of Dickens's novels in his own life, about the 'true' geographical location of his fictional settings, about the real-life 'models' for his characters, and about other socio-cultural minutiae as well. Mrs Joe's pride in having brought up Pip 'by hand' has recently been set against the widespread Victorian belief that dry-nursing deprived the child of nourishment and consolation.[69] Prototypes of Miss Havisham have been discovered in celebrated cases of mental illness in which Dickens took an interest,[70] while her wedding dress has been identified as of a Regency style which resulted in some widely reported cases of accidental death by fire.[71] The mesmeric powers of Jaggers have been linked to Dickens's acquaintance with John Elliotson, one of Mesmerism's pioneers.[72] Magwitch's Thames-side hide-out may have been uncovered.[73] And there has been debate as to whether Pip, as a visitor, could have smuggled in poison to Magwitch behind bars.[74]

By the 1920s this kind of work, with its strong emphasis on the historical contextualisation of Dickens's novels, was already being attacked by formalist literary critics as insufficiently interested in the novels for their own sake, and many later critics have continued to marginalise it as mere amateurism and antiquarianism, often with good reason. The best of it, however, is based on patient scholarship, often by acknowledged authorities in the field, and we are now entering a phase when something of the 'alternative' or semi-popular, historical discourse on Dickens can be unreservedly co-opted as an enrichment to criticism. It is part of the 'cases' of Dickens's novels not only in the sense that this is how many people actually talk about them. Often it also has a perfectly obvious relevance to readers' pragmatic processing. If Dickens's treatment of Miss Havisham was in fact realistic enough to make her 'recognisable' to early readers, this can complement or qualify interpretations which emphasise, say, the elements of Gothic grotesque. Furthermore, now that 'new historical' and 'cultural materialist' critics are extending their Marxist or post-Marxist critique from Shakespeare to other writers, we can expect them to establish new and surprising connections between Dickens and society by using just the kind of miscellaneous socio-cultural detail which has always been *The Dickensian*'s forte.

Both the pragmatic relevance and the ideological significance of such detail are already clearly grasped in a piece on Miss Havisham by Linda Raphael (essay 12 below). Raphael is anything but a historical purist. On the contrary, she roundly declares that the stature of *Great Expectations* consists in its relevance to ages later than the one in which it was written, and that readers today will never interpret it in the same way as Dickens's own contemporaries.[75] Her essay, fully committed to current modes of psychological, sociological and ideological analysis, concludes that the pathos of Miss Havisham lies in her own conception of her fate as a merely personal affair between herself and those who have cheated her, whereas in fact it is typical of a systematic social injustice connected with the passive role of daughters, sisters, spinsters and wives within the Victorian economy, which forced women into the psychological postures of repression and aggressive narcissism. This analysis, reinforced by suggestive intertextual comparisons, draws on the concepts and terminology of a structuralist feminism that was quite unavailable to the Victorians themselves. Yet the title of Raphael's essay signals an interpretative convergence of horizons: 'A Re-vision of Miss Havisham: Her Expectations and Our Responses'. Partly by drawing on the *Dickensian* type of historical minutiae, Raphael explicitly interrelates the present-day structuralist analysis of Victorian society with the intensely personal experience of that same society by a Victorian spinster, or by a reader with a Victorian perception of spinsters. Developing the two historically different viewpoints more or less in tandem, Raphael impugns the integrity of neither, so that her own reader is likely to end up, not only with a better understanding of Dickens, but with a heightened degree of culturally relativistic self-knowledge as well. Neither of these gains would actually be possible without the other.

In this kind of literary criticism, then, the reading of literature is seen as a meeting of minds, or of cultures, which become mutually defining, and the discourse of criticism itself interfaces both with historical scholarship and with the intellectual frameworks and mental processes of present-day readers. Among other things, this last point means that the gap between *Great Expectations* as the international popular classic, and *Great Expectations* as the canonical text pored over by critics and university students is at last beginning to narrow, a tendency which is possibly connected with increased access to higher education. To speak of a difference between 'ordinary' and 'educated' readers of literature has always been somewhat problematic, but nowadays it is more difficult than ever, since so many of the people who still read literature actually are 'educated', often by university literature departments. On the one hand there is now a far greater number of readers likely to think about Dickens in a 'serious' way. On the other hand scholars and critics now have to make themselves intelligible to a larger audience, and this at a time when critical thought is in any case beginning to be concerned with what the readers of literature actually do with it.

Given these far-reaching changes, any prediction about the future course of Dickens studies must be taken with a pinch of salt. But a perennial possibility in intellectual history is that scholars will begin to rethink some of the ideas that have been fruitful in the past. We have already seen how this is happening with 'character' and 'author', and Linda Raphael's essay sets up a particularly rich dialogue between Victorian and late-twentieth-century frames of reference. Another issue which could well re-emerge is the question of Dickens's humour, which in the case of *Great Expectations* has seldom received satisfactory treatment. If Dickens's own description of his new novel as 'exceedingly droll' was a strategic half-truth, then much twentieth-century academic criticism, with notable exceptions such as Anny Sadrin's discussion of the romantic irony, has been the equal and opposite half-truth. Assuming, if we may, that we do still have a sense of humour, there are many questions to be asked. Is it a matter of our 'individual personality', to the extent that we still believe in such a thing, or is humour quite inconceivable except as a communal phenomenon? In so far as it *is* communal, how and why does humour nowadays converge with, and diverge from, Victorian humour? How do readers negotiate humour which they feel is not like their own? How, as an entertainer, does Dickens compete with rival attractions in our culture? Which serves to raise the more fundamental question: What, as a matter of fact, *is* Dickens's social role at present?

NOTES

1. The first two paragraphs are based on John Forster, *The Life of Charles Dickens* (London, 1872–74), Book Ninth, ch. 3.

2. Ibid.

3. This is the assessment of Mowbray Morris, 'Charles Dickens', *Fortnightly Review*, 32 (1882), 762–99. Another suggestive piece of evidence is that *Great Expectations* is listed as a 'minor work' in James Cook, *Bibliography of the Writings of Charles Dickens and Many Curious and Interesting Particulars Relating to His Works* (London, 1879), p. 26.

4. [Edwin Whipple], Review of *Great Expectations*, *Atlantic Monthly*, 8 (1861), 380–2.

5. [? Meredith Townsend], Review of *Great Expectations*, *Spectator*, 34 (1861), 785–6.

6. For the distinction between a classic text and a canonical text see Joel Weinsheimer, *Philosophical Hermeneutics and Literary Theory* (New Haven, 1991), pp. 124–57.

7. Algernon Charles Swinburne, 'Charles Dickens', *Quarterly Review*, 196 (1902), 20–39; Andrew Lang, 'Charles Dickens', *Fortnightly Review*, 64 (1898), 944–60; George Gissing, *Charles Dickens: A Critical Study* (rev. edn London, 1903).

8. Thomas E. Connolly, 'Technique in *Great Expectations*', *Philological Quarterly*, 34 (1955), 48–55; John Hagan, 'Structural Patterns in Dickens's *Great Expectations*', *Journal of English Literary History (ELH)*, 21 (1954), 54–66; Joseph A. Kestner, *The Spatiality of the Novel* (Detroit, 1978), pp. 116–21.

9. Rowland McMaster, introduction to Macmillan College Classics edition of *Great Expectations* (Toronto, 1965), repr. in Rowland and Juliet McMaster (eds), *The Novel from Sterne to James: Essays in the Relation of Literature to Life* (London, 1981), pp. 71–87; J. Hillis Miller, *Charles Dickens: the World of his Novels* (Cambridge, Mass., 1958), pp. 249–78; Robert Barnard, 'Imagery and Theme in *Great Expectations*', *Dickens Studies Annual*, 1 (1970), 238–51; William F. Axton, '*Great Expectations* Yet Again', *Dickens Studies Annual*, 2 (1972), 279–93, 373–4; Barbara Hardy, *The Moral Art of Dickens* (London, 1970), pp. 139–55, and Sarah Gilead, 'Barmecide Feasts: Ritual, Narrative, and the Victorian Novel', *Dickens Studies Annual*, 17 (1988), 225–47, esp. 233–8; Elliot L. Gilbert, '"In Primal Sympathy": *Great Expectations* and the Secret Life', *Dickens Studies Annual*, 11 (1983), 89–113; David Gervais, 'The Prose and Poetry of *Great Expectations*', *Dickens Studies Annual*, 13 (1984), 85–114.

10. John Forster, *The Life of Charles Dickens* (London, 1872–74), Book Ninth, ch.3.

11. Published for the Limited Editions Club [of New York] by R. and R. Clark, Edinburgh.

12. G. H. Lewes, 'Dickens in Relation to Criticism', *Fortnightly Review*, 17 (1872), esp. 143–51.

13. In Edmund Wilson, *The Wound and The Bow* (Boston, 1941), pp. 1–104.

14. *Studies in English Literature, 1500–1900*, 19 (1979), 689–704.

15. Dorothy Van Ghent, 'The Dickens World: A View from Todgers's, *Sewanee Review*, 58 (1950), 419–38. Incorporated into her *The English Novel: Form and Function* (New York, 1953), pp. 125–38.

See also Roger D. Sell, 'Projection Characters in *David Copperfield*', *Studia Neophilologica*, 55 (1983), 19–30.

16. Julian Moynaham, 'The Hero's Guilt; the Case of *Great Expectations*', *Essays in Criticism*, 10 (1960), 60–79. Of the many subsequent accounts influenced, not always explicitly, by Moynaham a recent one is Brian Cheadle, 'Sentiment and Resentment in *Great Expectations*', *Dickens Studies Annual*, 20 (1991), 149–74.

17. A. L. French's essay (essay 1 in the present volume), 'Beating and Cringing: *Great Expectations*', was first published in *Essays in Criticism* 24 (1974), 147–60.

18. Lucy Frost's essay (essay 2 in the present volume), 'Taming to Improve: Dickens and the Women in *Great Expectations*', was first published in *Meridian*, 1 (1982), 11–20.

19. See, for example, Michal Peled Ginsburg, 'Dickens and the Uncanny: Repression and Displacement in *Great Expectations*', *Dickens Studies Annual*, 13 (1984), 115–24.

20. See Albert Hutter, 'Crime and Fantasy in *Great Expectations*', in Frederick Crews (ed.), *Psychoanalysis and the Literary Process* (Cambridge, Mass., 1970), pp. 25–65.

21. Curt Hartog, 'The Rape of Miss Havisham', *Studies in the Novel*, 14 (1982), 248–65.

22. Hutter. See note 20 above.

23. Ian Watt, 'Oral Dickens', *Dickens Studies Annual*, 3 (1974), 165–81, 240–2.

24. Jack Rawlins's essay (essay 3 in the present volume), 'Great Expiations: Dickens and the Betrayal of the Child', was first published in *Studies in English Literature, 1500–1900*, 23 (1983), 667–83.

25. Anny Sadrin, *Great Expectations* (London, 1988), pp. 118–38. An extract from Sadrin's book – though not from this part – is reprinted as essay 10 in the present volume.

26. Peter Brook's account was first published as an article entitled 'Repetition, Repression, and Return: *Great Expectations* and the Study of Plot' in *New Literary History*, 11 (1980), 503–26. In the present volume it appears (as essay 4) in a somewhat shortened form. It is reprinted in full as a chapter in Brooks's *Reading for the Plot: Design and Intention in Narrative* (Oxford, 1984; second edn Cambridge, Mass., 1992).

27. See Edgar Johnson, *Charles Dickens: His Tragedy and Triumph* (London, 1953), p. 859.

28. For instance, there has been discussion of the sexual relationship – or lack of one – between Dombey and his second wife. See Alan

Horsman's introduction to the World's Classics edition of *Dombey and Son* (Oxford, 1982), esp. p. x, and Roger D. Sell, 'Dickens and the New Historicism: the Polyvocal Audience and Discourse of *Dombey and Son*', in Jeremy Hawthorn (ed.), *The Nineteenth-Century British Novel* (London, 1986), pp. 62–79, esp. p. 72.

29. Beth F. Herst, *The Dickens Hero: Selfhood and Alienation in the Dickens World* (London, 1990).

30. John Carey, *The Violent Effigy: a Study of Dickens's Imagination* (London, 1973), p. 14.

31. Humphrey House, 'G.B.S. on *Great Expectations*', *Dickensian*, 44 (1948), 63–70 and 183–86; George Orwell, 'Charles Dickens', in his *Inside the Whale* (London, 1940), pp. 9–85.

32. Lionel Trilling, 'Manners, Morals, and the Novel', in his *The Liberal Imagination* (New York, 1950), pp. 205–22.

33. Robin Gilmour, *The Idea of the Gentleman in the Victorian Novel* (London, 1981), pp. 104–48. (Essay 5 in the present volume is made up of extracts from these pages.)

34. John Lucas, *Charles Dickens: the Major Novels* (London, 1992), p. 131. Lucas discusses the double-edged Cockney idyll in his earlier study as well: *The Melancholy Man: A Study of Dickens's Novels* (London, 1970), pp. 312–13.

35. F. S. Schwarzback, *Dickens and the City* (London, 1979).

36. Murray Baumgarten, 'Calligraphy and Code: Writing in *Great Expectations*', *Dickens Studies Annual*, 11 (1983), 61–72.

37. James M. Brown, *Dickens: Novelist in the Market-Place: A Sociological Reading* (London, 1982). For other accounts of Dickens's relationship with his audience see: George H. Ford, *Dickens and his Readers: Aspects of Novel Criticism since 1836* (Princeton, 1955); Philip Collins, 'The Popularity of Dickens', *Dickensian*, 70 (1974), 5–20; J. D. Jump, 'Dickens and his Readers', *Bulletin of the John Rylands Library* 54 (1971–2), 384–97. For the possibility that Dickens needed his audience almost like a drug or a mistress, see the account of his public readings in David Ponting, 'Charles Dickens: The Solo Performer', in Robert Giddings (ed.), *The Changing World of Charles Dickens* (London, 1983), pp. 109–34.

38. Q. D. Leavis, 'How we must read *Great Expectations*', in Q. D. and F. R. Leavis, *Dickens the Novelist* (London, 1970), pp. 277–331.

39. E.g. John Lucas, *Charles Dickens: the Major Novels* (London, 1992), p. 136, and *The Melancholy Man: A Study of Dickens's Novels* (London, 1970), p. 304.

40. A. J. Greimas, *Sémantique structurale* (Paris, 1966), p. 173.

41. Anny Sadrin, *Great Expectations* (London, 1988), pp. 146–60. (Essay 10 in the present volume is an extract from this.)

42. Jeremy Tambling's essay (essay 6 in the present volume) was first published in *Essays in Criticism*, 36 (1986), 11–31.

43. Pam Morris, *Dickens's Class Consciousness: A Marginal View* (London, 1991), esp. pp. 103–19.

44. David Trotter, *Circulation: Defoe, Dickens, and the Economies of the Novel* (London, 1988), esp. 124–36.

45. Philip W. Martin, *Mad Women in Romantic Writing* (Brighton, 1987), pp. 113–22. Cf. Katharine M. Rogers, *The Troublesome Helpmate: A History of Misogyny in Literature* (Seattle, 1966), pp. 195, 201; Richard Brickman, Susan MacDonald and Myra Stark, *Corrupt Relations: Dickens, Thackeray, Trollope, Collins and the Victorian Sexual System* (New York, 1982), pp. 59–110, esp. 68–75.

46. E.g. in 'Discourse in the Novel', in M. M. Bakhtin, *The Dialogic Imagination: Four Essays* (Austin, 1981), pp. 259–422, esp. 301–8.

47. Eiichi Hara's essay (essay 7 in the present volume), 'Stories Present and Absent in *Great Expectations*', was first published in *ELH*, 53 (1986), 593–614.

48. Christopher Morris, 'The Bad Faith of Pip's Bad Faith: Deconstructing *Great Expectations*', *ELH*, 54 (1987), 941–55.

49. Steven Connor, *Charles Dickens* (Oxford, 1985), esp. pp. 109–44. (Essay 8 in the present volume is an extract from this.)

50. Stein Haugom Olsen, *The End of Literary Theory* (Cambridge, 1987).

51. For further discussion of the relevance of pragmatics to the writing, reading and teaching of literary texts, see Roger D. Sell, 'Teaching Shakespeare on Literary Pragmatic Principles', in Per Serritslev Petersen (ed.), *Literary Pedagogics After Deconstruction: Scenarios and Perspectives in the Teaching of English Literature* (Aarhus, 1992), pp. 7–27; 'Literary Gossip, Literary Theory, Literary Pragmatics', in Roger D. Sell and Peter Verdonk (eds), *Literature and the New Interdisciplinarity: Poetics, Linguistics, History* (Amsterdam, 1994); and 'The Difficult Style of *The Waste Land*: a Literary Pragmatic Perspective on Modernist Poetry', in Peter Verdonk (ed.), *Twentieth-Century Poetry: From Text to Context* (London, 1993), pp. 134–58.

52. See Stanley Fish, *Surprised by Sin: the Reader in Paradise Lost* (New York: Macmillan, 1967); and Wolfgang Iser, *The Implied Reader: Patterns of Communication in Prose Fiction from Bunyan to Beckett* (Baltimore: Johns Hopkins University Press, 1954).

53. James A. Davies, *The Textual Life of Dickens's Characters* (London, 1989), esp. pp. 94–102.

54. John O. Jordan, 'The Medium of *Great Expectations*', *Dickens Studies Annual*, 11 (1983), 73–88.

55. James Phelan, 'Reading for the Character and Reading for the Progression: John Wemmick and *Great Expectations*', was first published in *Journal of Narrative Technique*, 19 (1989), 70–84. (Essay 9 in the present volume is an extract from this.) The affective poetics of the Chicago critics is represented by R. S. Crane (ed.), *Critics and Criticism: Ancient and Modern* (Chicago, 1952), which includes Crane's essay on *Tom Jones*.

56. E.g. respectively: Michael Hollington, *Dickens and the Grotesque* (London, 1984); Jerome H. Buckley, *Season of Youth: The Bildungsroman from Dickens to Golding* (Cambridge, Mass., 1974), esp. pp. 28–62; Lars Hartveit, *Workings of the Picaresque in the British Novel* (Oslo, 1987), esp. pp. 104–29; Lawrence Lerner, 'Literature and Social Change', *Journal of European Studies*, 7 (1977), 231–52; *Ghosts of the Gothic; Austen, Eliot, & Lawrence* (Princeton, 1980), esp. pp. 99–120; Edwin M. Eigner, 'The Absent Clown in *Great Expectations*', *Dickens Studies Annual*, 11 (1983), 11–33; Iain Crawford, '"Large was his bounty, and his soul sincere" – Gray's *Elegy*, Theme, and Intertextuality in *Great Expectations*', *Dickens Quarterly*, 4 (1987), 195–9; William A. Wilson, 'The Magic Circle of Genius: Dickens's Translations of Shakespearian Drama in *Great Expectations*', *Nineteenth-Century Fiction*, 40 (1985), 154–74; Susan Schoenbauer Thurin, 'The Seven Deadly Sins in *Great Expectations*', *Dickens Studies Annual*, 15 (1986), 201–20; Naomi Lightman, 'The Vulcanic Dialect of *Great Expectations*', *Dickensian*, 82 (1986), 33–8.

57. See note 41 above.

58. Stanley Fish's later work on reading communities is represented by his *Is There a Reader in This Class? The Authority of Reading Communities* (Cambridge, Mass., 1980). A helpful introduction to Gadamer is Georgia Warnke, *Gadamer: Hermeneutics, Tradition and Reason* (Cambridge, 1987). For the relevance of Gadamer to literary study, see Joel Weinsheimer, *Philosophical Hermeneutics and Literary Theory* (New Haven, 1991), and Roger D. Sell, 'Simulative Panhumanism: A Challenge to Current Linguistic and Literary Thought', *Modern Language Review*, 88 (1993), 545–58.

59. Harry Stone, *Dickens and the Invisible World: Fairy Tales, Fantasy and Novel-Making* (Bloomington, 1979), esp. 298–339.

60. Jerome Meckier, *Hidden Rivalries in Victorian Fiction: Dickens, Realism, and Revaluation* (Lexington, 1987), esp. pp. 122–52. Cf. Harold Bloom, *The Anxiety of Influence: A Theory of Poetry* (New York, 1973).

61. Thomas Loe's essay (essay 11 in the present volume), 'Gothic Plot in *Great Expectations*', first appeared in *Dickens Quarterly*, 6 (1989), 102–10.

62. John Butt and Kathleen Tillotson, *Dickens at Work* (London, 1957).

63. This kind of work has been facilitated by the Pilgrim Edition of Dickens's Letters, edited by Madeline House, Graham Storey and Kathleen Tillotson (Oxford, 1965–   ), and by Harry Stone (ed.), *Dickens's Working Notes for his Novels* (Chicago, 1987).

64. Jerome J. McGann, *The Beauty of Inflections: Literary Investigations in Historical Method and Theory* (Oxford, 1985).

65. Edgar Rosenburg, 'A Preface to *Great Expectations*: The Pale Usher Dusts his Lexicons', *Dickens Studies Annual*, 2 (1972), 294–335, 374–8.

66. Edgar Rosenburg, 'Last Words on *Great Expectations*: A Textual Brief on the Six Endings', *Dickens Studies Annual*, 9 (1981), 87–115.

67. Anny Sadrin, *Great Expectations* (London, 1988), pp. 28, 169, 172–5.

68. Claire Tomalin, *The Invisible Woman: The Story of Nelly Ternan and Charles Dickens* (New York, 1990; paperback, London, 1991).

69. Virginia Phillips, '"Brought up by Hand": Dickens's Pip, Little Paul Dombey, and Oliver Twist', *Dickensian*, 74 (1978), 144–7; Susan Schoenbauer Thurin, 'To Be Brought up "By Hand"', *Victorian Newsletter*, 64 (1983), 27–9.

70. Susan Shatto, 'Miss Havisham and Mr Mopes the Hermit: Dickens and the Mentally Ill', *Dickens Quarterly*, 2 (1985), 43–50 and 79–84. See also Anny Sadrin, *Great Expectations* (London, 1988), pp. 215–41.

71. Richard Witt, 'The Death of Miss Havisham', *Dickensian*, 80 (1989), 151–6.

72. Fred Kaplan, *Dickens and Mesmerism: the Hidden Springs of Fiction* (Princeton, 1975), esp. pp. 133–4, 156–8.

73. Gwen Major, 'The Magwitch Hide-out', *Dickensian*, 67 (1971), 31–4.

74. Robert A. Stein, 'Pip's Poisoning Magwitch, Supposedly: The Historical Context and its Implications for Pip's Guilt and Shame', *Philogical Quarterly*, 67 (1988), 103–16.

75. Linda Raphael's essay (essay 12 in the present volume) was first printed in *Studies in the Novel*, 21 (1989), 400–12.

1

Beating and Cringing:
Great Expectations

A. L. FRENCH

Everyone remembers Mr Wopsle's performance of *Hamlet* in chapter 31 of *Great Expectations*: it is the funniest thing in a book not otherwise much distinguished by humour, and it joyfully undermines Pip by suggesting, long before Magwitch's return, that the Expectations which have – or ought to have – disappointed Mr Wopsle by the way in which they have been realised may eventually turn out, in Pip's case, to be just as untrustworthy. I don't want to suggest that, in picking *Hamlet* for Mr Wopsle to be dreadful in, Dickens was consciously interested in how he might use a play some of whose concerns are relevant to his novel: indeed, I'm inclined to think that it was precisely his unconsciousness of the possible connections between the two that enabled him to leave them inexplicit – to use them without inflating or underlining them.

Hamlet is (among many other things) about the way in which the past influences the present: Hamlet can no more free himself from what his ghostly father wants him to do and be than Claudius can help having been the late King's unrespected brother, than Polonius and Laertes can help being Claudius' instruments, or Ophelia her father's. One question put by the play is: How can Hamlet help being what his father, or his stepfather, or his aunt-mother, want him to be? How can he 'be' – be himself? Now, the story of *Great Expectations* largely turns on the same sort of issue; and it's no accident, I think, that when Magwitch comes back (ch. 39) he, like the Ghost in *Hamlet*, comes in the dark and is heralded, not by a 'bell ... beating' the hour but by the church clocks of London striking it. Pip has the same kind of difficulty as Hamlet in deciding *what* his visitor is; when he has finally found out he comments 'I doubt if a ghost could have been more terrible to me ...' (ch. 40). On Herbert's return, later in the same chapter, Magwitch makes him *swear*, on a 'greasy little clasped black Testament', not to reveal anything – 'Now you're on your oath, you know'. What is more, Magwitch, like the Ghost, reveals to Pip something crucial but hitherto unknown about the past, and lays on him an obligation as to the future (just as, on his first appearance, right at the beginning of the book, he had terrified the little Pip into stealing, as a kind of duty). Pip in fact finds that he has become what he is largely because of Magwitch's desires; and the rest of his life, including his leaving England to make his own way in Herbert's business (financed by Miss Havisham's money as well as by Magwitch's), follows inevitably from the mere fact of his benefactor's return from 'the darkness beneath' (ch. 39).

The *Hamlet* parallels offer no more than a way into thinking about the recurrent human situations that Dickens is interested in. *Great Expectations* is, for instance, full of situations in which parents, or their substitutes, dominate and indeed determine their children – not merely what the children do but also what they are. Pip himself is exposed to four such influences: Joe, Mrs Joe, Miss Havisham and Magwitch – all of them being pretty unsatisfactory. Herbert Pocket perhaps owes his decency to his having been allowed to 'tumble up' instead of having been 'brought up by hand'; Clara, his fiancée, is waiting, quite openly, for her detestably domineering father to die. And if Pip, when Magwitch comes back, feels like a Frankenstein in reverse – pursued by the creature who has made him – Miss Havisham, before she is burnt to death, realises she has created a monster, Estella, feels 'pity and remorse' (ch. 44), and begs Pip's forgiveness (ch. 49). Estella, like Pip, is the victim, or beneficiary, of another's wishes; although in her case there seems little prospect of her being able to free herself from Miss Havisham's influence. About the only normal relationship between a parent and child in the novel is that between Wemmick and the Aged P.: but that exists only behind a raised drawbridge and, besides, the Aged P., being stone deaf, can't really communicate with his son, nor his son with him. The tone of the novel when Walworth sentiments are in question is indulgent, not cynical, but the implication – which Dickens chose not to follow up – is that affection may even depend on *not* communicating. Nor does the novel explore the real problems of having an aged parent, at least in reference to Wemmick, though Old Bill Barley (Clara's rum-and-pepper father) starts some uncomfortable reflections which Dickens couldn't perhaps afford to pursue (ch. 46).

We see the foundations of Pip's nature being laid early in the book: the experience with Magwitch in the churchyard merely plays in an even harsher key the tune he is used to at home, from Mrs Joe, Pumblechook, and the Hubbles: his life is largely a matter of being threatened, bullied, knocked around, and made to feel ashamed of eating and being alive. Pip himself gives this account of the effect on him of his upbringing:

> My sister's bringing up had made me sensitive. In the little world in which children have their existence whosoever brings them up, there is nothing so finely perceived and so finely felt, as injustice.... Within myself, I had sustained, from my babyhood, a perpetual conflict with injustice. I had known, from the time when I could speak, that my sister, in her capricious and violent coercion, was unjust to me. I had cherished a profound conviction that her bringing me up by hand, gave her no right to bring me up by jerks. Through all my punishments, disgraces, fasts and vigils, and other penitential performances, I had nursed this assurance; and to my communing so much with it, in a solitary and unprotected way, I in great part refer the fact that I was morally timid and very sensitive.   (ch. 8)

Of course, being 'morally timid and very sensitive' is not the only possible reaction to injustice; Pip, if he had been born with a different temperament, could have responded in Magwitch's way to the injustice he met: by becoming 'hardened', getting his own back (ch. 42). But Pip takes the way of submission, shrinking from or flowing round difficulty and violence rather than fronting up to it. That in itself doesn't call for criticism, given that there is no proper way to deal with such a situation; whatever we do with Pip, we are not (usually) meant to use him as an occasion for feeling moral superiority. But perhaps our sympathy with his timidity and sensitivity is put in a slightly different light when we have taken, in the previous chapter, the kind of unaware self-justification that Joe offers him as an explanation of why he doesn't protect him against Mrs Joe. The whole episode is intensely interesting, but for my present purposes I shall only look at the central passage. Having made Pip feel deeply grateful for having been taken in ('I said to your sister, "there's room for *him* at the forge!"'), Joe goes on to explain why Pip must teach him to read and write 'on the sly': because Mrs Joe is 'given to government' – she domineers and won't have Joe being a 'rebel'; she is a 'master-mind'. All this seems to suggest that Joe feels his subservience to his wife is not only inevitable, but right: as though a slave should defend his not rebelling on the grounds that his master is wiser. One's sense that these thoughts are questionable becomes stronger when Joe goes on to connect his marriage with his parents':

> I see so much in my poor mother, of a woman drudging and slaving and breaking her honest hart and never getting no peace in her mortal days, that I'm dead afeerd of going wrong in the way of not doing what's right by a woman, and I'd fur rather of the two go wrong the t'other way, and be a little ill-conwenienced myself. I wish it was only me that got put out, Pip; I wish there warn't no Tickler for you, old chap; I wish I could take it all on myself; but this is the up-and-down-and-straight on it, Pip, and I hope you'll overlook shortcomings.   (ch. 7)

The suggestion seems to be that he doesn't want to put Mrs Joe in the position of his mother (his father, we have heard, was a drunk who stopped Joe from going to school and 'hammered' him and his mother), so that the only course of action for Joe is to let her have her way. But obviously, what he is doing is reliving his parents' marriage in his own, except that now it is the man who never gets no peace and the woman who does the hammering: the sexes are reversed but the relationship is the same. And if Joe can believe, nevertheless, that 'my father were that good in his hart', he can also believe – and get Pip to agree – that his wife is 'a fine figure of a woman', a 'master-mind', and so on. Pip's reaction to this self-justification of Joe's is significant: 'Young as I was, I believe that I dated a new admiration of Joe from that night. ... I had a new sensation of feeling conscious that I was looking up to Joe in my heart.' The older Pip, who is narrating the story, not only renders but apparently also approves this 'new sensation'; at least, I see no sign that he is dubious about it or about Joe. And while Pip, in chapter 8, sees clearly enough that his sister's regime is a matter of 'injustice', he has got from Joe a powerful confirmation of his own tendency to deal with it by not dealing with it and by feeling 'admiration' for the inner voice (as it becomes) which rationalises inaction into a higher courage than action. The only time before

Magwitch's return when Pip squares up to things is in the boxing-match with the pale young gentleman; but he can't avoid that and it is, in any case, purely comic.

Pip's sensibility is thus fixed in early life: he is a kisser of rods. And when we ponder what Joe could have seen in Mrs Joe, to make him want to marry her (loneliness is the explanation he gives, unconvincingly), we might then make a further link: if there's something in Joe that enjoys being dominated, there is no less something in Pip which feels drawn to Estella for the very reason that she ill-treats him. No doubt it's true enough to say, as Mrs Leavis does,[1] that when he first meets her he adores her purely for what she represents; but to go on and claim that he never loves her for what she is, since she is 'unlovable and unloving', and that the whole relationship is clearly seen by Dickens to be merely unrealistic, is to overlook, or at any rate to slight, an important vein of feeling that runs through the whole book. Once Pip has come into his Expectations, after all, Estella can hardly go on representing for him the glamour of wealth, education and social status that he hasn't yet got. In fact, after he has gone up in the world there still remain two painfully conflicting feelings about her, which lead Pip to say rather different things at different times. On his first visit to his home town after removing to London (ch. 29), the clashing emotions come out in the form of a contradiction. First, near the start of the chapter, we have this:

> though [Estella] had taken such strong possession of me, though my fancy and my hope were so set upon her, though her influence on my boyish life and character had been all-powerful, I did not, even that romantic morning, invest her with any attributes save those she possessed. I mention this in this place, of a fixed purpose, because it is the clue by which I am to be followed into my poor labyrinth. According to my experience, the conventional notion of a lover cannot be always true. The unqualified truth is, that when I loved Estella with the love of a man, I loved her simply because I found her irresistible. Once for all; I knew to my sorrow, often and often, if not always, that I loved her against reason, against promise, against peace, against hope, against happiness, against all discouragement that could be. Once for all; I loved her none the less because I knew it, and it had no more influence in restraining me, than if I had devoutly believed her to be human perfection.

This feeling is the hardest thing in the novel for the modern reader to take, because it looks embarrassingly Victorian; and so we tend to whisk it out of sight by calling it 'sentimental' or 'unrealistic', with the implication that Dickens sees it so, as part of his 'keen exposure of Pip's case'.[2] Yet, since Dickens is a nineteenth-century novelist, it would scarcely be surprising if he believed as whole-heartedly as Pip does in the value, or at least the interestingness, of a passion whose distinguishing mark is that it is unreciprocated and wholly unsatisfying (in the normal sense of 'satisfying'). The situation is so common in Victorian fiction as to be conventional; and if the paragraph just quoted stood alone, we would be justified in accusing Dickens of having allowed a cliché to do his novelist's work for him. That his intentions in this book were serious and intelligent is shown, I think, by the fact that the slack rhetoric of this paragraph ('often and often …') is countered by what we find a little later in the same chapter, where we get a very different account of Estella's irresistibility:

> Proud and wilful as of old, she had brought those qualities into such subjection to her beauty that it was impossible and out of nature – or I thought so – to separate them from her beauty. Truly it was impossible to dissociate her presence from all those wretched hankerings after money and gentility that had disturbed my boyhood – from all those ill-regulated aspirations that had first made me ashamed of home and Joe – from all those visions that had raised her face in the glowing fire, struck it out of the iron on the anvil, extracted it from the darkness of night to look in at the wooden window of the forge and flit away. In a word, it was impossible for me to separate her, in the past or in the present, from the innermost life of my life.

The partial contradiction between the implication, here, that he loves Estella because he can't escape from his childhood impressions, and the implication, in the passage quoted earlier, that he loves her for her own sake and not for what she represented, certainly testifies that Pip very much wants to believe himself free from early influences. Yet, as soon as he enters Miss Havisham's unearthly domain, those influences reassert themselves potently: 'I fancied, as I looked at her, that I slipped hopelessly back into the coarse and common boy again.' That is, the relationship remains arrested in the form it first took, when they were both children; and while, in the earlier passage, Pip avows that he didn't invest her 'with any attributes save those she possessed', and that he has come 'to love Estella with the love of a man' (normal sexual love), he very quickly grasps, if not altogether consciously, that he can't break the fixed pattern and that 'the love of a man' merely means superadding sexual love to his other feelings of abject dependence. Dickens clearly relates Pip's feelings for Estella's 'irresistibility' to his early impressions and to his consequent tendency to enjoy being hurt – to find his emotional satisfactions in casting other people as Mrs Joe or the Convict or Pumblechook. It's not merely that he loves Estella although she isn't 'human perfection' or anything like it; he loves her precisely because she is more like the reverse and, as she frankly implies herself, is, in her lack of normal affections, scarcely human at all. The kind of 'love' Pip would inevitably experience is exactly the sort of love he is virtually ordered to feel by Miss Havisham, later in the same chapter:

> 'I'll tell you', said she, in the same hurried passionate whisper, 'what real love is. It is blind devotion, unquestioning self-humiliation, utter submission, trust and belief against yourself and against the whole world giving up your whole heart and soul to the smiter – as I did!'

It is clear that Miss Havisham, having brought Estella up to take revenge on men, is casting Pip in the role of victim, confirming him in the part he has always played; the sort of relationship she wants him to have with Estella is analogous to that between a very small child and a brutal parent. (I presume there is always some kind of infantilism in such self-abasement: Dickens has the insight but not the vocabulary.) And Miss Havisham is pushing – or leading – Pip into this position with something of the authority of a parent as well as a supposed patron.

When that night Pip goes back to the Blue Boar, he lies awake and gives a characteristic emphasis to Miss Havisham's words:

> Far into the night, Miss Havisham's words, 'Love her, love her, love her!' sounded in my ears. I adapted them for my own repetition, and said to my pillow, 'I love her, I love her, I love her!' hundreds of times. Then, a burst of gratitude came upon me, that she should be destined for me, once the blacksmith's boy. Then, I thought if she were, as I feared, by no means rapturously grateful for that destiny yet, when would she begin to be interested in me? When should I awaken the heart within her, that was mute and sleeping now?

What 'love' means to Pip, we have already seen; he is now himself rapturously acquiescing in his destiny of being an innocent Lycius to a Lamia or a 'wretched wight' to Estella's Belle Dame sans Merci.

'Adapting' Miss Havisham's words means he accepts that role while refusing absolutely to see that Estella's being 'by no means rapturously grateful for that destiny' is an intended and inevitable corollary of it; 'yet' contrives to insinuate that, at some time, Estella will be grateful and will be able to return his love in, presumably, the normal adult way – a thought brought out further by Pip's reference to 'awakening' her heart. But Estella herself has warned him, only a few pages before: 'I have no heart.' (At the end of the book we meet an Estella whose heart has apparently been battered into sensibility by Bentley Drummle; there is a parallel with Mrs Joe's being battered into submissive idiocy – a second childhood – by Orlick, whom she then tries, like a frightened child, to propitiate.)

The run-out of the chapter goes as follows:

> Ah me! I thought those were high and great emotions. But I never thought there was anything low and small in my keeping away from Joe, because I knew she would be contemptuous of him. It was but a day gone, and Joe had brought the tears into my eyes; they had soon dried, God forgive me! soon dried.

The rival claims of the two parent substitutes – Joe and Miss Havisham (her claim being made through Estella) – could hardly be more sharply put. Yet one may be dissatisfied by the suggestion that these emotions were *not* 'high and great': it isn't clear how far Pip the narrator is simply dismissing what he felt for Estella and how far he wants to say that, though the feelings were not as grand as he thought, they were nevertheless real and significant. Yet if the reader is dissatisfied, that may perhaps be because the Pip who is writing the novel can't be altogether clear what significance to attach to his earlier life.

The remainder of Pip's relationship with Estella follows the groundwork already laid down; it would be surprising if there were any real growth on either side, though both come to understand better why they are what they are. The whole of chapter 38 is intensely interesting, as showing a further realisation on the part of Pip and Miss Havisham just what Estella is – though to Pip's feelings this can make no difference. Indeed, near the start of the chapter he says:

> I suffered every kind and degree of torture that Estella could cause me. The nature of my relations with her, which placed me on terms

of familiarity without placing me on terms of favour, conduced to my distraction. She made use of me to tease other admirers, and she turned the very familiarity between herself and me, to the account of putting a constant slight on my devotion to her. If I had been her secretary, steward, half-brother, poor relation – if I had been a younger brother of her appointed husband – I could not have seemed to myself, further from my hopes when I was nearest to her.

It makes no difference precisely because, to Pip, love *is* 'every kind and degree of torture', and the conditional sentence concedes that, in essence, he is still a 'poor relation' emotionally and morally, though factually he is nothing of the kind. The suggestion about being her 'half-brother' or prospective brother-in-law testifies, at one level, to the as yet unrevealed fact that both Pip and Estella are creatures of Magwitch's; but it also suggests Pip's sense of something perverse in the relationship. His realisation of the perversity comes out more sharply a moment later: 'I never had one hour's happiness in her society, and yet my mind all round the four-and-twenty hours was harping on the happiness of having her with me unto death.' The analogy between Pip's feelings and Miss Havisham's emerges a little further on: when they arrive at Satis House, Miss Havisham

> was even more dreadfully fond of Estella than she had been when I last saw them together; I repeat the word advisedly, for there was something positively dreadful in the energy of her looks and embraces. She hung upon Estella's beauty, hung upon her words, hung upon her gestures, and sat mumbling her own trembling fingers while she looked at her, as though she were devouring the beautiful creature she had reared.

Every detail here (apart from the mumbled fingers) is strictly applicable to Pip's feelings; Pip's fondness, too, is likewise 'dreadful' in its monomaniac intensity, and his passion is also a devouring one (though, deprived of its object, it devours *him*). And while he hasn't 'reared' Estella, he has certainly been rearing – in effect creating – the image of her he adores.

It is fitting, then, that the rest of the chapter pursues the analogy, with a tact which should dispose at once of the notion of Dickens which sees him as having no interest in the inner life. Miss Havisham dwells on Estella's conquests with 'the intensity of a mind mortally hurt and diseased'; and in the spectacle she presents Pip sees 'the distinct shadow of the darkened and unhealthy house in which her life was hidden from the sun'. The next superb paragraph must be quoted in full:

> The candles that lighted that room of hers were placed in sconces on the wall. They were high from the ground, and they burnt with the steady dulness of artificial light in air that is seldom renewed. As I looked round at them, and at the pale gloom they made, and at the stopped clock, and at the withered articles of bridal dress upon the table and the ground, and at her own awful figure with its ghostly reflection thrown large by the fire upon the ceiling and the wall, I saw in everything the construction that my mind had come to, repeated and thrown back to me. My thoughts passed into the great room across the landing where the table was spread, and I saw it written, as it were, in the falls of the cobwebs from the centre-piece, in the crawlings of the spiders on the cloth, in the tracks of the mice as they betook their little quickened hearts behind the panels, and in the gropings and pausings of the beetles on the floor.

What Pip sees is the effect Miss Havisham has had on herself and therefore, by her potent ('large') influence, on him. She has stopped herself, like the clocks; Pip too is arrested in the earliest state of his 'love'. The 'withered articles of bridal dress' hint what marriage to Estella would be like. And the small creatures at the end, characterised both by 'little quickened hearts' and also by 'gropings and pausings', imply Pip's sense of having been reduced to something less than human. Pip mayn't explicitly make the inference that *his* mind has been 'mortally hurt and diseased', but the reader can't – and shouldn't – forbear. It is no accident that, immediately after this passage, Miss Havisham makes the appalled discovery that Estella no more loves her than she does Pip: the monster rounds on its Frankenstein. (That analogy, as we have seen, is used by Pip of Magwitch in ch. 40.)

If the novel works in the way I have been suggesting, we needn't make heavy weather of Pip's farewell to Estella (ch. 44) when he hears she is going to marry Bentley Drummle; his claim, for example, that 'you must have done me much more good than harm' is poignant in its absurdity; the book has clearly shown his capacity for feeling and living to have been laid as waste as Satis House. Nor need we have any difficulty in seeing how Miss Havisham is relevant. Far from being an engaging Dickens eccentric, or a 'picturesque convenience' (Mrs Leavis[3]), or a fairy-tale witch, or an example of the hypertrophy of Dickens's art, her 'case' is only the most striking of the many striking images Dickens finds of emotional arrest. Only this arrest isn't caused in a child by dominant parents, guardians or benefactors; it is a deliberate and conscious adult decision – a way (it is hinted) of ostensibly taking revenge on a world that has let one down, while in fact taking revenge on oneself for one's inadequacy, the inadequacy consisting in having *been* let down. Miss Havisham's self-destructiveness is, I take it, the point of the young Pip's hallucination, towards the end of chapter 8, when he sees her 'hanging ... by the neck' from 'a great wooden beam' in the deserted brewery, as though she had committed suicide – as, emotionally, she has. We learn from Herbert Pocket (ch. 22) that 'she was a spoilt child', whose 'mother died when she was a baby, and [whose] father denied her nothing': a scrap of information that makes it clear why she responds as she does to Compeyson's jilting her. She stops all life and normal feeling at the very moment in her life when she gets his letter, and proceeds to train Estella to do to men what a man has done to her, as well as training Pip to be to Estella what she has been to Compeyson. If Miss Havisham can only conceive of human relationships in terms of dominating or being dominated, of being a harsh parent or a submissive child, of being the smiter or the smitten, then it is shockingly appropriate that when (in ch. 49) she begins to see what she has done to those two young lives, she should slip into exactly the opposite role to the one she has been sustaining hitherto and become a pleading child:

> She turned her face to me for the first time since she had averted it, and, to my amazement, I may even add to my terror, dropped on her knees at my feet; with her folded hands raised to me in the manner in which, when her poor heart was young and fresh and whole, they must often have been raised to heaven from her mother's side.
> To see her with her white hair and her worn face kneeling at my feet, gave me a shock through all my frame.

What elsewhere in Dickens might have been a distasteful cliché of remorse ('they must often have been raised to heaven') here comes out as a really painful insight – not only into the Miss Havisham of this particular novel but also into the cliché on which, in earlier books, Dickens had been too ready to depend.

A good deal of *Great Expectations* therefore seems to me to be concerned with the ways in which a person is determined either by his upbringing or by a traumatic experience that happens before his character is fully formed. The novel is defining, long before modern psychology, the ways in which the child is father of the man; and there is a strong impulsion in its art to see the man as being exclusively and solely the offspring of the child – to see the characters as altogether determined by their earlier lives and being unable to 'bend the past out of its eternal shape' (ch. 56). In other words, the book is at this level an analysis of psychological and moral determinism, as *Hamlet* (in part) is. Yet there is obviously another drive: Dickens believes, or as a Victorian wants to believe, that the will is to some extent free, that there are possibilities of growth and maturing. A good many critics take this to be the main burden of the novel; present its *rationale* as a more or less naïve meliorism; and are therefore unable to account for its depressed and muted tone. And it's true that Dickens does want to believe the Pip who is writing the story to be, on the whole, a better and freer man than he would have been had he been left at the forge or, after leaving it, had not been made to suffer. Similarly, Miss Havisham is shown as winning through, shortly before she is burnt to death, to a genuinely clearer and more humane understanding of what she has done; Magwitch 'softens'; and Estella, at the very end, says that 'suffering has been stronger than all other teaching, and has taught me to understand what your heart used to be. I have been bent and broken, but – I hope – into a better shape', so that in her case the past *has* been unbent, by her being bent. Joe and Herbert Pocket find happiness in marriage; and Wemmick's marrying Miss Skiffins suggests that Walworth sentiments are finally stronger than Little Britain ones.

And there are subtler reasons, too, for thinking that the novel wants to work in this way. Despite the circumstances of Pip's childhood, which if they occurred in real life could properly be called horrific, there is something about the tone and poise of those early chapters which throws the horror sufficiently out of focus for us to be able to feel that it wouldn't have been at all impossible for the boy to grow up a free and independent spirit, despite that start. The thing is delicately done, and it is hard to put one's finger on how Dickens contrives to present the Mrs Joe menage and at the same time draw its sting. Perhaps what denatures the little boy's experience is the constant intervention of the middle-aged man's voice, which tends to admit the facts, but in a humorous manner. This is evident, as Mr T. B. Tomlinson showed some years ago,[4] even in the description of the convict in the fifth paragraph of the novel. And it comes out even more revealingly, I think, in things like the description of the Christmas dinner at the Gargerys' (ch. 4). Abstracted from the jolly tone that the narrator uses (if that were possible), the moral arm-twisting indulged in by all the adults (except Joe) at Pip's expense is perfectly sickening: Mr Hubble calls him 'naterally wicious', his sister gives him the worst bits of meat and Mr Pumblechook draws a sadistic contrast between Pip as he is and Pip as he would have been if he had been born a pig:

> 'Dunstable the butcher would have come up to you as you lay in your straw, and he would have whipped you under his left arm, and with his right he would have tucked up his frock to get a penknife from out of his waistcoat-pocket, and he would have shed your blood and had your life.'

This leads straight on to Mrs Joe's complaining of the trouble Pip has been to her:

> [She] entered on a fearful catalogue of all the illnesses I had been guilty of, and all the acts of sleeplessness I had committed, and all the high places I had tumbled from, and all the low places I had tumbled into, and all the injuries I had done myself, and all the times she had wished me in my grave, and I had contumaciously refused to go there.

By the time we get to the end of this sentence, the syntactical pattern ('all the ... all the ...') and the bouncing rhythm have so reduced our grasp of what is being said that we don't notice that Mrs Joe is publicly – and over Christmas dinner! – wishing Pip were dead. If this happened in real life it would be appalling and unpardonable; but from the novel we take away no more than a sense of unease; the child's reaction is 'placed', almost obliterated, by the narrator's avuncular geniality. Similarly, the horrible scraps of meat that Pip gets appear facetiously as 'those obscure corners of pork of which the pig, when living, had had the least reason to be vain'. A good deal of what happens in the first fifteen or so chapters is muffled in this way: even Pip's sense of guilt, after his sister has been struck down – a guilt that looks at first as though it is going to be deeply revealing about how Pip (we suppose) must have felt towards her – dissolves into a worry whether or not he should tell Joe of the ancient episode of the convict (ch. 16).

It's not altogether surprising, then, that when Pip starts to aspire beyond the dullness of the forge, when he begins to try and make himself different from Joe and Biddy, the kind of cruelty he shows them shouldn't be unforgivably gross: as Mrs Leavis rightly says, 'few in the circumstances could be confident of showing up better'. Though that is a healthy corrective to the notion of Pip as merely a snob, or merely anything, one wonders if it doesn't inadvertently reveal Dickens's problem. Mrs Leavis has just claimed that

> Pip himself, the mature recorder of his own exemplary history, does not deal tenderly with himself, recording mercilessly every least attractive impulse, but we should notice that these are mitigated always by generous misgivings, permeated by uneasy self-criticism, and contrary movements of feeling of a self-corrective kind.[5]

The consequence of this mingling of the mean act, the misgiving, and the self-criticism, is that the older Pip, whom we think of as having freed himself from his conditioning, must consequently be only *too* acute about his younger failings. By being concerned to show up his younger self, Pip the narrator puts himself in a position of moral superiority so great that it has the unfortunate effect of reducing the moral significance of his earlier experiences – of making the younger Pip into something too like a butt. The intention is no doubt that the older Pip shall show up the younger one's moral shortcomings; the actual effect is to make the younger Pip show up the older one's moral achievements. This comes out rather embarrassingly in the three chapters (17, 19 and 35) which deal with his relationship with Biddy. The kind of irony we get there at Pip's expense seems to me pretty crude – its crudity matches, in a way the older Pip doesn't realise, the crudeness of his younger self's behaviour. Pip indeed behaves callously and arrogantly to Biddy, but the irony underlines the point so heavily that one starts wondering about its motive: to be that 'merciless' (Mrs Leavis's word) to oneself is to call for admiration; the self-humiliation is a form of self-inflation. No one, of course, can quarrel with Dickens's undertaking to show the growth of a moral sensibility, but one may wonder whether he hasn't been tempted to think of the narrating Pip as *finally* mature or (as it were) saved, regenerate. If he is, then he casts the deepest doubts on the insights he himself appears to have about the importance of a human being's childhood.

Yet in an odd way we are invited by the novel to see Pip's improvement as happening, not despite, but because of, his upbringing: there is throughout a strong vein of suggestion that suffering (as Estella openly says right at the end, in a passage I've quoted) is beneficial, and that the benefit consists in making the beneficiary kinder, sweeter, more tolerant, and in general a member of the Lamb's party rather than the Tyger's. We are to regard Pip as better partly, at least, on the grounds that he has rooted out of himself all the darker impulses and every rationalisation by which people normally defend them. Morally that may have something to be said for it; in a work of fiction, the inevitable result is that the Pip who is better is at the same time less interesting and less recognisably human. Pip's progress is also a kind of regress: as a grown man he has learnt to live the ideal of being a well-behaved little boy.

An analogous fate overtakes some of the other characters. We're obviously meant to think Miss Havisham's remorse and prayer for forgiveness to be a testimony to a sort of Original Virtue: human nature can't be suppressed, and it has its own inward drive towards health, freedom and goodness. What I earlier suggested was a crowning irony – that Miss Havisham in chapter 49 becomes a suppliant child begging forgiveness from her 'father' – may just as easily be seen as a quite unironical implication by Dickens that this is the right way to be good. 'Whosoever shall not receive the kingdom of God as a little child shall in no wise enter therein' (Luke xviii.17) is a text that must have meant a great deal to Dickens; it is the optimistic obverse of Mr Hubble's 'naterally wicious', but it can lead us into some strange emotional places. Magwitch, too, once he goes to the Barleys' (ch. 46 onwards), turns from a figure who was terrifying to Pip because he told him what to do and made him what he is, into a figure who happily complies with Pip's suggestions: Pip becomes active, in determining how he shall be got out of the country, while Magwitch becomes passive ('softened'). After the convict is injured in the struggle with Compeyson and is lying in prison waiting for death, Pip comments:

> The kind of submission or resignation that he showed, was that of a man who was tired out. I sometimes derived an impression, from his manner or from a whispered word or two which escaped him, that he pondered over the question whether he might have been a better man under better circumstances. But, he never justified himself by a hint tending that way, or tried to bend the past out of its eternal shape. (ch. 56)

It is not that this development is implausible either in fictional terms or in terms of real life; the problem is rather that Magwitch, by becoming submissive, has lost that very powerful presence which the novel gave him: the nearer he comes to death, the better he gets. Goodness, that is, comes here to be associated with physical weakness; Magwitch's being 'tired out' is the condition of that goodness, but the reader regrets that he has lost the fierce will which made him a man, without having acquired any quality which can seriously be taken to replace it. Thus, he too has broken free from the conditioning imposed on him by his childhood (given to us with great vividness in ch. 42), and has ceased to be a 'warmint', but only at the cost of losing his manhood (he, like Mrs Joe and Miss Havisham, must be mortally hurt). It is no accident that, on Magwitch's death at the very end of chapter 56, Pip should refer to the Biblical text about the 'two men who went up into the Temple to pray', since in Luke xviii (the parable of the Pharisee and the publican) Christ says that 'he that humbleth himself shall be exalted' – a dictum that occurs only three verses before the remark about the 'little child', quoted above.

But there are, as everyone will point out, characters in *Great Expectations* who are neither shown to have been determined by their childhood nor suggested to have the power to free themselves (in however suspect a way) from that conditioning. Orlick, for example, comes into the novel from nowhere; Dickens produces him without antecedents in the very chapter where Mrs Joe is struck down. Of Mrs Joe's own background we know virtually nothing. Bentley Drummle, who appears in chapter 25, is given very little in the way of antecedents: 'He came of rich people down in Somersetshire, who had nursed this combination of qualities ["idle, proud, niggardly, reserved, and suspicious"] until they made the discovery that it was just of age and a blockhead.' Mr Jaggers, who significantly admires Drummle ('I like the fellow, Pip; he is one of the true sort' – end of ch. 26), similarly has nothing in the way of family background; and the only personal relationship he is capable of is with Molly, his housekeeper, who turns out to be Estella's mother and Magwitch's wife, so that we see Molly tamed by Jaggers in something of the same way as her daughter is tamed by Drummle. If then Orlick and Drummle – characters whom Pip detests – together with Jaggers, about whom the novel is at worst uneasy, are none of them allowed to give (or are given by the book) any explanation as to their brutal domination of others, we must suppose that there is another element altogether in Dickens's thinking about what makes a man what he is. Hitherto, as we have seen, there is a drive in the novel to see man as the victim of his upbringing, a drive that is qualified by the impulse to see him as to some extent capable of freeing himself. But the thoughts represented by these bad characters are only intelligible if we suppose Dickens to have also believed, with part of his mind, that some people are, in Mr Hubble's words, 'naterally wicious'; if Dickens felt that some kinds of bad temperaments were not explicable in any terms at all. In other words, despite both his psychological insights and his Victorian meliorism, Dickens couldn't help wondering about Original Sin. His interest in theology as such may have been slight, but it isn't surprising that a man so interested in Shakespeare should have been finally dissatisfied with psychological and social 'explanations' of human behaviour, as well as with the notion that the exercise of free will can save us. We may well regard these thoughts about sin as the deepest insights of all; but unfortunately the novel doesn't really support us. For apart from Mr Jaggers and Mrs Joe, the 'evil' characters are disappointingly unrealised and play a pretty peripheral part in the action. Orlick is produced when Mrs Joe must be struck down, when Biddy must be danced at, and when Pip must meet an accusing conscience at the lime-kiln; Bentley Drummle appears only to make the link with Jaggers (and hence with Estella and her mother) and then again when Estella needs to be married off (and the reasons Estella gives for marrying him, in chapter 44, are to me inadequate). And there is also the difficulty that, if the novelist wants to bring in characters whose very point is that their behaviour is inexplicable, he runs a serious risk of seeming arbitrary when he is writing a novel which is otherwise so rich in its psychological and social explanations. Mrs Joe is of course treated at greater length and in fuller detail than Orlick or Drummle; but in her case, the problem arises that I mentioned earlier: all her behaviour, from the merely mean and ungracious to the openly pathological (the 'rampages'), is as it were shot slightly out of focus, the sharp lines of the child's remembered perception being ever so subtly blurred by the humorous tones and asides of the mature narrator. Take, for example, this passage from near the beginning of chapter 2:

> She was tall and bony, and almost always wore a coarse apron, fastened over her figure behind with two loops, and having a square impregnable bib in front, that was stuck full of pins and needles. She made it a powerful merit in herself, and a strong reproach against Joe, that she wore this apron so much. Though I really see no reason why she should have worn it at all: or why, if she did wear it at all, she should not have taken it off, every day of her life.

The last sentence, in the present tense, clearly comes from the mind of Pip the narrator, not from a recalled thought of the child's; and its effect is to suggest that Mrs Joe's unreasonableness was something she might, perhaps, have been joked out of, or something which the narrator can at any rate afford to joke about now. No doubt he can; but if the aim of these early pages is to establish Mrs Joe as a potent and terrifying figure, the humour is at odds with that aim. It is true to say, with Mrs Leavis, that though Pip's 'sufferings are minimised by the amusement with which the adult Pip recounts his memories, there is sufficient poignancy in the recollections to make them moving as well as vivid';[6] yet the vividness is like that with which someone growing up during the War now remembers those insecure and frightening years; one jokes about having been cold and hungry: one mythologises it. So that, while Dickens in the early chapters of *Great Expectations* may seem to be doing something like what Gorki attempts in *My Childhood*, he never earns the right to say 'the truth is beyond all commiseration', and is unsure how far he is even trying to earn that right. He has therefore put himself in the uncomfortable position of endorsing, in regard to Mrs Joe, Orlick and Drummle, the notion of 'nateral wiciousness' which, when applied to Pip or Magwitch or Estella, is felt to be itself vicious.

It's in chapter 48 that Jaggers gives his opinion of Bentley Drummle, who is about to marry Estella: 'A fellow like our friend the Spider ... either beats, or cringes. He may cringe and growl, or cringe and not growl; but he either beats or cringes. Ask Wemmick *his* opinion.' And Wemmick (not the Walworth twin) agrees. Much of the world of *Great Expectations* sorts itself out into these two distasteful categories. One may beat because one has been beaten (Magwitch, Estella), or one may cringe for the same reason (Pip, Molly, Joe); or one may, because beaten, simultaneously beat *and* cringe (Miss Havisham); or one may beat for no apparent reason at all except that one happens to have been born that way (Orlick, Drummle, Mrs Joe). Dickens was obviously bent on pursuing some highly dismaying insights about the exercise of power – psychological as well as social and financial; but it is quite evident that he badly wanted, at the same time, to believe other things about the possibilities of human nature than that it classified itself only along these lines. The result is that the more attentively we read the book, the less we know whether Dickens really grasped just how dismaying the best things in it are.

From *Essays in Criticism*, 34 (1974), 147–68.

NOTES

[A. L. French's influential essay argues that relationships between the characters in *Great Expectations* are strongly coloured by sado-masochism. French belongs to that line of probingly psychoanalytical critics who, while admiring Dickens for his intuitive grasp of human nature, raise questions about his degree of self-knowledge or frankness (see Introduction pp. 3–7). In French's words, didn't Dickens realise 'just how dismaying the best things in ... [*Great Expectations*] are'?

On the one hand, the novel clearly endorses the common Victorian belief that human beings have a certain amount of free will and are capable of moral growth, sometimes against heavy odds. Dickens not only made Pip, Estella, Magwitch and Miss Havisham 'soften' and become 'better' people, but gave Pip the narrator an avuncular geniality of tone which plays down the horrors of his own upbringing at the hands of Mrs Joe. According to French, Dickens may even be hinting that the upbringing did Pip some good: that he was somehow immune to the psychological damage that might be expected to follow from such cruelty, and that it made him sweeter and more tolerant – in Blakean terms, 'a member of the Lamb's party rather than the Tyger's'.

On the other hand, the novel also exposes the pernicious nonsense of such an idea. French argues that *Great Expectations* is actually 'full of situations in which parents, or their substitutes, dominate and indeed determine their children – not merely what the children do but also what they are'. The sensibility of Pip, for instance, 'is ... fixed early in life: he is a kisser of rods' – a masochist. French also makes a further point: that Dickens's gut feeling seems to be that some people are simply born evil, and remain so from cradle to grave. In short, human beings are exactly what they are bred or born to be. It can be pretty nasty. And there's nothing to be done about it.

French's quotations are from *Great Expectations*, ed. Angus Calder, Penguin English Library (Harmondsworth, 1965). Ed.]

1. F. R. and Q. D. Leavis, *Dickens the Novelist* (London, 1970), p. 302.

2. Ibid.

3. Ibid., p. 324.

4. T. B. Tomlinson, *Melbourne Critical Review* (1960), 64–74.

5. F. R. and Q. D. Leavis, *Dickens the Novelist*, p. 304.

6. Ibid., p. 296. I have also found much general stimulus in Robert Garis, *The Dickens Theatre*, and in T. B. Tomlinson's 'Dickens and Individualism', *Melbourne Critical Review* (1960), 64–74.

2

Taming to Improve: Dickens and the Women in *Great Expectations*

LUCY FROST

In *Great Expectations* it is the psychologically aberrant women, not the admired models of Victorian womanhood, who engage Dickens's subtle and complex imagination. But after delineating precisely the inner lives of such deviant women as Mrs Joe, Miss Havisham and Estella, Dickens undermines his own insights by forcing upon the novel a grim moral logic of repentance and conversion. These women, whose behaviour he charts in richly inventive prose, present him with a problem in shaping the novel. Inflexible and destructive, they resist his efforts to mould Pip's world into a place where humane dreams come true, where sensitivity flourishes and the callous are without power. Women in such a landscape need to be meek and mild, like Herbert's Clara and Joe's Biddy. These are the women of received Victorian ideas, pale allegories animated from without. They are neither interesting nor memorable, and yet it is into their company that Dickens tries to drive his strong females. He does this by taming them, and he tames them by violence. The pattern of moral improvement is achieved, but at the cost of the credibility and consistency of the characterisation.

Mrs Joe illustrates the situation at its simplest. In her case, the extravagant prose of caricature embodies inner extravagances of character. Each detail of language and gesture suggests that what is a common enough mood in even the best-adjusted married women has completely taken over a personality. Out of the constrictions of her married life, Mrs Joe (who doesn't even have a name of her own) has hewn the angry and frustrated self she flamboyantly dramatises with her apron for a prop:

> a coarse apron, fastened over her figure behind with two loops, and having a square impregnable bib in front, that was stuck full of pins and needles. She made it a powerful merit in herself, and a strong reproach against Joe, that she wore this apron so much. Though I really see no reason why she should have worn it at all: or why, if she did wear it at all, she should not have taken it off every day of her life. (p. 9)

Feeling imprisoned by her domestic role, Mrs Joe constantly calls everyone's attention to her fate, always blaming her frustrations on a source outside herself, on someone or some circumstance over which she has no control. Language reinforces gesture as she laments being 'a blacksmith's wife, and (what's the same thing) a slave with her apron never off' (p. 19). She asks Joe 'why he had not married a Negress Slave at once' (p. 92), and assures Pip that 'it's bad enough to be a blacksmith's wife (and him a Gargery), without being your mother' (p. 7). This self-image of domestic slave with time off for nothing she would *like* to do – 'I'm rather partial to Carols myself, and that's the best of reasons for my never hearing any' (p. 19) – informs her whole life. In Mrs Joe's insistence that she has no scope for gratifying any desires, Dickens intuitively recognises the behaviour of a neurotic who clings to her neurosis. Whatever her protestations to the contrary, she is adept at finding ways of satisfying her compulsive need to enliven housewifely tedium. Life around her house will never be a quietly boring routine so long as it can be dramatised and spiced with such well-timed bits of violence as hurling Pip across the room, hacking up a loaf of bread for tea, or pouncing upon Joe by the two whiskers and knocking his head 'for a little while against the wall behind him' (p. 9). True, these are negative escapes and do not solve the problem of feeling imprisoned by the duties of scarcely varied household drudgery performed within the dull confines of a small town. It is not surprising, then, that she should be so easily gulled by Pip's outlandishly romantic vision of Miss Havisham taking cake and-wine on a gold plate while sitting in a black velvet coach in her room.

About sexual frustration nothing is said, although one can scarcely avoid recognising how unlucky Mrs Joe has been in marrying a blacksmith who turns out to be the male counterpart of those Dickensian child-brides – sexless and dependable. There seems to be no lasting help for any of Mrs Joe's frustrations until chapter 15 when Orlick surprises the reader with his belated appearance. By the end of the chapter he has got Mrs Joe permanently off 'the Rampage' and given her an entirely new personality. Mrs Joe is converted to placid goodness after she intrudes upon a male domain. 'Mastery' is the key issue. Orlick has demanded that if the apprentice Pip is to have a half holiday, then as a journeyman he deserves one too. Joe asserts his authority over the forge by 'refusing to entertain the subject until the journeyman was in a better temper...'. Only after Orlick has 'hammered himself hot' and a red-hot-bar of iron cold, does 'the master declare a "half-holiday for all"' (p. 106). Joe will be fair, but he will not relinquish control.

With order and temper restored, the fracas would have been over had Mrs Joe not interfered, berating her husband as a 'fool' for 'giving holidays to great hulkers like that' and asserting heatedly, 'I wish *I* was his master' (p. 106). This outburst unbalances the hierarchy of power within the world of men at work: it introduces sexuality into the dispute. Mrs Joe is a woman who has no business entering quarrels at the forge. Orlick responds to her as a usurper of sexual prerogative, taunting her with his retort, 'You'd be everybody's master if you durst', calling her a 'foul shrew', and offering his solution of mastery by violence – 'I'd hold you, if you was my wife. I'd hold you under the pump, and choke it out of you' (pp. 106, 107). In the face of Orlick's mockery, Mrs Joe is impotent. Cornered, she collapses into sexual stereotype, the hysterical woman. Self-dramatising as always, she hurls abuse at her husband the 'noodle' and at Orlick the 'rogue', and she 'consciously and deliberately' takes 'extraordinary pains to force herself' into a furious rage which presses the men into a fight because the husband must defend his wife's honour (p. 107). During the fight (or more probably after it) the termagant plays nineteenth-century lady and coyly faints away. Even insensible, however, she keeps up her struggle against the men. Unconsciousness does not relieve the violence so deeply embedded within self:

> Joe unlocked the door and picked up my sister, who had dropped
> insensible at the window (but who had seen the fight first, I think),

> and who was carried into the house and laid down, and who was
> recommended to revive, and would do nothing but struggle and
> clench her hands in Joe's hair.   (p. 108)

This is the last time Mrs Joe appears 'on the Ram-page' in the
novel. Orlick, angered by the manipulative woman, returns to take
his revenge. Now that his master is away he can deal with the
usurper without interference. His motivation is straightforward.
Mrs Joe's response is another matter. After the attack, we are told,
'her temper was greatly improved, and she was patient' (p. 115).
Orlick, by bashing Mrs Joe into imbecility (and, significantly, into
speechlessness), has become a catalyst for moral regeneration. At
her death, she is affectionate to her husband and for the first time
entertains some scruples about her behaviour toward him and Pip.
The prose in which Biddy recounts the scene to Pip is dull and
sentimental, and provides a disappointing finale to a memorable
character:

> She made signs to me that she wanted him to sit down close to her,
> and wanted me to put her arms round his neck. So I put them round
> his neck, and she laid her head down on his shoulder quite content
> and satisfied. And so she presently said 'Joe' again, and once
> 'Pardon', and once 'Pip'. And so she never lifted her head up any
> more.   (p. 269)

Dickens asks us to believe in a change of personality. But how can
such a change have occurred? Before the bashing, Mrs Joe is neither
affectionate nor worried about the effect she is having upon Joe or
Pip. Certainly she is never 'quite content and satisfied'. Out of what
potential came the moral growth? Perhaps Dickens is simply naïve,
believing that even the most obsessive, inflexible of personalities
retain some potential for moral regeneration. This could be a satisfactory explanation if it were not for Mrs Joe's bizarre attachment
to Orlick. What are we to make of that attachment? It might have
been further evidence of Mrs Joe's moral regeneration if it were
couched in terms of a victim extending forgiveness to her attacker,
but it isn't. Although by leaving Pip baffled Dickens keeps the
reader in the dark so far as articulated explanations go, there is a
subtext which offers a motive. When Mrs Joe takes pleasure in the
company of a man who has 'disturbed' her sight, 'greatly impaired'
her hearing and memory and left her speech 'unintelligible', her
behaviour is by no stretch of the imagination normal (p. 115).

Dickens knows this and makes Pip explicit about the peculiarity. What he does not seem to realise is the extent of sexual perversity, both Mrs Joe's and his own. He writes about her attachment to Orlick in prose which tries to accommodate the sexual elements within a picture of her new geniality:

> She manifested the greatest anxiety to be on good terms with him, was evidently much pleased by his being at length produced, and motioned that she would have him given something to drink. She watched his countenance as if she were particularly wishful to be assured that he took kindly to his reception, she showed every possible desire to conciliate him, and there was an air of humble propitiation in all she did, such as I have seen pervade the bearing of a child towards a hard master. After that day, a day rarely passed without her drawing the hammer on her slate, and without Orlick's slouching in and standing doggedly before her, as if he knew no more than I did what to make of it.   (p. 117)

The tone is bland enough to keep a full sense of the grotesquerie at bay, and there is vivid imagery for the reader to fix upon, but while Pip seems puzzled without being horrified the real dreadfulness of it all is not entirely concealed. The simile which draws Mrs Joe's determination to please into a context of children and hard masters raises the issue of cruelty which the passage otherwise seems to be ignoring. It also returns the narrative to that quarrel over mastery at the forge, the quarrel to which this is after all the finale. Far from wanting to 'be everybody's master if you durst', Mrs Joe is revelling in Orlick's mastery of her. In her violated mind, Orlick now *is* his tool and that tool has phallic properties almost embarrassingly obvious to a twentieth-century reader, if not to the pre-Freudian Dickens: 'She had lost his name, and could only signify him by his hammer' (p. 116). Apparently the memory of Orlick's violence offers lasting pleasure. Why else should Mrs Joe daily summon 'the hammer' to her mutilated presence? Her bashing gathers overtones of rape as therapy, the gratifying of a sex-starved woman. There is no real sexual gratification of course, only a taming through violence. Something similar will happen to Estella, who also watches with sexually-charged pleasure as two males fight, and who is later tamed by a man after he has used her 'with great cruelty' (p. 458).

Of course Estella is a far more complicated character than Mrs Joe, and her presence in the novel is felt quite differently. As victim and victimiser she inhabits a disturbing psychic area where callousness, no longer embodied within the exuberant comic prose which keeps Mrs Joe an essentially engaging figure, does not amuse. Too much is at stake both within and beyond the fictional world. Estella's aberrance is fuelled by Dickens's fear of childhood's potential for so warping a person's inner life that sexuality and intelligence are severed from feelings, and the capacity for love thereby destroyed.

As a child who is cut off from ordinary family life and from the mundane normality of the village, who is surrounded by emotional cannibals and is assigned the lead role in Miss Havisham's mono-tonously repetitive productions of revenge melodrama, Estella becomes self-protectively remote from affection. Even as a young girl she is a cynic. When she grows older, a disturbing passivity takes hold. She talks about herself as though she were an instrument obedient not just to Miss Havisham's will, but to inflexible laws of her own nature, laws which she seems to have no sense of shaping, only of observing with a strangely detached curiosity. Nothing in the novel offers to disabuse Estella of her fatalism, to suggest that the damaged psyche could be repaired if her attitude or circumstances should change. Nothing, that is, until the novel's conclusion with its fairy tale metamorphosis.

There, psychologically consistent character is wiped out by sentimental piety. Dickens simply abandons his previous under-standing of Estella's inner life. The essential point about her, whether as a maliciously impish child or sexually alluring snow queen, has always been emotional frigidity. Dickens has been adamant about the matter, persistently dissociating himself from Pip's naïve belief that anyone as beautiful and enticing as Estella cannot be impervious to love. Such coldness, as Pip protests to Estella, would not be 'in Nature' (p. 343). Maybe not, but every-thing within the novel supports Estella's rejoinder that it is 'my nature ... the nature formed within me' (p. 343). Experience can expunge Nature.

This is the notion about Estella which most fascinates Dickens. Never is she more vividly created than as a child beyond the pale. Later, as Pip's *femme fatale*, she seems a far less substantial cre-ation, disappointingly close to stereotype. She would have been reduced simply to a dull and predictable role as sexual bait if Dickens had not imagined her inner world, demonstrating again his genius for holding tightly to the inner lives of secondary characters while maintaining the narrative's central thrust. But this interest in

Estella pushes his talents hard. The observable detail, however tellingly selected, can reveal little about someone who has withdrawn into unresponsive aloofness, and yet this is the sort of person Dickens wants Estella to be on her return from Paris. Although central narrative action could proceed even if Estella were a wooden puppet (Pip's love by now is self-generating, quite detached from anything Estella may say or do), Dickens is not content to relinquish the world of Estella herself. He solves his problem by giving the older Estella perceptive intelligence and making her unusually adept at self-analysis. It is in the scenes where Estella's words open vistas into her psychic mutilation that she seems most vivid. Here her creator is inside his character. This is not to say that Dickens renders the nuances of sensibility with the precision of a Proust or James. And he need not do so because he has made Estella reflective by circumstances rather than temperament.

At the inn on the way to Richmond, for instance, Estella is pressured by Pip's perplexed reaction into explaining the spontaneously vindictive pleasure with which she laughs – not 'languidly, but with real enjoyment' – when she thinks of Miss Havisham's relatives made ridiculous in their wild jealousy of the presumed heir. Her explanation is concise, self-confidently knowing, her language attuned to her emotions:

> 'It is not easy for even you ... to know what satisfaction it gives me to see those people thwarted, or what an enjoyable sense of the ridiculous I have when they are made ridiculous. For you were not brought up in that strange house from a mere baby. – I was. You had not your little wits sharpened by their intriguing against you, suppressed and defenceless, under the mask of sympathy and pity and what not, that is soft and soothing. – I had. You did not gradually open your round childish eyes wider and wider to the discovery of that imposter of a woman who calculates her stores of peace of mind for when she wakes up in the night. – I did.'
>
> It was no laughing matter with Estella now, nor was she summoning these rememberances from any shallow place. I would not have been the cause of that look of hers, for all my expectations in a heap.   (p. 253)

In passages such as this, Estella's awareness of her own peculiarities, her ability to distinguish among versions of reality, her understanding of people whose feelings are not her own, all mark a character whose intellect is far less constricted than her emotions. Nevertheless, as Dickens insists over and over, awareness is not salvation and Estella's intellect is powerless to repair the emotional damage of childhood. To grasp intellectually the fact of Pip's 'sentiments, fancies' is not to experience them personally: 'When you say you love me, I know what you mean, as a form of words; but nothing more. You address nothing in my breast, you touch nothing there' (p. 343). Estella is severely limited by her frozen nerve ends.

Throughout the novel one feels keenly Dickens's awareness that although everybody's personality operates within a limited range of emotion and intellect, some ranges are far more restricted than others. Narrowness may be only a matter of degree, but degree can mean psychological mutilation and madness. Estella's range is defined most explicitly in chapter 38, when she mounts her defence against Miss Havisham's charge of being an 'ingrate' of 'stock and stone' with a 'cold, cold heart' (p. 289). With self-engrossed hysteria Miss Havisham demands a response appropriate to her own 'burning love', but of course for Estella 'fierce affection' is not something real. Although she feels what she understands is love for her 'mother by adoption', such love is something she can discuss with detachment, with nothing more disconcerting than the 'kind of calm wonder', which enables her to look at Miss Havisham 'with perfect composure', her face expressing 'a self-possessive indifference to the wild heat of the other, that was almost cruel' (p. 289, 91). Her words are alien to passion. In a chillingly incongruous metaphor, she imagines a daughter's love to be like a pupil's efforts in the schoolroom: 'When have you found me false to your teaching? When have you found me unmindful of your lessons?' (p. 291). The very choice of the schoolroom analogy underscores Estella's distance from ordinary emotional responses. Here again, Dickens is insistent on setting affection beyond her emotional range.

During the scene Estella puzzles her way toward comprehension. In a sense she doesn't learn anything she didn't know long before when she repeatedly told Pip that she neither loved him nor even knew what his love meant beyond a form of words. But her knowledge of a part (her inability to love Pip) becomes knowledge of the whole (her mutilated self) when she sees her inability to love as the inevitable outcome of being 'brought up in that strange house from a mere baby'. Suddenly the bitter import of her schoolroom lesson becomes clear: love is like sunshine from which she has been kept all her life, learning only untruths about it until now nothing can send her walking naturally into the daylight.

'I begin to think,' said Estella, in a musing way, after another moment of calm wonder, 'that I almost understand how this comes about. If you had brought up your adopted daughter wholly in the dark confinement of these rooms, and had never let her know that there was such a thing as the daylight by which she has never once seen your face – if you had done that, and then, for a purpose, had wanted her to understand the daylight and know all about it, you would have been disappointed and angry?'

Miss Havisham, with her head in her hands, sat making a low moaning, and swaying herself on her chair, but gave no answer.

'Or,' said Estella ' – which is a nearer case – if you had taught her, from the dawn of her intelligence, with your utmost energy and might, that there was such a thing as daylight, but that it was made to be her enemy and destroyer, and she must always turn against it, for it had blighted you and would else blight her; if you had done this, and then, for a purpose, had wanted her to take naturally to the daylight and she could not do it, you would have been disappointed and angry?'

Miss Havisham sat listening (or it seemed so, for I could not see her face), but still made no answer.

'So,' said Estella, 'I must be taken as I have been made. The success is not mine, the failure is not mine, but the two together make me.'

(pp. 291–2)

With painful precision Estella has seen her own deviation from what is natural. And behind her is Dickens, whose powerfully persuasive prose is endorsing his own way of knowing and creating truth within fiction. What has happened to Estella happens to his art. She has possessed a kind of understanding before, one she can express in the abstract language of her warnings to Pip. But full knowledge has had to wait until that understanding fused with her most deeply felt emotions and was then focused by her imaginative powers, the powers which can make real other selves in other worlds. Only then can she get at the core of what it is to be Estella. And this fusion within her self is signalled by a fusion within the prose: the concrete language of personal experience, the metaphors of the imagination, and the logic of the formulating mind coalesce.

To a reader persuaded by this characterisation of Estella, her ultimate transformation must come as a surprise. Pip describes her as changed in her very essence, the coldness gone: 'what I had never seen before, was the saddened softened light of the once proud eyes; what I had never felt before was the friendly touch of the once insensible hand' (p. 458). These details are supplied in the admittedly more sentimental second version of the ending, but both endings agree on the nature and process of the change and offer the metamorphosis in a prose which does nothing to enhance credibility. Estella is reduced to the victim of a Victorian domestic melodrama: her brute of a husband has 'used her with great cruelty' and she has improved. We are back in the world where Mrs Joe smiles and grows loving once Orlick bashes her over the head. Brutality in men is again breeding sensitivity and lovingness in women – this implication, however unconscious, is certainly there. Estella's case is especially unnerving because brutality seems to have succeeded where the intellect is impotent. Powerless to help herself, in spite of her impressively accurate self-analysis, Estella is freed from her emotional frigidity by the one character who most resembles Orlick in sheer loutishness. The fact that twice in one novel such brutes should tame women through violence suggests something more than the intricacies of a complicated plot.

The novelist seems again to be indulging in a kind of fantasy which wipes out the character who has gone before. Although Dickens has been at pains to locate Estella's arrogant behaviour within a context of the mutilated psyche, he abandons that context in favour of one centred on moral pietism, a context offered as unexpectedly and gratuitously as when Miss Havisham suddenly drops to her knees beseeching Pip's forgiveness. Estella is now to be seen as an arrogant (bad) woman who has been chastened into humility (goodness): 'in her face and in her voice, and in her touch, she gave me the assurance, that suffering had been stronger than Miss Havisham's teaching, and had given her a heart to understand what my heart used to be' (p. 461). In the second version, the language of this transformation is physical and brutal: 'I have been bent and broken, but – I hope – into a better shape' (p. 460). Both versions, then, make of extreme suffering a force for personal regeneration. In doing so, they ignore the nature of Estella's experience at Satis House. That experience, neutralised into the vagueness of 'Miss Havisham's teaching', is not something distinct from suffering: it is an excursion into the extremities of life where suffering is allowed exclusive domain. If suffering destroys the heart of Miss Havisham, under what circumstances can it give a heart to Estella? How can brutality breed humanity? Dickens skirts these serious questions and retreats into a banal generalising prose, its tone so distanced and detached that the experience created by the novel's most disturbing (and often most vivid) sections fades from memory, leaving the reader peacefully reassured of humanity's essential goodness, believing that no matter how obsessive and cruel an individual may be, his sensitivity may at any moment return. And yet in order to make distorted personalities whole again, Dickens must conclude with an imbecilic Mrs Joe, a grovelling Miss Havisham, and a sentimentalised Estella.

One explanation for this may be the novelist's sense of the threat posed by women with strong personalities. The unbelievably good women, like Clara and the grown-up Biddy, give proof of their goodness partly by doing nothing that will call attention to themselves, will require much notice. They are there to help and sympathise. Lightweight cartoon characters – Mrs Pocket and Miss Skiffens, for instance – amuse, but do not influence central issues. There are no women who are at once interesting and basically sensitive, no counterparts to Pip or even to secondary characters like Magwitch and Wemmick. The women with strong personalities, the women who must be noticed, are destructive. Or at least they are so until men manage to humble them, to render them inoffensive. Behind Mrs Joe, Miss Havisham, and Estella, there hovers the image of the once very handsome and hot-blooded murderess, Molly. Thanks to Jaggers, she has become 'a wild beast tamed' (p. 371). By the time Pip first sees her serving at Jaggers's dinner party, the man she calls 'Master' has virtually mesmerised her into subservience. Nevertheless, something about her makes Pip think of witches. After lightly dismissing that fancy as the influence of having watched *Macbeth* the night before, he returns to it almost immediately with a curious remark couched in vivid and highly-charged language: 'I always saw in her face, a face rising out of the cauldron. Years afterwards, I made a dreadful likeness of that woman, by causing a face that had no other natural resemblance to it than it derived from flowing hair, to pass behind a bowl of flaming spirits in a dark room' (p. 201). Why should Pip say this? His adult presence is rarely felt in the novel, and certainly never as that of a man who would experiment with strange and occult images of women. Surely the voice speaking through Pip is that of the novelist for whom a woman who fascinates may be imagined most fittingly as 'a face rising out of the cauldron'. One need not be a student of psychoanalysis to perceive within *Great Expectations* a deep-seated fear of women. The strong women are created vividly and are unquestionably memorable, but because their strength is negative and is associated with the ability to inflict pain on men, they must be 'bent and broken' (p. 460) before they can win approval, before they can stop being outsiders and can achieve the proper, tensionless relationship with Pip. The novel has a subtext which Dickens never consciously intended. Or so we can assume when the subtext is so consistent in itself and so clearly at odds with the consciously asserted point of view.

Tension between conscious and unconscious attitudes toward women affects most seriously the way Dickens handles the conversion of Miss Havisham. Of all the women she is undoubtedly the most mulitated. From the first glimpse of the recluse at Satis House the reader feels himself in the presence of a haunted mind within a haunted world. The village itself had held Mrs Joe in perspective and reined in her powers, but Miss Havisham can control her own world within the grounds of Satis House and the fear is that she may be able to spread her corrosive influence beyond the garden walls. Dickens imagines her as a particularly horrible cannibal who devours the people she loves as well as those for whom she cares nothing. In a passage where repetitions and prose rhythms create an aura of fascinated abhorrence, Pip describes Miss Havisham's mad delight as she listens to her accomplished protégé's account of the men she has fascinated:

> She was even more dreadfully fond of Estella than she had been when I last saw them together; I repeat the word advisedly, for there was something positively dreadful in the energy of her looks and embraces. She hung upon Estella's beauty, hung upon her words, hung upon her gestures, and sat mumbling her own trembling fingers while she looked at her, as though she were devouring the beautiful creature she had reared. (p. 288)

In Dickens's own words, Miss Havisham dwells upon the roll of Estella's victims 'with the intensity of a mind mortally hurt and diseased' (p. 288).

Given the accumulated evidence of her severely traumatised state, this judgement seems only too obvious. Intense suffering, unnaturally prolonged, has thoroughly destroyed – 'mortally hurt' – her capacity for responding with the moral sensitivity of an even vaguely normal person. It is therefore with some astonishment that we shortly afterwards find her acquiring two characteristics utterly at variance with her earlier self: a sense of responsibility for the effects of her behaviour on other people, and with it a sense of guilt. True, she has demonstrated an unexpected sensitivity to Joe when he comes to discuss Pip's apprenticeship, but that makes no sense either – her ability to look far enough beyond her own obsessive needs to understand the discomfort of the village blacksmith and to treat him kindly is inconsistent with her usual behaviour. The main thrust of the scene is obviously to highlight Pip's excessive shame and not Miss Havisham's latent humanity. Her sudden horrified recognition of what she has done to Pip and Estella is another matter.

This outbreak of humanity may be intended to convince, but how can it? It is radical, abrupt and totally out of character. For well over twenty years Miss Havisham has been untroubled by compassion or guilt. She has refused to acknowledge the individuality of other people, much less their moral claims upon her. Indeed, if anyone or anything (even time) exists beyond her self-dramatised life of embittered revenge, she prefers not to know. Throughout the English novel there is no better example of an ingrown mind and yet, at her long-prepared moment of triumph over Pip, her inflexible mind sees beyond itself. Even granting that Miss Havisham might feel for Pip because she suddenly identifies with him, the text makes our credulity seem foolish. At the beginning of chapter 49 when Miss Havisham sends for Pip to ask his forgiveness and make reparation, there occurs a scene which can be moving and persuasive only for extra-literary reasons. The original Miss Havisham vanishes. The dialogue discards her distinctive voice, and bald statements replace the evocative prose. Religious language and sentimental pietism, completely out of keeping with her former character, are pushed forward in the service of emotional drama just as they might be in any third-rate novel of the period. When Miss Havisham kneels before Pip the gesture is described in flat, maudlin prose, culminating in an astonishingly unlikely image of her childhood:

> She turned her face to me for the first time since she had averted it, and to my amazement, I may even add to my terror, dropped on her knees at my feet; with her folded hands raised to me in the manner in which, when her poor heart was young and fresh and whole, they must often have been raised to Heaven from her mother's side.
>
> (p. 377)

They must? Hasn't this picturebook girlhood been appropriated from the shallowest platitudes of Victorian sentimentality? And how could it be remotely true if, as Herbert Pocket says, her mother died when she was a baby? Even Satis House itself has gone out of focus. Although we are told that Miss Havisham 'was not in her own room, but was in the larger room across the landing' (p. 374), no detail reminds the reader that this is the room where the wedding feast lies mouldering amidst spiders and beetles. The ghoulishness of the setting, which might be expected to cast some shadow over the conversation, is obliterated. Since no mention is made of Miss Havisham's clothes either, the evidence of her behaviour over the past decades subsides into vagueness.

Furthermore, the act of atonement itself is suspect. Miss Havisham will give money to Pip to pay off the cost of buying a partnership for Herbert Pocket. Pip has asserted before this, and will repeat later, that buying the partnership was an unequivocal good, an act of unblemished moral value, and Dickens never asks the reader to doubt Pip's judgement. And yet there are enough parallels with Pip's experience to raise doubts of some importance. Pip, having recently learned the identity of his own benefactor, should be aware that money bestowed in secrecy can be a very mixed blessing indeed. Surely Herbert after years of assuming that the basis for his partnership was his personal merit might well be distressed when he eventually discovers that his position was bought for him. Dickens glosses over this possibility and has Pip blithely report that 'Herbert was as much moved as amazed, and the dear fellow and I were not the worse friends for the long concealment' (p. 455). Moreover, in the case of Magwitch Dickens is at pains to show that however generous a benefactor may believe himself, the gift of money from secret sources creates complicated moral and psychological dilemmas for the recipient who is of course expected to be grateful to the benefactor. Shouldn't the reader wonder whether the money given by Pip and Miss Havisham to atone for their own selfishness might not be considerably more soothing to themselves than to the recipient, and thus paradoxically yet another act of selfishness? While there are significant differences between the gifts of money to Pip and to Herbert, the parallels remain disturbing.

And yet Dickens shows no more awareness of such problems than of what he is doing with Miss Havisham. At some unconscious level the scene may not have rung true to him, however. This would explain the second half of the chapter, which has an entirely different feel about it and reads like an alternative to the pietistic conversion and atonement. The action in this part of the chapter is easy to summarise – Pip returns to Miss Havisham's room, sees her catch fire and smothers her flaming clothes – but the details make the action by no means straightforward. Once Pip leaves Miss Havisham after their conversation about forgiveness he returns to the garden of Satis House and there becomes himself again, the young man whose intense emotional involvement with the past has been ignored in the interest of approved behaviour. With the ruined garden vividly detailed once more, the novel re-enters Miss Havisham's world as it originally existed, a unique psychic location where Pip's emotional life has been manipulated outrageously. It is as though Dickens, having advanced his moral argument, were relaxing into the logic of his imagination. The problem – of which he is aware – is one of plot rather than substantive vision: it is time to get rid of Miss Havisham. He does so, but critics have not asked many questions about what happens to the narrative in the process.

They do not seem to notice how odd it is that, having just struck a blow for normal and reasonable behaviour, Dickens should immediately return to the haunted world of bizarre dreams, terrorising Pip with the reappearance of a boyhood horror, the image of Miss Havisham hanging by the neck from a beam in the decaying brewery. Pip can try to rationalise the sight, call it 'a fancy', but not before he has reacted to it, 'shuddering from head to foot' (p. 380). And the labelling, conscious mind does not help much anyway; it cannot obliterate the fear and it is, moreover, wrong in dismissing the reality. Miss Havisham's moment of destruction has come – or rather, is coming. Pip is not responsible for it, or is he? It is *his* fancy which comes true, after all, and yet the fire is an accident, something he sees from outside the room. This is not the earlier version of a world in which the distanced narrative voice assumed that one could apportion blame, solicit forgiveness and concoct reparation. This is the mirror image of fears and desires shaping in confusion a subterranean world conveyed to the reader through the highly particularised voice of Pip, intensely involved, indeed swept away by acts and feelings he experiences without understanding. Dickens details this grotesque scene by using a montage of images brilliant in their controlled ambivalence: the hanging woman, suicide and criminal; the blazing figure who rushes at Pip, victim frantic for help and demonic spectre threatening a blazing engulfment; Pip struggling with Miss Havisham, heroic rescuer and yet one who himself says, 'we were on the ground struggling like desperate enemies' (p. 380). The language of the prose creates an atmosphere charged with violence – Pip's violence. He imagines himself as aggressor (though the nature of the action will exonerate him from guilt) and when he says that he acted unconsciously, the claim is less an excuse than an assertion of basic, primitive forces released under pressure. Those forces, without being specified, are surely hinted at in the unexpected reference to a prisoner, a reference which in the context of struggle against a foe carries eerily ironic echoes of the festering bitterness which drove Magwitch to struggle with Compeyson on the moor: 'I still held her forcibly down with all my strength, like a prisoner who might escape; and I doubt if I even knew who she was, or why we had struggled, or that she had been in flames, or that the flames were out' (p. 381). Pip has been lucky. No Orlick or Bentley Drummle, he needed an act which could be construed as morally affirmative if he were to release his destructive feelings for Miss Havisham. Otherwise his conscious mind, held in check by moral considerations, would control his behaviour. This is an interesting psychological insight which probably came to Dickens intuitively. If he had been more self-aware, he would have perceived an affinity with Pip in his own impulse to destroy fictional women in the guise of improving them. Social morality can be, paradoxically, a nice cover-up for an individual's socially unacceptable needs. It cannot, however, simply take the place of those needs as Dickens asks it to do in Pip's initial conversation with Miss Havisham where there is no acknowledgement that forgiveness must strain to triumph over bitterness, no sense of that hard-won control over strongly opposed feelings which makes the reunion with Magwitch powerful and convincing. Dickens is falsifying Pip as well as Miss Havisham.

Conceptually unsophisticated, he cannot think through the implications of the prose. In creating Miss Havisham's world he has constructed subterranean passages for the irrational. Like Daedalus, he is threatened by his own creation. He tries to think away a world where reason is lost, but he cannot. At bottom, as the portrayal of Estella also suggests, he does not have faith in the redemptive powers of the intellect. Perhaps his own intellectual limitations vex him, or perhaps they seem to him signs of a general truth, or perhaps (most likely) his fiction can suggest notions he would not consciously formulate into ideas. In any case, he gets rid of Miss Havisham's power most persuasively when he gives up all pretence to reason and morality, and offers within melodramatic action disjointed images fused together by a highly emotional narrative voice which cannot be attributed to the novelist but is by no strategy distinguished from him either. The novelist himself seems unable to get free of Miss Havisham without investing her violent punishment with something of his own psychic distress, while never admitting his involvement, or even acknowledging that the violence is indeed a punishment and not part of a gratuitous accident. The problem is Pip's, after all. In the room where that vindictive wraith has held power over him for years, distorting disastrously the way he sees himself and the way he believes he is entitled to see the world, Pip at last gains the release of mastery. Circumstances created by the novelist rather than the character cloak that mastery with revenge and allow Pip to overcome Miss Havisham physically while he remains strong himself, recovering his psychic equilibrium while her mind breaks irretrievably. Now the plea for forgiveness is placed after the struggle and is thus made consequent upon it, not upon moral revelation. This time Miss Havisham's words of horrified self-realisation and her plea for absolution echo hauntingly from the tortured nerves of a broken eccentric instead of falling with flabby sentimentality from the lips of a reformed sinner who weeps and grovels upon the floor.

Once more Satis House is in focus as it has not been when Dickens tries to stage Miss Havisham's conversion within her grotesque and self-indulgently filthy rooms. At that point he backed away from physical detail for reasons easy to understand. The place was not quite suitable to the occasion, but if he changed Miss Havisham's clothes and tidied up the rooms, he would be giving away the utterly fantastic nature of that internal cleaning-up he was trying to wish into existence. When Miss Havisham catches fire, physical details again chart psychic action. Dickens keeps his language and insight precise so that the prose is again vivid and persuasive. 'The faded bridal dress' cannot be regenerated. Nevertheless, its burning into 'patches of tinder ... falling in a black shower around us' (p. 381) is a disintegration which frees because the dress is part of a general filth, part of a physical dimension which he has given to Miss Havisham's morally reprehensible life. The prose is impelled by an almost atavistic need to get rid of the filth as though moral and physical repugnance were inseparable. Pip, throwing Miss Havisham to the floor and wrapping his coats around her, 'dragged the great cloth from the table for the same purpose, and with it dragged down the heap of rottenness in the midst, and all the ugly things that sheltered there' (p. 380). The images resonate with meaning which the prose need not assert. Within Satis House adaptation and renewal are not genuine possibilities. The house will later be torn down not renovated by new owners, and if Miss Havisham is to be purified, the logic is fire, not piety. Her mind is light years away from the flexibility and resilience Pip drew upon to reconcile himself gradually to Magwitch and to his lost expectations. Dickens understands Miss Havisham's severely limited capacity for change as long as he writes within the details used to particularise her and allows those details to shape meaning. In describing her altered appearance, there is no attempt to give her a new personality without connection to her past:

> Though every vestige of her dress was burnt, as they told me, she still had something of her old ghastly bridal appearance; for, they had covered her to the throat with white-cotton wool, and as she lay with a white sheet loosely over-lying that, the phantom air of something that had been and was changed was still upon her.
>
> (p. 381)

Change has been horrifying. Self-awareness and contrition have been bought at the expense of a violent shock from which she will not recover. Dickens says specifically that 'the danger lay mainly in the nervous shock', not in the physical burns, and presumably it is from the shock that she dies (p. 381).

This, then, is strikingly different from the optimistic version of moral rescue offered at the beginning of the chapter and from the generally positive notions about life which the novel by this point is promoting. Although Dickens would not be saying explicitly the kinds of things which I think are implied when one analyses the text with an eye to fictional strategies instead of being taken in entirely by explicit surfaces, this is not to claim that the 'real' meaning lies at the subterranean level. The point is that while *both* conscious and unconscious elements appear in the work (the best and the worst of the novel depends upon this fact), the unconscious drives of the novelist have not been accommodated convincingly within his conscious vision. Dickens may believe in the human capacity for moral improvement but in the case of women this belief has a psychological basis to which, understandably, he does not admit. Because he associates energy in women with destructiveness and psychic unbalance he can conceive of their goodness only as broken submissiveness. He uses the socially acceptable notion of conversion as a cover-up for his own vicious desire to punish and break. His inability to be honest shows up in the prose as a split between asserted and subtextual meaning. Because his imaginative powers depend so heavily on intuition, suppression affects his creativity. Astray from the truth about himself, he loses hold of the truth within his fiction, and whenever this happens the novel's verbal brilliance gives way to maudlin prose and the voice of highly inflected rhetoric. The cutting edge of imaginative intuition is precarious.

From *Meridian*, 1 (1982), 11–20.

NOTES

[In Lucy Frost's powerful article the line of disturbing psychoanalytical criticism converges with a particular type of feminist criticism. Her overall concern is with the ways in which author psychology affects the images of women in literature. She suggests that Dickens himself, in his activities as a novelist – in his descriptions, in his treatment of character, in his plotting – is caught up in the same sado-masochistic cycle of 'beating and cringing' as Pip and other characters in the story.

One of her main points is that Dickens is not particularly interested in the 'admired models of Victorian womanhood'. On the contrary, some of his most perceptive writing is about psychologically aberrant 'strong' women. At the same time, however, he is terrified by these women's ability to inflict pain on men, and would therefore like to force on them a 'grim moral logic of repentance and conversion'. In other words, he wishes that Mrs Joe, Estella and Miss Havisham would settle quietly down beside the admirable but unexciting Clara and Biddy, in a world where 'humane dreams come true, where sensitivity flourishes and the callous are without power'. When the strong women resist such pacification, Dickens tries to tame them by a kind of violence, but is not fully aware of what he is doing. As a result, his prose deteriorates and his story loses consistency and credibility.

Frost's quotations are taken from an edition of *Great Expectations* published by Oxford University Press (London, 1974). Ed.]

3

Great Expiations: Dickens and the Betrayal of the Child

JACK RAWLINS

> As I walked along, the times when I was a little helpless creature,
> and my sister did not spare me, vividly returned.
>
> (Pip, at Mrs Joe's funeral)

Traditionally, Pip's progress in *Great Expectations* has been interpreted in one of two ways. Some critics have focused on Pip's personal moral failure, whereupon the novel becomes a myth of error, purgation, and salvation. Pip's ever-increasing tendency to self-blame is seen as the vehicle by which Dickens engineers his moral recovery from the sins of pride, snobbery, vanity, or fantasy (depending on the individual critic). Pip's sense of guilt is then awareness of his own sin, and moves him to reformation.[1] Other critics have focused on society's moral failure, whereupon the novel becomes a myth of original sin and scapegoat atonement. Pip's habitual guilt is seen as an awareness within himself of society's universal error – that there are good people and bad people, victims and oppressors, people of gentility and low-class people. Pip's guilt grows until he is ready to be beaten and burned into insight and to realise that we are all brothers in crime or in love.[2] In both interpretations Pip's guilt is a vehicle to growth and self-awareness; the myth of *Great Expectations* is curative.

I would like to suggest a third interpretation, in which the novel has its source in another myth. In this myth Pip has nothing to learn, his

guilt does not lead him to health, and the two conventional interpretations, with which the societal Dickens would certainly agree,
constitute a betrayal of the novel's original ego-centred impetus.

Writers are dreamers, and their work often serves the function of
dreaming for them, allowing them to meet psychic needs that
cannot be met in the conscious daytime. Dickens is apparently an
unsuccessful dreamer; his literary dreams bring him no peace, and
the longer he lives the more he resembles a man denied the release
of dreaming. In his last years, the demons of his childhood tear at
him with increasing violence; with increasing desperation he seeks
escape in self-destructive behaviour.

If we look at *Great Expectations* as Dickens's attempt to dream a
healthy relationship with the child within him, we can see how the
dream not only denies him peace, but actually turns on the dreamer
and sides with the demons by reaffirming his guilt. The novel begins
with Pip, Dickens's child, methodically wronged by the adult world
around him, but ends with him doing penance; it begins with him
as victim of society's corruption, and ends with him as the single
unforgiven source of it. By the end of the novel Pip has internalised
his tormentors – Jaggers, Orlick – and has become his own most
vindictive prosecutor. And this revaluation of Pip's responsibilities
is forced by Dickens at the expense of the novel's own evidence and
dramatic logic.[3]

The psychological horrors of Dickens's childhood are well known
and need not be detailed here. More significant for us than the pain
itself – the horrors of the blacking factory and an imagined life
trapped there, the apparent betrayal and abandonment by his
parents, the torment at the hands of a whimsical Maria Beadnell –
is Dickens's inability to share the pain with anyone else, and so
accept it. Dickens knew that his parents were acting unnaturally –
but no one else could see it. He knew his lover was inexplicably
torturing him – but no one else could see it. Dickens learned so well
that his experience of the world could not be shared that his
immediate family learned about his days in the blacking factory by
reading Forster's biography after his death,[4] and he was so unable
to confront his past himself that his attempt at autobiography
ended when the Beadnell episode proved unwritable.[5]

Every child learns that his world is not the world others see.
Dickens's way of dealing with this ego/superego conflict is a common and unhappy one: 'What's wrong with me, that I don't see
things the way I should? I must be bad.' That Dickens, given a

choice between the two voices (one saying, 'You hurt' and the other saying, 'You shouldn't'), would feel compelled to choose the second is not surprising, since his age equates the first voice with vanity, anarchy, and madness; rather, it is the clarity with which that first voice is allowed to speak through the opening chapters of *Great Expectations*, before it is silenced, that amazes us.

One's shadow, the part of oneself one learns can't be looked at, insists on being seen. Fantasy has traditionally been a theatre where the demands of the superego can be circumvented and one's shadow be allowed to triumph. *Great Expectations* seems to set out determined to provide Dickens with such absolution, but the novel changes its mind, and ends up arguing that Pip hurts only because he's a bad boy – that is, his feeling the pain at all is a measure of his corruption.

The novel begins with Pip caught in Dickens's own childhood nightmare: he looks at the world and sees everything out of joint, corrupt and unfair, but the adult world assures him that everything's fine. Mrs Joe seems 'in [Pip's] young eyes' (to use Pip's habitual phrase) to be cruel, selfish and mad: the world sees a devoted wife, guardian and housekeeper. Miss Havisham and her household seem psychotic; the world sees only eccentricity. And so with Jaggers, Pumblechook, and the entire crew: Pip looks and sees what is – and sees that things are terribly wrong; the world looks and sees that all is well – but we know they see with lying eyes. One adult, Joe, might seem not to fit the pattern: he can't lie, and he can accept Pip's pain. But in fact he does fit it. He lies, but from a good heart. He insists against fact that his father was a good man and that Mrs Joe is a good woman, in fact that everyone is good and that in general the sun is shining brightly when Pip knows it's raining. Like the Aged P., he sees no evil, and thus is unable to validate Pip's vision of the world. Joe cannot rage, and so reinforces the lesson of the Pumblechookian perspective: a good person wouldn't feel what Pip is feeling.

Pip is tormented by the dissonance between his vision and society's and he habitually wonders if there is something wrong with him to account for the disparity, but we know surely where the fault lies. The first third of the novel rests on a bedrock of the child's congenital egocentric moral rightness. The child sees truly; adults have learned to see falsely. And, as is the way in wish-fulfilling fantasies, the voice of the serpent, the seducer who invites the dreamer to doubt and betray the self, is transparent and inept:

society is spoken for by Mrs Joe and Pumblechook, and we are not tempted to believe them.

Throughout the novel, 'as if' similes represent the discord between Pip's view of things and the world's. The 'as if' simile is a life-long stylistic device of Dickens, and many critics have offered interpretations of it,[6] but in *Great Expectations* similes multiply and take on a special emblematic significance. For Pip, the force of the simile is almost the opposite of its traditional function in poetry. Customarily, similes make connections between like things; the simile-maker fosters community by revealing likeness between things we saw as separate. Pip's similes do something like the reverse of this: they bring unlikes together, not because they have something in common, but because they don't, yet the world has perverted the tenor into something like the vehicle, and hence into something not itself. Pip witnesses an adult world where inauthenticity makes everything like something it is not like.

> 'Swine,' pursued Mr Wopsle, ... pointing his fork at my blushes, as if he were mentioning my christian name.
>
> (p. 58)

> A hackney-coachman ... packed me up in his coach and hemmed me in with a folding and jingling barrier of steps, as if he were going to take me fifty miles.
>
> (p. 187)

> The great numbers on [the convicts'] backs, as if they were street doors.
>
> (p. 249)

To the objective eye, the world makes no sense. 'Swine' isn't Pip's name – why does Wopsle act as if it is? Pip is riding a block or two to Jaggers's – why does the coachman seem to prepare for a long journey? Of course, as adults, we have answers: the coachman is trying to impress Pip with his labours and thus increase his tip, for instance. Generally, things look 'as if' they were something they're not because the world is populated with posturing, dehumanised, compulsive confidence men. Pip finds the world incomprehensible to the extent to which he is innocent of its corruptions. Similes measure the extent to which the world has gone wrong, and so they flourish in scenes of extreme unnaturalness – the *Hamlet* performance, Mrs Joe's funeral, and Joe's meeting with Miss Havisham, where Pip gives us the lesson of the simile directly by saying 'I could hardly have imagined dear old Joe looking so unlike himself or so like some extraordinary bird' (p. 128).

Pip's vision is naturally true. It is also naturally just. Pip is not good; he is fair. In this novel, Joe is good, Biddy is good, the Aged P. is good – what we now call 'nice'. For Dickens, the essential act of goodness is Joe's dead wrong insistence that his father was a good man (p. 77). The goodness is all in Joe, who imposes it on the world by the simple act of assuming it. Pip is immune to this kind of goodness in the beginning, as he makes clear in his response to Joe's judgement of his father – the man wasn't good, and nothing can make Pip overlook that. It is precisely this refusal to commit himself to Dickens's virtuous blindness that makes Pip Dickens's best hope for solving the puzzle of living in a world curiously good and bad at the same time. The dramatic question at this point in the book seems clear: can Pip continue to acknowledge the wrong he sees in the world, and still find a means to moral living without sealing himself off from the flawed human race in a private fantasy society of innocents, as Dickens's other heroes tend to do?

Pip's true judgement tells him he is victimised by exploitive adults who deny his humanity. 'In the little world in which children have their existence ... there is nothing so finely perceived and so finely felt, as injustice', he says in response to Estella's injustice to him; 'Within myself, I had sustained, from my babyhood, a perpetual conflict with injustice. I had known, from the time when I could speak, that my sister ... was unjust to me' (p. 92). He unerringly spots the unfairness of a Pumblechook torturing Pip with sums 'while he [sits] at his ease guessing nothing' (p. 84). Who else but Dickens encourages a child to such a sense of self-worth? Who else would grant a child the right to feel violated by an adult rumpling his hair without his permission (p. 125)? Indeed, Pip is not good. A good boy, reflecting upon his guardian's death, thinks of her virtues, however slight, his debt to her, however small, and the infinite mercy of God. Pip, meditating on Mrs Joe's death, says, 'the times when I was a little helpless creature, and my sister did not spare me, vividly returned' (p. 298). In most literature, children are things for moulding and shaping; in the opening chapters of *Great Expectations*, this child is a thing for defending – a thing that must battle with guts and spite against the adult forces that constantly demand a renunciation of the self.

Thus the novel begins less like a *bildungsroman* than like a quest, and Pip is more knight errant than vessel to be filled: Pip is perfectly, selfishly intact at the novel's beginning, and, as with Gawain or Parsifal, the question is, can he hold fast in a world of doubt? A series of sirens and dragons will bribe, torture and argue in attempts to make him fail to persist. The world will offer only opportunities for straying.

Like all defenders of the right who aren't divine, Pip is racked by guilt. Sometimes he knows where the guilt comes from – Mrs Joe and others drum it into him.

> 'Trouble?' echoed my sister; 'trouble?' And then entered on a fearful catalogue of all the illnesses I had been guilty of, and all the acts of sleeplessness I had committed, and ... all the injuries I had done myself, and all the time she had wished me in my grave, and I had contumaciously refused to go there.
>
> (p. 59)

But righteous people, however clearly their integrity tells them the world is wrong, tremble at their audacity. A part of Pip knows that, 'through all [his] ... penitential performances' Mrs Joe invents to teach him another answer (p. 92), he's right and she's wrong, but another part of Pip fears that Mrs Joe is right – he is guilty of being sick, of not going to his grave when asked to. The adult world encourages Pip to cultivate a sense of original sin; they know he's guilty, because he's a boy – they're just waiting for the crime to be manifested.

Pip learns to see himself through this adult perspective, and moments when he chooses without external reason to convict himself are frequent in the novel. When he hears George Barnwell's history, he feels somehow responsible for the murder (p. 145). When Mrs Joe is struck down, Pip assumes for a moment that he did it (p. 147). When Mrs Pocket rages at her children, Pip remarks without justification, 'I felt quite abashed: as if I myself had done something to rouse' her anger (p. 217). Pip's guilt complex is part of a larger picture, where guilt, crime and violence are so confused in his mind that the sequence of act–consequence–reward breaks down. Pip doesn't strike Mrs Joe down but he is guilty of the act, in that Orlick does it and Orlick acts out the life of Pip's bestial self. And others are as susceptible as Pip himself to sudden, violent retribution for non-crimes: Wopsle is executed, in Pip's imagination, for wet pants. He sits in the damp, and Pip concludes, 'the circumstantial evidence on his trousers would have hanged him if it had been a capital offence' (p. 72).

The novel's opening action, Pip's encounter with Magwitch, makes clear what the novel originally sees Pip as guilty of: he is tormented by fears that he will be caught in the act of charity.[7] And throughout the novel, Pip's natural humanity leads him to do what's right, only to sweat out nightmares in which he is shipped off to the Hulks for refusing to obey the adult world's corrupt commands. Pip feels guilty because his ego isn't strong enough for him to outface the adult world and say, 'I know you're all wrong'. But to such a place we hope he will grow.

Thus far Dickens seems to have created in Pip a perfect vehicle for the exorcism of his childhood demons. Pip sees the truth of things; he is born with a rage for justice and a commitment to the preservation and nurture of the ego; he is racked with guilt, but we see that the guilt is the result of his attempt to integrate the dissonant voices of true ego and false superego. He is subjected to the horrors of the Dickensian childhood – he is stripped of his rights, found guilty of being himself, and rendered invisible – but he's not Oliver Twist this time, and he has the grit to decry his treatment and the determination to right his wrongs by his own hand. If the myth is played out, he will be tempted to forswear the self, but will hold fast; those in the adult world who are open to truth will be converted and will gather around him in a new community of authentic spirits, and those who are not will be expelled or destroyed. There are traces of this myth in the second half of the novel (most clearly with Miss Havisham, who is explicitly punished for her crimes to Pip, in front of Pip, and to whom alone Pip is allowed to express his pain and see it empathetically confirmed), but the novel principally abandons it for another. Pip discovers he really is at fault, that he is the bad boy the adults have been foretelling since his birth, and he ends up doing most of the expiating. From a focus on adults' injustice to him, we move to a focus on his injustice to Joe and Magwitch. Dickens works it out so that Pip's lifelong guilt is finally justified by his own apparent badness, and Pip is saved through cultivated self-loathing. Crying, 'Strike me, Joe. Tell me of my ingratitude. Don't be so good to me' (p. 472), he strips himself of money (i.e. worth and power) and dedicates himself to service – first to Magwitch, then to Herbert. Finally, after years spent breaking the spirit of fantasy at a clerk's desk, Pip can say with Estella, 'I have been bent and broken, but – I hope – into a better shape' (p. 493).

And it is more than Pip simply discovering his own imperfection. As the novel relocates the source of the problem, from a corrupt world to a vain and foolish Pip, it revalues many of the adult characters – Jaggers, Havisham, Magwitch, Joe – and excuses their former behaviour. As Pip discovers the fault in himself, he discovers the relative faultlessness of others, so that the very fact that Pip originally saw wrongness in them becomes evidence at his own sentencing. This pattern is clearest in the treatment of Jaggers, because he seems so thoroughly beyond salvation. In the beginning, Jaggers is very nearly the Devil. He works from a desk chair like a coffin, 'sets man-traps' for everyone (p. 221), hires false witnesses, torments Molly for his own amusement in front of his dinner guests while boasting of his courtroom dishonesty, and generally in his dealings with the human race 'has 'em, soul and body' (p. 283). He is the archetypal adult in Pip's world: a puppet-master the world smiles on, who controls by inducing groundless guilt in others. Pip fears that the wine whispers to Jaggers things to Pip's disadvantage (p. 264), but with Jaggers the world shares Pip's paranoia: Herbert, whose conscience is clear, meets Jaggers and concludes that Herbert himself 'must have committed a felony and forgotten the details of it, he [feels] so dejected and guilty' (p. 311), and Jaggers has a similar effect on Wopsle and everyone else at the Three Jolly Bargemen (p. 163). Thus Jaggers personifies what Pip must learn to retain his integrity in the face of, and with Jaggers much of the rest of the world is ready to support Pip in his perception that the adult's relationship with the world is askew.

The lesson is told clearly in Joe's single encounter with Jaggers. Others accept Jaggers's poor opinion of them, but Joe knows who Joe is, and he knows just as plainly that Jaggers is trying to beat him up. He responds appropriately: 'Which I meantersay ... that if you come into my place bull-baiting and badgering me, come out!' (pp. 168–9). Something like this is what Pip needs: a confrontation with the hypercritical parent and an exorcising of the negative self-concept through a raging attack on the icon.

The confrontation takes place. Pip, armed with incriminating secret knowledge about Jaggers – that is, when the power balance between them seems finally to have tipped in Pip's favour – calls Jaggers to account. But the scene goes horribly wrong, and Pip is forced to exonerate Jaggers of all charges. Jaggers explains that his behaviour in Estella's case has been humane; he 'saved' her from the fate of the criminal's child, he 'sheltered' Molly and 'kept down the old wild violent nature', and so on (pp. 424–6). Finally Jaggers persuades Pip to keep Jaggers's secret, thus making him an accessory and winning from him tacit sanction for Jaggers's behaviour. The oppressive parent has been discovered to be wise and loving – and what of Pip? He looked and saw the devil – there must be something wrong with him. Dickens saves Jaggers, but this salvation isn't Dickens's conventional rebirth through drowning, explosion, or whatever, and the psychological consequences for Pip are dire. Jaggers is not reborn; he is revealed *to have always been* benevolent – so apparently Pip saw falsely. Dickens has to cheat to bring this off – Jaggers cannot be benevolent, as the emotional truth of scenes like the brutalising of Molly attests. Our grown-up tormenters know best, Dickens concludes, but he must lie to himself before he's convinced.[8]

As the novel continues, Dickens exonerates other characters, in each case forcing Pip to recant the supposed error of his original perception. Joe, who was a poor guardian, explains how his failure to protect Pip from Mrs Joe was really wise and humane (p. 478), and Pip again acknowledges the parental wisdom: Joe asks, 'Is he right, that man?' (meaning himself), and Pip responds, 'Dear Joe, he is always right'.[9] Herbert, who has been benevolent but self-deceiving and ineffective throughout the novel, turns out to be 'always right' too, and Pip takes all responsibility for his ever appearing otherwise:

> I often wondered how I had conceived that old idea of his inaptitude, until I was one day enlightened by the reflection, that perhaps the inaptitude had never been in him at all, but had been in me.
>
> (p. 489)

Dickens's determination to find the world 'always right' even embraces Trabb's boy, who is allowed to play hero at the sluice-house, after which Pip absolves him of all traces of 'malignancy', discovers that he is merely a case of 'spare vivacity', and expresses his regret at ever thinking ill of him (p. 443).

And Pip is factually wrong in these cases. Just as Jaggers is a devil, so Herbert is a fool, and Joe was wrong – when he allowed Mrs Joe to destroy Pip's ego, when he assured Pip that Pip was right to follow the money to London and forget the forge. Pip becomes his own Jaggers, his own prosecuting adult, convicting himself of imaginary crimes. He has now internalised his attackers so successfully that he can do to himself what they did to him, and his lectures to himself in the second half of the book are exactly the texts of Mrs Joe's sermons: you're congenitally bad, you're always in the way, everything you do makes trouble for your betters. Now the lesson of the simile is reversed: the distance between the vehicle and the tenor is the measure of Pip's viciousness. The responsibility for wrong-doing lies with the person who creates the wrong by seeing it.[10]

Pip spends the last third of the novel visiting the adults he dared find at fault, exonerating each, and by implication accepting responsibility for their weakness or cruelty. He is a scapegoat, but Dickens seems to think the goat literally committed the sin in the first place. Thus Pip must do more than Christ; he must not only suffer for the sins of the world, he must believe he caused them. Christ is free of guilt, but Pip isn't, so, while Christ is willing to be crucified, Pip crucifies himself.

The conventional view of *Great Expectations* says in rebuttal to all this, No – Pip is guilty; he does indeed have much to expiate. This view, which accepts the older Pip's judgement of his young self, must now be examined. What does the young Pip do that is so bad? The elder Pip says, he fell victim to a vain dream of worldly glory. He wanted to be rich and grand, to impress the vacuous star Estella and win her love. This sin – call it vanity, egoism, fancy – led him to abandon his friends, devote his life to idleness, and deny his fundamental Christian brotherhood with Magwitch. When he is awakened to his error, he embraces Magwitch as his spiritual equal, acknowledges Joe's lack of striving, his acceptance of the world as it is, as a model for moral behaviour, realises that fancy is a betrayer, and puts himself to useful work. In this view, Pip's crimes begin with his love for Estella and are proven by his treatment of Magwitch. Yet the novel offers us the means to rebut Pip's interpretation of these actions.

In terms of the novel's original vision, Magwitch is the epitome of a basic adult perversion: the desire to create, own and exploit human beings as property and extensions of the ego. When he and Pip meet in Pip's London apartments, Magwitch speaks in pure form the doctrine by which adults relate to children in Dickens's world: I made you; you exist only as an extension of me.[11] His view of the world is among the farthest from genuineness in the novel – he prizes books in foreign languages for his inability to read them, for instance (p. 338). Pip has been intentionally prevented from learning a profession to satisfy Magwitch's twisted but all too conventional sense of what makes a gentleman (pp. 219–20), so Pip would be justified in seeing him as the head of a conspiracy, joined by every adult in the novel, to blind Pip, stuff his pockets with money, inflate his head, and send him off to London to run up debts, while assuring him he's thriving all the time. The older Pip often sounds as if young Pip defiantly embraced a life of vanity in the face of sound adult counsel to the contrary, but sometimes he knows better: 'I acquiesced, of course, knowing nothing to the contrary' (p. 220).

When Magwitch returns to England, the nature of the conspiracy is revealed to Pip. How does he react? We might expect one of two reactions. An ego-centred response would be to rage at his puppet-master. A more mature reaction would be to acknowledge the puppet strings that manipulate the manipulator. Magwitch is of course not the source of the corruption that destroys Pip, any more than our parents invent the lies they teach us. Typically children move through their rage at the imperfect parent to sympathetic understanding. But Pip's response poisons his opportunity for either insight. He loathes Magwitch, but for reprehensible reasons. He does not respond to the moral horror of what Magwitch has done to him, or to what the world is doing to Magwitch and all of us, but is instead repulsed by the man's poor breeding and coarse manners. Thus he is able later to fault himself for being repulsed and do penance. Dickens avoids the ego-strengthening response to Magwitch and fixes on the rare one that facilitates Pip's self-loathing. Later, Pip is unable to see any but the single aspect of his relationship with Magwitch – that he was repulsed by him out of snobbishness. Pip is indeed guilty, but that sin treacherously prohibits Pip from dealing with the rest of the complex relationship – Pip can't be angry with Magwitch, because he now owes him. Again Pip has had the opportunity to confront one of the architects of his misery, and has been forced to accept responsibility for all evil and do penitential service.

This is a crucial loss for Pip, because Magwitch, more than Jaggers, is at the centre of young Pip's complex and baffling relationship with the world. Pip's benevolence is first established by his helping Magwitch on the moors, his sense of guilt blossoms when he becomes a criminal for Magwitch's sake, and his sense of being ethically at odds with the world is focused by the world's indifference to the plight of convicts and Magwitch particularly. As the father of Estella, Magwitch is the physiological as well as financial maker of Pip's Expectations. He is Pip's symbolic father and child, benefactor and destroyer, supporter and exploiter, society's victim and a caricature of its vices. Given all this, the central moral question of the novel is, how should Pip feel toward Magwitch?

And how has Pip served him? He has fed him, stolen for him, risked his life attempting to effect his escape from England, sympathised with him and acknowledged his inherent human integrity from the beginning – and is shocked by his lowness in London. Out of all this, Pip finds a kernel with which to nourish a sense of his own error, and he takes it. And to perfect his own culpability, he does with Magwitch what he does with Herbert, Jaggers and company: he redefines him free of blame. He says that Magwitch returned to England 'for [Pip's] sake' (p. 468), which is at best a gross oversimplification of some very questionable motives ('that there hunted dunghill dog ... got his head so high that he could make a gentleman' [p. 337]), and he sums up the lesson of the relationship by saying, 'I only saw in him a much better man than I had been to Joe' (p. 457).

The older Pip's perspective on his love for Estella is similarly narrow and oddly slanted to his own detriment. To him his love is simply proof of his folly, and is the constant target of his best mocking irony. He should love Biddy, he tells us. 'It would be very good for [him]' to 'get Estella out of [his] head' he says (p. 157); when he sees things clearly, he knows that Biddy is 'immeasurably better than Estella' and that the forge offers 'sufficient means of self-respect and happiness' (p. 159). His turning from Biddy and the forge is thus a rejection of goodness in favour of splendid surface. That his preference for Estella is a matter for the most severe contrition is made clear by the terms of his planned proposal to Biddy: 'humbled and repentant', Pip hopes to be received 'like a for-given child' and allowed to submit to her guidance (p. 481). Nothing could be more serious in the context of this novel than that Pip should seek a wife who will serve as authoritarian mother – that after a series of disastrous parent figures, Pip should abase himself before another parent, and this one someone he should, in Victorian terms, rule over – a wife. Perhaps we are never so aware of how much Dickens's late view of Pip differs from ours as when he denies Pip his Biddy and intends it as a bitter pill – and we gasp with relief.

We gasp because we know – the novel has let us know firmly – that, however much Pip should love Biddy, he doesn't, and for good reason: she, like the forge world, is good, but only good. She can't dream. The forge offers 'simple faith and clear home-wisdom' (p. 486), but Pip needs more in life, and we applaud his reaching out, however inadequately the world rewards the reaching out, however insistently the older Pip characterises the reaching out as vanity. Biddy and Joe are archetypes of Christian passivity; they endure everything cheerfully, and it is precisely Pip's unwillingness to devote his life to such mere endurance that makes him great, and dangerous. Pip is here much like Clarissa. In the midst of his problems with Magwitch, Pip cries, 'I would far far rather have worked at the forge all the days of my life than I would ever have come to this!' (p. 358). Similarly Clarissa longs for her oppressive household when she is in Lovelace's grip. Both Pip and Clarissa momentarily see themselves as over-reachers who got justly burned and now regret their aspirations, but Clarissa probably returns to a more just estimate of things than Pip. Pip's words here acknowledge that life at the forge is a sentence – a death of the spirit. Both Clarissa and Pip think they have won a victory over pride when they own a fault they don't have.

The premise of the two novels is that Clarissa and Pip must hold out for a life that nurtures their spiritual greatness. Anna Howe and Biddy say, learn to want less – but we know they say this out of the sorry conventionality of their souls; they're satisfied with less because they can't dream. Clarissa says, 'I'll never disobey my parents again'; Pip says, 'I'll never dream again' – and we shake our heads as our heroes forsake exactly what has won our allegiance.

That Pip's love for Estella is an argument for his greatness shows when he learns of her plans to marry Drummle. She assures him that she will be out of his thoughts soon, and he replies with an outburst of which I will only quote the beginning.

> Out of my thoughts! You are part of my existence, part of myself. You have been in every line I have ever read. ... You have been in every prospect I have ever seen since. ... You have been the embodiment of every graceful fancy that my mind has ever become acquainted with.
>
> (p. 378)

The rhetoric is thick, but the force is clear: here is what makes Pip glorious. And Estella, however unworthy of such feeling, is the nearest thing to a worthy object of aesthetic worship the world of the novel provides. Pip, like other artists, writes love sonnets to someone dwarfed by the poetry.[12] But, because Estella cannot bear the weight of Pip's sublime passion, he should marry Biddy, and forswear passion, and be merely good and happy? Never. Pip forgets why he knew he must leave home, but the convicts don't. One asks the other what Pip's country is like, and the other replies, 'A most beastly place. Mudbank, mist, swamp, and work; work, swamp, mist and mudbank' (p. 251). Pip need only add, 'And no poetry'.

In short, the older Pip, by thinking in terms of goodness, misses his own greatness. And what finally is his crime? To love grandly, despite the failure of women to deserve it; to aspire, despite society's failure to provide anything worth aspiring to; to dream, despite society's insistence that all dreams be in terms of money or social status. Pip is presented with a noble problem: can a poetic spirit fulfil himself and remain authentic in Dickensian society? Pip tries. He is wide open to the world, and the world fails to provide a woman worth adoring, a deed worth doing, an adult worth emulating.[13] Pip looks at the rubble that is his life and concludes, I should have been a Joe. But we know better. Pip is destined to be Dickens.

Why Dickens must find Pip to blame is made clearer by a modern analogy. Pip is like a great-souled woman in America in the 1950s. She is born to two options: stay at home and not really exist, or marry, and be a housewife. She will marry of course, and of course find it empty. When her soul cries out against the spiritual poverty, she will seek to escape to a life where her dreams can be lived, but society will offer her only one set of terms for such escape – sexual ones. She will have an affair. It won't work, because society lied when it assured her that sex is what she needed, but when her experiment at self-fulfilment fails she will blame herself. She was guilty, she will suppose, for dreaming at all; she should have been content with the housework. She will contritely return to make the marriage work. The boredom will now be seen as a measure of her depravity – good people don't feel bored. Why was I such a fool as to want more than what's right, she will ask herself, especially since when I got it I didn't really want it? If she is lucky, she will abase herself before her husband too late, only to discover that he has abandoned her for someone who knows her place enough not to dream.

This is exactly Pip's experience. His affair is with wealth and social position instead of sex, because he is of another age, but the real agent of the fiasco is the same: a society that says to the large-souled, this (money or sex) is what your dreams are really seeking. Pip and our imaginary housewife are both victims of 'a certain spiritual grandeur ill-matched with the meanness of opportunity', as George Eliot says of her Victorian saint. Pip is much like Dorothea Brooke, but Dickens is not like George Eliot; his need to exonerate the parents is stronger. Finally, he saddles Pip with the same guilty message that therapists emasculated women with in the years before the women's movement: the fault is in you for feeling dissatisfied;

feel less. Look at Joe: he's so 'good' his wife can torture him, and he doesn't feel a thing.

In the Victorian period, Dickens's recantation must be expected. For him to maintain the validity of Pip's pain in the face of a unanimous adult assurance that he shouldn't hurt, Dickens would have to declare triumphant the subjective reality of the ego. But in a shared sense of what is lies society's last anchor in the winds of change. To presume the inherent validity of feelings is to make an idol of the self, as Tennyson's career reminds us again and again. Tennyson's protagonists risk loss of sanity through immersion in the self, and with luck find salvation in a commitment to externals. The object of devotion may be an illusion or (as in the case of the Crimean War) an atrocity, but it takes the protagonist out of himself, and thus the commitment is healthy – like Joe's devotion to a bad father and a bad wife.

So Dickens saves his community by silencing the seer of unpalatable truths and convincing him that he is somehow responsible for the evils by seeing them. Dickens plays Orlick, stringing Pip up for crimes like being 'in the way' (p. 436), seeing through masks, being genuine ('They writes fifty hands; they're not like sneaking you, as writes but one' [p. 438]), and being responsible for what others have done. The poetic Pip dies then, survived by a clerk. But in his suffering he speaks more directly than Dickens ever was able to do of the agony of living in a society that demands a recantation of the self. Pip foresees his death, and considers the consequences:

> Estella's father would believe I had deserted him, would be taken, would die accusing me; even Herbert would doubt me ... ; Joe and Biddy would never know how sorry I had been that night; none would ever know what I had suffered, how true I had meant to be, what an agony I had passed through. The death close before me was terrible, but far more terrible than death was the dread of being misremembered after death. ... I saw myself despised by unborn generations.
>
> (p. 436)

'None would ever know what I had suffered.' At the heart of Pip's regret is his sense that he, like Dickens, feels unknown to the world. I know of no more powerful expression in literature of the child's idea that his sense of himself clashes inexplicably, horribly with the adult world's image of him. And as is typical in cases of such self-contempt, Pip and Dickens grow to be admired, loved, and cherished by others, and remain misremembered and accused only by themselves.

Dickens takes his son upon the mountain, in what generations of critics have found a heroic sacrifice. For those who disagree, Dickens allows Pip a small ego victory. A man who has sacrificed his inner child the better to serve in society's militia often finds that child reborn in the body of his offspring. Pip has no children, but Joe and Biddy have one for him, a child taken for Pip's own by Estella (in the original ending). Thank God, Pip likes him. Perhaps this Pip will never have to cry, 'Don't be so good to me'.

Dickens is not so lucky. Unable to ask for recognition of his shadow self, unable to find service that is expiation enough, unable to infatuate enough women, sell enough copies, wow enough audiences to justify self-esteem, he finishes Orlick's task, and kills himself with overwork. None ever knew what he had suffered.

From *Studies in English Literature, 1500–1900*, 23 (1983), 667–83.

NOTES

[Jack Rawlins's exuberant essay illustrates a tendency in some recent criticism of *Great Expectations* to meet psychoanalytical critics on their own ground, borrowing their terminology, but moderating the harshness of their verdicts. Rawlins's main target is criticism which has blamed Dickens and Pip for their psychological formation as if they themselves were entirely responsible for it. Like some sociological and structuralist critics, he emphasises the pressures of society on the developing mind, though he also strongly believes that Dickens and Pip could have shaken society off their backs.

Even critics who see Pip's shortcomings as representative of Victorian society as a whole have argued that Pip's oppressive sense of guilt is a healthy prerequisite to full self-understanding and awareness. This view is presumably close to Dickens's own conscious intentions, but Rawlins will have none of it. For him, Pip's guilt is part of a self-destructive process by which both Pip and Dickens punish the honest, child's-eye view of the world, in this way distorting the psyche into socially acceptable patterns of bad faith. In Rawlins's Freudian terminology, this is a betrayal of the novel's strong original focus on the ego. In the more old-fashioned gloss which Rawlins also offers: 'the older Pip, by thinking in terms of goodness, misses his own greatness'. Pip's only crimes are to love grandly, to aspire, and to dream, and the book traces the repression of his poetic altruism beneath the prejudices of Victorian society, prejudices which Dickens himself regrettably condones.

Rawlins's quotations are from *Great Expectations*, ed. Angus Calder, Penguin English Library (Harmondsworth, 1965). Ed.]

1. For interpretations of *Great Expectations* along these lines, see Barbara Hardy, 'The Change of Heart in Dickens' Novels', *Victorian Studies*, 5 (September, 1961), 49–67; Dorothy Van Ghent, *The English Novel: Form and Function* (New York, 1953); J. Hillis Miller, *Charles Dickens: The World of his Novels* (Cambridge, Mass., 1958); and Harry Stone, *Dickens and the Invisible World* (Bloomington, Indiana, 1979). That *Great Expectations* is an 'implicit critique of fantasy' is stated as a critical truism by Robert Ransom in a review of Stone, in *Dickens Studies Annual 9*, ed. Michael Timko, Fred Kaplan and Edward Giuliano (1981), 270. For a classic expression of the idea that *Great Expectations* is a morality play about a fantasist brought to reality's heel, see Paul Pickrel's classroom guide to the novel, in *Dickens: A Collection of Critical Essays*, ed. Martin Price (Englewood Cliffs, New Jersey, 1967), pp. 158–68.

2. For interpretations along these lines, see Taylor Stoehr, *Dickens: The Dreamer's Stance* (Ithaca, New York, 1965), esp. pp. 91–4; Van Ghent, *The English Novel*; and Stone, *Dickens and the Invisible World*. Critics commonly observe both patterns simultaneously, and they need not be mutually exclusive.

3. It has been recognised by most critics that Pip is Dickens, in a way that's striking even in terms of Dickens's habitually autobiographical art. See Stone, *Dickens and the Invisible World*, p. 309, and E. Pearlman, 'Inversion in *Great Expectations*', *Dickens Studies Annual*, 7 (1978), 190–202, on *Great Expectations* as inverted *Copperfield*. That *Great Expectations* is an attempt to redo the autobiographical business of *Copperfield*, but this time closer to the nub, is a critical commonplace, and Miller, *Charles Dickens* (pp. 252 ff.) argues that Pip is the archetypal Dickens hero. It is also frequently noted that *Great Expectations* is Dickens's first serious attempt to 'get the good and bad together', in Edmund Wilson's famous phrase (in *The Wound and the Bow*) – that is, to deal with the notion that good and bad in the real world run complexly through the same plot lines, the same characters, and the same social milieux. Given this consensus view of *Great Expectations* as essential confrontation by Dickens with the issues of self and morality, it seems odd that Pip is so unliked – by himself, by his creator it appears, and by the novel's readers. And he is disliked for reasons opposite to the conventional dislike modern readers have for Dickens's good people: typically we find Dickensian heroes cloying in their niceness – they are too comfortably superego-dominated. Pip is ego-dominated, and generations of critics have been ready with Dickens to condemn him for not serving well enough. He is too proud (Miller, *Charles Dickens*, p. 274), and pride is exactly what we wish Esther and her ilk had more of.

4. Edgar Johnson, *Charles Dickens: His Tragedy and Triumph*, 2 vols (New York, 1952), 1:44. See also 1:132.

5. Johnson, ibid., 2:659–60. That Dickens could neither confront his past nor reveal it to anyone else is a major thesis of Johnson's biography and is developed in several passages beyond those cited here. The idea that Dickens uses his novels as dream vehicles for coming to terms with an intolerable, unfaceable past is a central theme of Stoehr, *Dickens: The Dreamer's Stance*, esp. pp. 91–4.

It can be argued that Dickens, at the time of writing *Great Expectations*, might be more preoccupied with the agonies of the present, most notably his affair with Ellen Ternan and the resultant potential destruction of his familial, social and professional life, but his handling of the affair makes it clear that it is not a new problem – rather, it is a projection of lifelong demons, especially his search for a love that satisfies, and his belief that what he most centrally is unfaceable and must therefore be hidden and hysterically denied. He is, in effect, acting out Pip's bad boy image.

6. See Stoehr, *Dickens: The Dreamer's Stance*, p. 105, for a recent interpretation.

7. Critics are divided on the character of Pip's first service to Magwitch. Some see him motivated, as I do, by charity; others see him motivated by fear. It hardly matters, since fear equals self-preservation and charity is a recognition of the communal self one shares with others. Pip is acting rightly, either in terms of morality or in terms of the ego.

8. For another discussion of a manifestly malicious parent-figure whose benignity is insisted on for political reasons, see Harry Keyishian, 'Griselda on the Elizabethan Stage: The *Patient Grissil* of Chettle, Dekker, and Haughton', *Studies in English Literature*, 16 (Spring 1976), 253–61. And for an alternative interpretation of Jaggers's apparent contradictions, see Anthony Winner, 'Character and Knowledge in Dickens: The Enigma of Jaggers', *Dickens Studies Annual* 3, ed. Robert B. Partlow, Jr (1974), 100–21, where Winner argues that Pip grows by his ability to understand Jaggers's moral ambiguities. Winner argues that Dickens's heroes see things in moral blacks and whites, and Pip is morally superior to Dickens's other heroes because the lesson of Jaggers leads him out of a fantasy world of allegorical absolutes into the real world of moral greys, means vs ends, and expediencies. Winner's argument is based on the common critical assumption, which I obviously do not share, that Dickens's characters are *supposed* to grow from the fantasy principle to the reality principle – that Pip's fancy is something to be fixed.

9. Pearlman, 'Inversion in *Great Expectations*' (p. 195) discusses Dickens's dramatic difficulties in promoting Joe as worthy of emulation despite his failure as guardian, and offers a unique resolution of the difficulty.

10. Stone, *Dickens and the Invisible World* (p. 337) and others note the basic unreason in Pip's 'accepting responsibility for ... his fellow's sins',

but argue that in the unreason lies Dickens's message: that one must recognise the original sin shared by us all, expressed in a social sickness not of anyone's making, and awaiting a scapegoat expiation. Thus Van Ghent, *The English Novel*, argues that Dickens's enlightened characters purposely bow down before those who have trespassed against them, not before those they have trespassed against – Mrs Joe bows down before Orlick, not Pip, for instance (p. 138). This myth of Christian redemption is of course in the novel, and seems to have the societal Dickens's full support, but still seems a betrayal of the novel's original impetus. The central question is, is Pip's guilt, which all critics have recognised is the essence of his character, a congenital guiding light to wisdom, or is it something bred by the adult world and best unlearned?

11. *Great Expectations* apparently grew in Dickens's imagination from the seminal image of Magwitch as tragi-comic puppet-master of Pip's vain fortunes (Miller, *Charles Dickens: The World of his Novels*, p. 250). Of course Dickens may have shifted his focus later, and critics agree that if the world of the novel has a source of evil it is Compeyson, but Compeyson does not represent this particular childhood horror as well as Magwitch, because Compeyson's brand of manipulation is not so clearly a need to extend one's ego, to clone oneself, and so deny the separate existence of the manipulated party.

12. Criticism of *Great Expectations* traditionally tests itself by interpreting the novel's two endings in light of its thesis. I will attempt something of the sort. Estella cannot be a fit wife for Pip, because she cannot share his dreams. She is a symbol, and as such is more fit to pursue than Biddy, but she is fit only for pursuit. The first ending, though low-key, works because we can be convinced that Estella can be beaten into humble goodness and then married to a merely good man. But for her to marry Pip, we would need to know she had discovered more than goodness – she would need a firing of the poetic spirit, not a chastisement of the ego, and this we don't believe beating can produce. Dickens seems to realise, though faintly, what Pip really needs, because in both endings Estella suggests that at last she has suffered enough to empathise with Pip. She has learned 'to understand what [Pip's] heart used to be', and this phrase is almost the only thing the two endings share. To this point in the novel, no character could claim to share Pip's vision of the world beyond bits and pieces. With that benediction, the novel can end. If we thought that Estella meant it in any profound way, perhaps they could wed, but we don't.

13. Miller, *Charles Dickens: The World of his Novels* (p. 254) to my knowledge is alone in acknowledging that Pip's path to Great Expectations is the most sensible choice among the alternatives society provides for him.

4

Repetition, Repression, and Return: *Great Expectations* and the Study of Plot

PETER BROOKS

I

Great Expectations is exemplary for a discourse on plot in many respects, not least of all for its beginning. For what the novel chooses to present at its outset is precisely the search for a beginning. As in so many nineteenth-century novels, the hero is an orphan, thus undetermined by any visible inheritance, apparently unauthored. This clears away Julien Sorel's problems with paternity. There may be sociological and sentimental reasons to account for the high incidence of orphans in the nineteenth-century novel, but clearly the parentless protagonist frees an author from struggle with pre-existing authorities, allowing him to create afresh all the determinants of plot within his text. He thus profits from what Gide called the 'lawlessness' of the novel by starting with an undefined, rule-free character and then bringing the law to bear upon him – creating the rules – as the text proceeds. With Pip, Dickens begins as it were with a life that is for the moment precedent to plot, and indeed necessarily in search of plot. Pip when we first see him is himself in search of the 'authority' – the word stands in the second paragraph of the novel – that would define and justify – authorise – the plot of his ensuing life.

The 'authority' to which Pip refers here is that of the tombstone which bears the names of his dead parents, the names that have already been displaced, condensed and superseded in the first paragraph, where Pip describes how his 'infant tongue' (literally, a speechless tongue: a catachresis that points to a moment of emergence, of entry into language) could only make of the name, Philip Pirrip, left to him by the dead parents, the monosyllabic Pip. 'So, I called myself Pip, and came to be called Pip.' This originating moment of Pip's narration and his narrative is a self-naming that already subverts whatever authority could be found in the text of the tombstones. The process of reading that text is described by Pip the narrator as 'unreasonable', in that it interprets the appearance of the lost father and mother from the shape of the letters of their names. The tracing of the name – which he has already distorted in its application to self – involves a misguided attempt to remotivate the graphic symbol, to make it directly mimetic, mimetic specifically of origin. Loss of origin, misreading, and the problematic of identity are bound up here in ways we will further explore later on. The question of reading and writing – of learning to compose and to decipher texts – is persistently thematised in the novel.[1]

The decipherment of the tombstone text as confirmation of loss of origin – as unauthorisation – is here at the start of the novel the prelude to Pip's *cogito*, the moment in which his consciousness seizes his existence as other, alien, forlorn:

> My first most vivid and broad impression of the identity of things seems to me to have been gained on a memorable raw afternoon towards evening. At such a time I found out for certain, that this bleak place overgrown with nettles was the churchyard; and that Philip Pirrip, late of this parish, and also Georgiana, wife of the above, were dead and buried; and that Alexander, Bartholomew, Abraham, Tobias, and Roger, infant children of the aforesaid, were also dead and buried; and that the dark flat wilderness beyond the churchyard, intersected with dykes and mounds and gates, with scattered cattle feeding on it, was the marshes; and that the low leaden line beyond was the river; and that the distant savage lair from which the wind was rushing, was the sea; and that the small bundle of shivers growing afraid of it all and beginning to cry, was Pip.
>
> 'Hold your noise!' cried a terrible voice.
>
> (p. 1)

The repeated verbs of existence – 'was' and 'were' – perform an elementary phenomenology of Pip's world, locating its irreducible objects and leading finally to the individual subject as other, as aware of his existence through the emotion of fear, fear that then appears as the origin of voice, or articulated sound, as Pip begins to cry: a cry that is immediately censored by the command of the convict Magwitch, the father-to-be, the fearful intrusive figure of future authorship who will demand of Pip: 'Give us your name.'

The scenario is richly suggestive of the problem of identity, self-consciousness, naming, and language that will accompany Pip throughout the novel, and points to the original decentring of the subject in regard to himself. For purposes of my study of plot, it is important to note how this beginning establishes Pip as an existence without a plot, at the very moment of occurrence of that event which will prove to be decisive for the plotting of his existence, as he will discover only two-thirds of the way through the novel. Alien, unauthorised, self-named, at the point of entry into the language code and the social systems it implies, Pip will in the first part of the novel be in search of a plot, and the novel will recount the gradual precipitation of a sense of plot around him, the creation of portents of direction and intention.

II

The novelistic middle, which is perhaps the most difficult of Aristotle's 'parts' of a plot to talk about, is in this case notably characterised by the return. Quite literally: it is Pip's repeated returns from London to his home town that constitute the organising device of the whole of the London period, the time of the Expectations and their aftermath. Pip's returns are always ostensibly undertaken to make reparation to the neglected Joe, an intention never realised; and always implicitly an attempt to discover the intentions of the putative donor in Satis House, to bring her plot to completion. Yet the returns also always bring his regression, in Satis House, to the status of the 'coarse and common boy' (ch. 29, p. 222) whose social ascension is hallucinatorily denied, his return to the nightmare of unprogressive repetition; and, too, a revival of the repressed convict association, the return of the childhood spell. Each return suggests that Pip's official plots, which seem to speak of progress, ascent and the satisfaction of desire, are in fact subject to a process of repetition of the yet unmastered past, the true determinant of his life's direction.

The pattern of the return is established in Pip's first journey back from London, in chapter 28. His decision to visit Joe is quickly

thrown into the shade by the presence on the stagecoach of two
convicts, one of whom Pip recognises as the man of the file and the
rum and water, Magwitch's emissary. There is a renewed juxta-
position of official, genteel judgement on the convicts, voiced by
Herbert Pocket – 'What a vile and degraded spectacle' – and Pip's
inward avowal that he feels sympathy for their alienation. On the
roof of the coach, seated in front of the convicts, Pip dozes off while
pondering whether he ought to restore the two one-pound notes that
the convict of the file had passed him so many years before. Upon
regaining consciousness, the first two words he hears, continuing his
dream thoughts, are: 'Two one-pound notes.' There follows the convict's account of his embassy from 'Pip's convict' to the boy who
had saved him. Although Pip is certain that the convict cannot recognise him, so changed in age, circumstance, and even name (since
Herbert Pocket calls him 'Handel'), the dreamlike experience forces
a kind of recognition of a forgotten self, refound in fear and pain:

> I could not have said what I was afraid of, for my fear was altogether
> undefined and vague, but there was great fear upon me. As I walked
> on to the hotel, I felt that a dread, much exceeding the mere
> apprehension of a painful or disagreeable recognition, made me
> tremble. I am confident that it took no distinctness of shape, and that
> it was the revival for a few minutes of the terror of childhood.
>
> (ch. 28, p. 217)

The return to origins has led to the return of the repressed, and vice
versa. Repetition as return becomes a reproduction and re-enactment
of infantile experience: not simply a recall of the primal moment,
but a reliving of its pain and terror, suggesting the impossibility of
escape from the originating scenarios of childhood, the condemna-
tion forever to replay them.

This first example may stand for the other returns of the novel's
middle, which all follow the same pattern, which all double return
to with return of and show Pip's ostensible progress in the world to
be subverted by the irradicable presence of the convict-communion
and the Satis House nightmare. It is notable that toward the end of
the middle – as the novel's dénouement approaches – there is an
acceleration in the rhythm of these returns, as if to affirm that all
the clues to Pip's future, the forward movement of his plot, in fact
lie in the past. Repetition as return speaks as a textual version of
the death instinct, plotting the text, beyond the seeming dominance
of the pleasure principle, toward its proper end, imaging this end as

necessarily a time before the beginning. In the moment of crisis before the climax of the novel's action, Pip is summoned back to the marshes associated with his infancy to face extinction at the hands of Orlick – who has throughout the novel acted the role of Pip's 'bad double', a hateful and sadistic version of the hero – in a threatened short-circuit of the text, as Pip indicates when he thinks how he will be misunderstood by others if he dies prematurely, without explanation: 'Misremembered after death ... despised by unborn generations' (ch. 53, p. 404). Released from this threat, Pip attempts to escape from England, but even this voyage out to another land and another life leads him back: the climax of Magwitch's discovery and recapture are played out in the Thames estuary, where 'it was like my own marsh country, flat and monotonous, and with a dim horizon' (ch. 54, p. 416). We are back in the horizontal perspectives and muddy tidal flats that are so much a part of our perception of the childhood Pip.

But before speaking further of resolutions, I must say a word about the novel's great 'recognition scene', the moment at which the latent becomes manifest, the repressed convict plot is forcibly brought to consciousness, a scene that decisively re-enacts both a return of the repressed and a return to the primal moment of childhood. The recognition scene comes in chapter 39, and it is preceded by two curious paragraphs at the end of chapter 38 in which Pip as narrator suggests that the pages he has just written, concerning his frustrated courtship of Estella, constitute, on the plane of narration itself, a last binding of that plot in its overt version, as a plot of romance, and that now he must move on to a deeper level of plot – reaching further back – which subsumes as it subverts all the other plots of the novel: 'All the work, near and afar, that tended to the end had been accomplished.' That this long-range plot is presented as analogous to 'the Eastern story' in which a heavy slab of stone is carved out and fitted into the roof in order that it may fall on 'the bed of state in the flush of conquest' seems in coded fashion to suggest punishment for erotic transgression, which we may want to read as return of the nightmare plot of Satis House, forcing its way through the fairy tale, speaking of the perverse, sadistic eroticism that Pip has covered over with his erotic object choice – Estella, who in fact represents the wrong choice of plot and another danger of short-circuit. To anticipate later revelations, we should note that Estella will turn out to be approximately Pip's sister – natural daughter of Magwitch as he is Magwitch's adoptive son – which lends force to the idea that she, like so many Romantic maidens, is marked by the interdict, as well as the seduction, of incest, which, as the perfect androgynous coupling, is precisely the short-circuit of desire.[2]

The scene of Magwitch's return operates for Pip as a painful forcing through of layers of repression, an analogue of analytic work, compelling Pip to recognise that what he calls 'that chance encounter of long ago' is no chance, and cannot be assigned to the buried past but must be repeated, re-enacted, worked through in the present. The scene replays numerous details of their earlier encounter, and the central moment of recognition comes as a re-enactment and revival of the novel's primal scene, played in dumb show, a mute text which the more effectively stages recognition as a process of return to the inescapable past:

> Even yet I could not recall a single feature, but I knew him! If the wind and the rain had driven away the intervening years, had scattered all the intervening objects, had swept us to the churchyard where we first stood face to face on such different levels, I could not have known my convict more distinctly than I knew him now, as he sat in the chair before the fire. No need to take a file from his pocket and show it to me; no need to take the handkerchief from his neck and twist it round his head; no need to hug himself with both his arms, and take a shivering turn across the room, looking back at me for recognition. I knew him before he gave me one of those aids, though, a moment before, I had not been conscious of remotely suspecting his identity.
>
> (ch. 39, p. 301)

The praeterition on which the passage is constructed – 'no need ... no need' – marks the gradual retrieval of the past as its involuntary repetition within the present. The repetition takes place – as Magwitch's effective use of indicative signs may suggest – in the mode of the symbolic, offering a persuasive instance of Freud's conception of repetition as a form of recollection brought into action by repression and resistance to its removal. It becomes clear that the necessity for Pip to repeat and work through everything associated with his original communion with Magwitch is a factor of his 'forgetting' this communion: a forgetting that is merely conscious. The reader has undergone a similar process through textual repetition and return, one that in his case has had the function of not permitting him to forget.

The scene of Magwitch's return is an important one for any study of plot since it demonstrates so well how such a novelist as Dickens can make plotting the central vehicle and armature of meaning in the narrative text. All the issues raised in the novel – social, ethical, interpretive – are here simultaneously brought to climax through the peripety of the plot. Exposure of the 'true' plot of Pip's life brings with it instantaneous consequences for all the other 'codes' of the novel, as he recognises with the statement, 'All the truth of my position came *flashing* on me; and its disappointments, dangers, disgraces, consequences of all kinds' (ch. 39, p. 303 – my italics). The return of the repressed – the repressed as knowledge of the self's other story, the true history of its misapprehended desire – forces a total revision of the subject's relation to the orders within which it constitutes meaning.

Magwitch poses unanswerable questions, about the origins of Pip's property and the means of his social ascent, which force home to Pip that he has covered over a radical lack of original authority. Like Oedipus – who cannot answer Tiresias's final challenge: who are your parents? – Pip does not know where he stands. The result has been the intrusion of an aberrant, contingent authorship – Magwitch's – in the story of the self. Education and training in gentility turn out to be merely an agency in the repression of the determinative convict plot. Likewise, the daydream/fairy tale of Satis House stands revealed as a repression, or perhaps a 'secondary revision', of the nightmare. That it should be the criminally deviant, transgressive plot that is shown to have priority over all the others stands within the logic of the model derived from *Beyond the Pleasure Principle*, since it is precisely this plot that most markedly constitutes the detour from inorganic quiescence: the arabesque of the narratable. One could almost derive a narratological law here: the true plot will be the most deviant. We might be tempted to see this deviant arabesque as gratuitous, the figure of 'pure narration'. Yet we are obliged to remotivate it, for the return of the repressed shows that the story Pip would tell about himself has all along been undermined and rewritten by the more complex history of unconscious desire, unavailable to the conscious subject but at work in the text. Pip has in fact misread the plot of his life.

III

The novel in fact toward its end appears to record a generalised breakdown of plots: none of the schemes machinated by the charac-

ters manages to accomplish its aims. The proof *a contrario* may be
the 'oversuccessful' result of Miss Havisham's plot, which has turned
Estella into so heartless a creature that she cannot even experience
emotional recognition of her benefactress. Miss Havisham's plotting
has been a mechanical success but an intentional failure, as her final
words, during her delirium following the fire, may suggest:

> Towards midnight she began to wander in her speech, and after that
> it gradually set in that she said innumerable times in a low solemn
> voice, 'What have I done?' And then, 'When she first came, I meant
> to save her from misery like mine.' And then, 'Take the pencil and
> write under my name, "I forgive her"!' She never changed the order
> of these three sentences, but she sometimes left out a word in one or
> other of them; never putting in another word, but always leaving a
> blank and going on to the next word.
>
> (ch. 49, pp. 381–2)

The cycle of three statements suggests a metonymic movement in
search of arrest, a plot that can never find satisfactory resolution,
that unresolved must play over its insistent repetitions, until
silenced by death. Miss Havisham's deathbed scene transmits a
'wisdom' that is in the deconstructive mode, a warning against plot.

We confront the paradox that in this most highly plotted of
novels, where Dickens performs all his thematic demonstrations
through the manipulation of plot, we witness an evident subversion
and futilisation of the very concept of plot. If the chosen plots turn
out to be erroneous, unauthorised, self-delusive, the deep plots
when brought to light turn out to be criminally tainted, deviant,
and thus unusable. Plot as direction and intention in existence
appears ultimately to be as evanescent as Magwitch's money, the
product of immense labour, deprivation and planning, which is in
the end forfeit to the Crown. Like money in its role as universal
modern (capitalist) signifier as described by Roland Barthes in *S/Z*,
tied to no referent (such as land), defined only by its exchange
value, capable of unlimited metonymic circulation, the expectations
of fortune, as both plot and its aim or intention, as vehicle and
object of representation, circulate through inflation to devaluation.

The ultimate situation of plot in the novel may suggest an approach to the vexed question of Dickens's two endings to the novel:
the one he originally wrote and the revision (substituted at Bulwer
Lytton's suggestion) that was in fact printed. I think it is entirely
legitimate to prefer the original ending, with its flat tone and refusal

of romantic expectation, and find that the revision, with its tentative promise of reunion between Pip and Estella, 'unbinds' energies that we thought had been thoroughly bound and indeed discharged from the text. We may also feel that choice between the two endings is somewhat arbitrary and unimportant in that the decisive moment has already occurred before either of these finales begins. The real ending may take place with Pip's recognition and acceptance of Magwitch after his recapture – this is certainly the ethical dénouement – and his acceptance of a continuing existence without plot, as celibate clerk for Clarrikers. The pages that follow may simply be *obiter dicta*.

If we acknowledge Pip's experience of and with Magwitch to be the central energy of the text, it is significant that the climax of this experience, the moment of crisis and reversal in the attempted escape from England, bears traces of a hallucinatory repetition of the childhood spell – indeed, of that first recapture of Magwitch already repeated in Mr Wopsle's theatrical vision:

> In the same moment, I saw the steersman of the galley lay his hand on the prisoner's shoulder, and saw that both boats were swinging round with the force of the tide, and saw that all hands on board the steamer were running forward quite frantically. Still in the same moment, I saw the prisoner start up, lean across his captor, and pull the cloak from the neck of the shrinking sitter in the galley. Still in the same moment, I saw that the face disclosed was the face of the other convict of long ago. Still in the same moment, I saw the face tilt backward with a white terror on it that I shall never forget, and heard a great cry on board the steamer and a loud splash in the water, and felt the boat sink from under me.
>
> (ch. 54, pp. 421–2)

If this scene marks the beginning of a resolution – which it does in that it brings the death of the arch-villain Compeyson and the death sentence for Magwitch, hence the disappearance from the novel of its most energetic plotters – it is resolution in the register of repetition and working through, the final effort to master painful material from the insistent past. Pip emerges from this scene with an acceptance of the determinative past as both determinative and as *past*, which prepares us for the final escape *from* plot. It is interesting to note that where the 'dream' plot of Estella is concerned, Pip's stated resolution has none of the compulsive energetic force of the passage just quoted, but is rather a conventional romantic fairy-tale ending, a conscious fiction designed, of course, to console the dying Magwitch, but possibly also a last effort at self-delusion: 'You had a child once, whom you loved and lost.... She lived and found powerful friends. She is living now. She is a lady and very beautiful. And I love her!' (ch. 56, p. 436). If taken as anything other than a conscious fiction – if taken as part of the 'truth' discovered by Pip's detections – this version of Pip's experience leads straight to what is most troubling in Dickens's revised version of the ending: the suggestion of an unbinding of what has already been bound up and disposed of, an unbinding that is indeed perceptible in the rather embarrassed prose with which the revision begins: 'Nevertheless, I knew while I said these words, that I secretly intended to revisit the site of the old house that evening alone, for her sake. Yes, even so. For Estella's sake' (ch. 59, p. 458). Are we to understand that the experience of Satis House has never really been mastered? Is its nightmare energy still present in the text as well? The original end may have an advantage in denying to Pip's text the possibility of any reflux of energy, any new aspirations, the undoing of anything already done, the unbinding of energy that has been bound and led to discharge.

As at the start of the novel we had the impression of a life not yet subject to plot – a life in search of the sense of plot that would only gradually begin to precipitate around it – so at the end we have the impression of a life that has outlived plot, renounced plot, been cured of it: life that is left over. What follows the recognition of Magwitch is left over, and any renewal of expectation and plotting – such as a revived romance with Estella – would have to belong to another story. It is with the image of a life bereft of plot, of movement and desire, that the novel most appropriately leaves us. Indeed, we have at the end what could appropriately be called a 'cure' from plot, in Pip's recognition of the general forfeiture of plotting, his renunciation of any attempt to direct his life. Plot comes to resemble a diseased, fevered state of the organism caught in the machinery of a desire which must eventually be renounced. Plot, we come to understand, was a state of abnormality or deviance, suggested thematically by its uneasy position between Newgate and Old Bailey, between criminality and the law. The nineteenth-century novel in general – and especially that highly symptomatic development, the detective story – regularly conceives plot as a condition of deviance and abnormality, the product of cities and social depths, of a world where *récit* is *complot*, where all stories are the result of plotting, and plotting is very much machination. Deviance is the very condition for life to be 'narratable': the state of normality is devoid of interest, energy and the possibility for narration. In between a beginning prior to plot and an end beyond plot, the middle – the plotted text – has been in a state of *error*: wandering and misinterpretation.

From *New Literary History*, 11 (1980), 503–26.

NOTES

[First appearing as an essay in 1980, Peter Brooks's account of *Great Expectations* was quick to establish a claim on subsequent critics' attention and in 1984 was republished as a chapter in his wide-ranging study of narrative in general: *Reading for the Plot: Design and Intention in Narrative* (Oxford; re-issued in 1992 by Harvard University Press). Brooks gives an interesting new twist to the Freudian tradition in Dickens studies, and at the same time attacks structuralist narratology, the intellectual background of which is sketched in the Introduction (pp. 11–13). What Brooks objects to is the premise of some narratologists that plotting is mainly a matter of drawing on received story paradigms, or of reshaping a story (*fabula*) into a plot (*sjuzet*). According to him, this ignores a vitally dynamic psychological dimension, which he seeks to illustrate by using Freud's *Beyond the Pleasure Principle* as a kind of master narrative.

Brooks suggests that all plots begin with the pleasure principle or Eros, which entails a desire for activity and movement, which in turn can set up tensions and be narrated. No less universally, plots end with the death wish or Thanatos, which connotes quiescence, non-happening, non-narratability. Yet a plot has to keep Eros and Thanatos in some sort of balance, and this means that the plot's middle, as well as being a stage on the path towards its end, will also be a kind of detour, delay or arabesque, which doubles back upon its beginning.

Essay 4 is made up of three extracts from Brooks's account. The first part deals with the opening pages of *Great Expectations*, where Pip is 'an existence without a plot', a being for whom plotting has still to begin. Yet before long a beginning is under way, with four different plot-lines rapidly gathering momentum around him. These are: the pressure of his secret communion with the convict; the equal and opposite pressure on him to conform with society's norms; the dream of his actually breaking the spell on Satis House, to become a fine gentleman married to Estella; and the nightmare counter-indications of erotic frustration and broken faith, with Miss Havisham figuring as a kind of witch. Once all this has been set in motion, the novel arrives at the doublings-back of the middle phase, discussed by Brooks in the second part of the essay. The plotting insistently returns to memories and associations long since repressed, 'serving to bind the energy of the text so as to make its final discharge more effective'. Two different versions of Pip's origins are for ever circling round, the one seeing him as naturally vicious, the other seeing him as a fairy-tale hero. But at the same time he also keeps returning from London to the village and the marshes, and finally the suppressed Magwitch himself returns. With this, which Brooks sees as the reinstatement of Pip's psychologically truest origin, the perplexities of the middle become less distressing. The third part of the essay argues that when the end is drawing near, all attempts to plot life into some sort of coherence and significance begin to seem beside the point. This is a sign that Eros is finally giving way to Thanatos, and Brooks's most striking claim is that Pip is actually 'cured' of plotting.

Brooks's quotations are from *Great Expectations* (Oxford University Press, London, 1975). Ed.]

1. On the theme of reading in the novel, see Max Byrd, '"Reading" in *Great Expectations*', *PMLA*, 91 (1976), 259–65. [See also Murray Baumgarten, 'Calligraphy and Code: Writing in *Great Expectations*', *Dickens Studies Annual*, 11 (1983), 61–72. Ed.]

2. See Harry Stone, 'The Love Pattern in Dickens' Novel', in *Dickens the Craftsman*, ed. Robert B. Partlow (Carbondale, 1970), pp. 1–20; and Albert G. Guerard, *The Triumph of the Novel* (New York, 1976), p. 70.

5

Pip and the Victorian Idea of the Gentleman

ROBIN GILMOUR

I

The greatness of *Great Expectations*, as Lionel Trilling observed, begins in its title: 'modern society bases itself on great expectations which, if they are ever realised, are found to exist by reason of a sordid, hidden reality. The real thing is not the gentility of Pip's life but the hulks and the murder and the rats and the decay in the cellarage of the novel.'[1] Much modern criticism of the novel has been rightly preoccupied with the relationship between cellarage and drawing-room, between the gentility of Pip's life and the criminal outcast who makes it possible; and discussion has tended to focus on the hero's seemingly excessive sense of guilt and the encompassing 'taint of prison and crime' (ch. 32) which pervades his upward rise. 'Snobbery is not a crime', Julian Moynahan points out in an influential article and asks 'Why should Pip feel like a criminal?'[2]

It is an important question, because Pip's guilty conscience is the link between cellarage and drawing-room in the novel, but the terms in which Moynahan and others have phrased and answered it are questionable on both intrinsic interpretive and extrinsic historical grounds. How true is it, for instance, to say that Pip is a snob? The words 'snob' and 'snobbery' are used by Dickens's critics but not by Dickens himself in the text of the novel, although Thackeray and *Punch* had made them widely current by the time *Great*

Expectations was written. One has only to compare Pip with the compulsive toadies in Thackeray's *Book of Snobs* to see how very different he is. The real snobs in *Great Expectations*, the characters blinded to human considerations by the worship of wealth and social position, are Pumblechook and Mrs Pocket, and Pip sees through them both from the start. What the view of the novel as a 'snob's progress' ignores, as Q. D. Leavis has convincingly demonstrated, is the sympathy and complexity with which Dickens treats Pip's predicament: to call him a snob is to suggest that he was wrong to feel discontented with life on the marshes and could have chosen to act otherwise than he did, whereas much of the energy of Dickens's imagination in the early part of the novel goes in showing how mean and limiting that life is, and how helpless Pip himself is in face of the contradictory forces at work on him. Similarly with Pip's great expectations, the burden of most modern criticism has been to stress that these are *only* illusory, that the 'real thing' (as Trilling says) is not Pip's gentility but what goes on in the cellarage of the novel, that his expectations are indeed even dangerous and anti-social, as Moynahan argues. But such arguments are in varying degrees unhistorical, ignoring the fact that Pip's desire to become a gentleman is 'real' too and has a representatively positive element, in the sense that it is bound up with that widespread impulse to improvement, both personal and social, which is a crucial factor in the genesis of Victorian Britain. Here, indeed, *Great Expectations* partakes of a contemporary meaning which we have largely lost with the passage of time, some such meaning as Frederic Harrison shared when he looked back on the nineteenth century in 1882, and found it to be 'the age of great expectation':

> Mr Carlyle, Mr Ruskin, the Aesthetes, are all wrong about the nineteenth century. It is *not* the age of money-bags and cant, soot, hubbub, and ugliness. It is the age of great expectation and unwearied striving after better things.[3]

It may be that we still have a tendency to see the Victorian age through the eyes of Carlyle and Ruskin, and that in our readiness to discern a criminal potential in Pip's expectations we overlook that sense of hopefulness and promise, even idealism, to which Harrison testifies. For the optimism inherent in his description of the nineteenth century as 'the age of great expectation and unwearied striving after better things' plays an important part in *Great Expectations*, as it did in the real world out of which the book was written.

At this stage it may be relevant to recall Samuel Smiles's *Self-Help* and Dinah Mulock's popular novel *John Halifax, Gentleman*. Ellen Moers has called Pip a dandy, but his dandyism is surely minimal: the immediately relevant context is self-help, which was very much in the air at the time with the publication of Smiles's famous book in 1859, the year before Dickens started work on *Great Expectations*. Dickens even makes an ironic reference to self-improvement literature in the 1868 edition of the novel, where 'The pursuit of Knowledge under difficulties' is the running title to the scene in chapter 2 in which Pip gets into trouble for asking persistent questions about the convict-hulks. The reference is of course to *Pursuit of Knowledge under Difficulties* (1831) by George Lillie Craik, who subsequently married the author of *John Halifax, Gentleman*. Dickens is making a familiar joke, but it might also alert a reader to the ways in which his story of the poor boy who wants to become a gentleman falls into a classic nineteenth-century pattern. Like Newcomen and Faraday, two of Smiles's heroes, Pip is a blacksmith's boy with a 'hunger for information' (ch. 15) which the dame-school in his narrow provincial world fails to satisfy. The fictional John Halifax had been ashamed of his ugly hands and employment as a tanner's lad, and wanted to marry a lady; Pip also learns to feel shame at his 'coarse hands and … common boots' (ch. 8), and his social ambitions are similarly confused with a sexual motive.

But it is the Smilesian notion of 'self-culture', in relation to the idea of the gentleman in self-improvement literature, that is most relevant to *Great Expectations*. Instead of talking of snobbery, we should see the young Pip as engaged in an attempt as self-culture, and note that his efforts to improve himself precede his visits to Satis House and are sympathetically handled by Dickens:

> There was no indispensable necessity for my communicating with Joe by letter, inasmuch as he sat beside me and we were alone. But, I delivered this written communication (slate and all) with my own hand, and Joe received it as a miracle of erudition.
> 'I say, Pip, old chap!' cried Joe, opening his blue eyes wide, 'what a scholar you are! An't you?'
> 'I should like to be,' said I, glancing at the slate as he held it.
>
> (ch. 7)

There is a representative pathos and comedy here, and it establishes a sympathetic attitude towards Pip's struggle for self-culture which is never entirely absent from Dickens's conception of his character. He means us to see Mr Wopsle's great-aunt's dame-school as the hopelessly inadequate and frustrating educational institution Pip finds it to be, and to respect Pip for his determination to make something of it; even in the midst of debt and dissipation in London, Pip reminds us, 'through good and evil I stuck to my books' (ch. 25).

Humour plays an essential part too in defining Pip's predicament and awakening our sympathies for him. *Great Expectations* is an unequalled record of the small daily pains, embarrassments, gauchenesses, involved in self-culture for the poor boy trying to become a gentleman. From the moment when Estella's scorn awakens shame in Pip – '"He calls the knaves, Jacks, this boy!" said Estella with disdain ... "And what coarse hands he has! And what thick boots!"' (ch. 8) – Dickens brings a wonderful comic tact to the portrayal of his education in etiquette and manners. There is Herbert's unobtrusive gentlemanly introduction to table manners:

> We had made some progress in the dinner, when I reminded Herbert of his promise to tell me about Miss Havisham.
> 'True,' he replied. 'I'll redeem it at once. Let me introduce the topic, Handel, by mentioning that in London it is not the custom to put the knife in the mouth – for fear of accidents – and that while the fork is reserved for that use, it is not put further in than necessary. It is scarcely worth mentioning, only it's as well to do as other people do. Also, the spoon is not generally used over-hand, but under. This has two advantages. You get at your mouth better (which after all is the object), and you save a good deal of the attitude of opening oysters, on the part of the right elbow.'
> He offered these friendly suggestions in such a lively way, that we both laughed and I scarcely blushed.
>
> (ch. 22)

And there is the comedy of Joe's awkward struggles with his hat when he comes to visit Pip in London, a scene which makes us share Pip's embarrassment at Joe's embarrassment, his uneasiness at this awkward reminder of his own recent awkwardness:

> [His hat] demanded from him a constant attention, and a quickness of eye and hand, very like that exacted by wicket-keeping. He made extraordinary play with it, and showed the greatest skill; now, rushing at it and catching it neatly as it dropped; now, merely stopping it midway, beating it up, and humouring it in various parts of the room

and against a good deal of the pattern of the paper on the wall, before he felt it safe to close with it; finally splashing it into the slop-basin, where I took the liberty of laying hands upon it.

(ch. 27)

I am sure, incidentally, that Dickens is poking fun here at his old enemy Lord Chesterfield and his exaggerated horror at displays of clumsiness. There is a passage in one of Chesterfield's letters which this scene seems to comment on:

> When an awkward fellow first comes into a room, it is highly prob-able that his sword gets between his legs and throws him down, or makes him stumble at least; when he has recovered this accident, he goes and places himself in the very place of the whole room where he should not; there he soon lets his hat fall down; and, taking it up again, throws down his cane; in recovering his cane, his hat falls a second time; so that he is a quarter of an hour before he is in order again ... At dinner, his awkwardness distinguishes itself particularly, as he has more to do: there he holds his knife, fork, and spoon differently from other people; eats with his knife to the great danger of his mouth, picks his teeth with his fork, and puts his spoon, which has been in his throat twenty times, into the dishes again ... His hands are troublesome to him, when he has not something in them, and he does not know where to put them; but they are in perpetual motion between his bosom and his breeches ... All this, I own, is not in any degree criminal; but it is highly disagreeable and ridiculous in company, and ought most carefully to be avoided by whoever desires to please.

(25 July 1741)

Physical clumsiness, and the difference between a working-class hand and a gentlemanly hand, are much emphasised in *Great Expecta-tions*. Dickens uses Joe's clumsiness both as a means of indicating how far Pip has come (for good and bad) from the forge, and to make the anti-Chesterfield point that these rough blacksmith's hands, of which Pip has started to feel ashamed in himself, are truly gentle: the comedy of clumsiness modulates into Joe's dignified exit at the end of the chapter, when he gives Pip his hand and 'touched me gently on the forehead, and went out' (ch. 27).

But if Dickens was capable of doing justice to the positive moral dimension in self-culture, he was also aware of the ways in which it tended to overlap with class and sexual aspirations. One can argue that there is a basic ambivalence in self-help literature towards the notion of 'getting on'. The moral emphasis in Smiles is admirable:

self-culture is to be pursued as the road to self-respect, dignity, the independence that comes from self-discipline, and so on; its end is character, not wealth or success. But he never faces squarely the possibility that these moral ends might be inseparable from more narrowly social and marital ambitions, nor does he seem to recognise the extent to which his own examples encourage the equation of self-help with worldly success. It was all very well for Smiles to say that 'even though self-culture may not bring wealth, it will at all events give one the companionship of elevated thoughts',[4] when often the motive behind self-culture, and its consequence, was to fit the self-helper for elevated companionship of a different kind – the company of gentlemen, in whose ranks, as Smiles argued in his final chapter, 'Character: The True Gentleman', the successful self-helper naturally belonged. In *Great Expectations* the ambivalence in the concept of self-culture is brought into the open. Dickens shows how, after Pip's visit to Satis House, his admirable ambition to improve himself gets caught up in social and sexual fantasies, which are then brought near to realisation by the news of his financial expectations. The real-life self-helpers elevated themselves by dint of perseverance and self-discipline, whereas Magwitch's anonymous gift instantly provides Pip with the economic basis for the genteel life. It is a significant twist, for by giving his hero the fruits of self-culture without the labour, Dickens is able to concentrate upon the social and sexual implications, and the inherent paradoxes, of the self-improvement idea.

Dickens's exploitation of these attitudes in *Great Expectations* is intimately related to his perception of another important feature of the contemporary scene. The struggle for individual refinement reflects a larger movement in society as a whole; men like Smiles were influential chiefly because they spoke to a generation which was itself acutely conscious of having made enormous advances in the civilisation of everyday life. Dickens's novel, it may help to recall, was published in the same year as the second volume of H. T. Buckle's *History of Civilization in England*, with its proclaimed faith in the 'laws of Progress' and the 'mighty career' of English civilisation. The belief in progress which inspired Buckle and his contemporaries was something more than vulgar optimism or self-congratulation, impressive as the record of social reform must have seemed to mid-century observers; behind it lay an awareness that the state of civilisation they had achieved was a unique and recent development, something that had taken place substantially within the lifetime of a large section of the Victorian public.

This historical fact suggests further ways in which Pip's story can be seen as representative of early nineteenth-century experience. His exaggerated allegiance to the concept of refinement is entirely characteristic of a culture which had barely emerged from the crude and violent society of the eighteenth century. The Victorians were proud, and rightly, of the improvements they had worked in the texture of daily living. As early as 1836 John Stuart Mill was contrasting the civilisation of his day to the 'rudeness of former times', and he noted that 'the spectacle, and even the very idea of pain, is kept more and more out of sight of those classes who enjoy in their fulness the benefits of civilisation', whereas in former times everyone had been habituated to 'the spectacle of harshness, rudeness, and violence, to the struggle of one indomitable will against another, and to the alternate suffering and infliction of pain'.[5] By mid-century this process of civilisation had become so consolidated that G. R. Porter could write, in the 1851 edition of his *Progress of the Nation*, that 'it is in itself a proof, of no slight significance, as to the general refinement of manners, that in a work of this nature there would be found an impropriety in describing scenes that were of every-day occurrence formerly, and without which description it is yet impossible adequately to measure the advance that has been made'.[6]

The proximity to the Victorian age of a violent past, and the contrast which this made with the age's most treasured social achievements, is of the utmost relevance to *Great Expectations*. On the one hand there is the England of 1860, relatively stable, relatively prosperous, conscious and rightly proud of the considerable advances in civilisation which the previous forty years had seen; and on the other there is the recent memory of a very different world, the harsh and brutal society of the eighteenth century which the Victorian reformers set out to transform and which still survived as a background to their efforts – a source of congratulation but also of uncertainty and anxiety. Here one can begin to see the contemporary significance of the social ironies in the novel. By making Pip's benefactor a transported convict, and thereby setting his effort at self-culture within a framework of criminality, Dickens was touching the very nerve of a characteristic mid-Victorian dilemma. For if anything seemed to contradict the new civilisation it was the continued existence within it of violent crime: this raised the vexing question of the relationship between those classes who were 'civilised' and those who were manifestly not. (Magwitch is, of course, only a criminal in a technical sense, and Dickens sympathises with him because he has been neglected and oppressed by society. But the important point about him, in terms of the novel's treatment of 'civilisation', is the fact that he is violent and animal, and that for much of the book he is invested with the horrors of Pip's childhood vision of him as 'a desperately violent man', whom he had seen 'down in the ditch, tearing and fighting like a wild beast' [ch. 39].) What responsibility did the civilised middle classes bear for the barbarity which still persisted at the fringes of their society? Was it a blot on their upward progress, or merely the work of a criminal underworld which the march of civilisation would eradicate?

These issues are raised in an article by W. R. Greg in the *Edinburgh Review* of 1851. Greg was reviewing William Johnston's *England as It Is* (1851) and, anxious to counter what he considered to be the pessimistic tenor of the book, set out to explain the increased crime figures Johnston had cited in support of his theory of national decadence. An increase in crime, Greg argued, did not necessarily betoken an increase in criminality, for *'crime is, for the most part, committed, not by the community at large, but by a peculiar and distinct section of it'* (his italics); these *'professional* criminals' constituted in Greg's view *'a class apart'*, and although they might have increased in number this 'in no degree militates against the idea of the progress of morality and civilisation among all other classes'. The 'swollen return of crime is undoubtedly a blot upon our escutcheon and a drawback on our progress; not as impeaching the general honesty and virtue of the nation, but as showing the existence of a class among us which the advance of civilisation ought to have eradicated or suppressed.'[7] This view of the criminal as belonging to a *'class apart'* is a typical contemporary attitude and one which Dickens is holding up to scrutiny throughout *Great Expectations*; we encounter it in Herbert's response to the convicts on the coach, and Pip's uneasiness on this and subsequent occasions may be seen as a dramatisation of the ambiguity inherent in such a response. Greg might reassure his middle-class readers with the comforting view of an altogether separate and self-contained criminal population, but Dickens's vision reveals a world in which the hero owes his respectability to his involvement with a criminal outcast.

No amount of background material can take the place of a careful critical reading, but it can provide the context for such a reading; in the case of *Great Expectations* it puts us back into a world more sympathetic to the idea of self-culture than ours, where the dream of 'great expectation' – that 'unwearied striving after better things' which Harrison noted – had its positive side too. Moreover, these contemporary attitudes mirror the subconscious hopes, fantasies and uncertainties of a society which is still very close to a more primitive past: Pip's hankering after gentility takes on a dimension of pathos when we realise that Victorian snobbery and prudishness were often (to quote from Dr Kitson Clark) 'the result of a struggle for order and decency on the part of people just emerging from the animalism and brutality of primitive society'.[8] His extreme sense of class division should be related to the intensity of his need to civilise himself, and in this Pip is a true child of the early nineteenth century, his awareness of the civilised life sharpened by a knowledge of its very precariousness.

What has been said so far points to an interpretation of *Great Expectations* which sets it rather apart from Dickens's other novels, certainly from the great social satires of his middle and late period. *Bleak House, Little Dorrit* and *Our Mutual Friend* are frontal assaults on the ills of Victorian society, and while *Great Expectations* is still concerned with the nature of that society, it is concerned in a different way. The novel is unique among his fiction in that its real subject is not a specific social abuse, or a series of related abuses, but nothing less than civilisation itself; more accurately, it is a study in social evolution, a drama of the development of conscience and sensibility in a child who grows up in the early years of the nineteenth century. And in this, as I have argued, Pip's story is truly a representative one. Behind *John Halifax, Gentleman, Self-Help* and *Great Expectations* – works otherwise so different in attitude and imaginative quality – lies the social experience of the first generation of the Victorian age. *Great Expectations* is a novel of memory in a double sense: it deals with one man's recollection of his past, and in doing so goes to considerable lengths to re-create a period of the immediate past which must have survived in the memory of many of Dickens's original readers. This historical dimension reveals further ways in which the story of Pip is the 'classic legend' of the nineteenth century.

II

The deepest irony of *Great Expectations* is Dickens's location of gentility in a context of violence – a violence that is defined in symbolic, almost Blake-like terms, as both creative and destructive, having its positive source in the life of instinct, energy, physical passion, as well as its negative manifestation in the barbarism of a brutal society. Pip wants to become a gentleman because he wants – rightly and, as I have argued, inevitably – to become a gentle man, to escape from the brutality and intimidation that characterise life on the marshes. But gentlemanliness in the nineteenth-century world involves exclusion and repression for someone like Pip, alienation from Joe and the warmth of instinctive life which the blazing forge symbolises. The novel is full of a wonderful unobtrusive poetry which suggests this beneath the level of narrative and character. In chapter 8, where Pip makes his first visit to Satis House, he stays with Pumblechook and notices the seeds tied up in little packets in the seedman's shop: 'I wondered ... whether the flower-seeds and bulbs ever wanted of a fine day to break out of those jails and bloom'; and the image anticipates and reinforces the sense of deadened life in that other jail, Satis House, where 'there were no pigeons in the dove-cot, no horses in the stable, no pigs in the sty, no malt in the store-house, no smells of grains and beer in the copper or the vat', and where he sees Estella 'pass among the extinguished fires' of the old brewery. Gentility is associated with the repression and defeat of instinct and vital energy. On his next visit to Satis House Pip fights and beats the 'pale young gentleman', Herbert, and when he meets him again in London Pip notices 'a certain conquered languor about him' (ch. 22); but Pip at this stage is neither pale nor a gentleman, and our sense of his instinctive vitality, and its associations with his blacksmith's arm, is underlined at the end of the chapter when we see the 'bright flush' on Estella's face and the light from Joe's furnace 'flinging a path of fire across the road' (ch. 11). One thinks of Blake and *The Marriage of Heaven and Hell*: 'The Giants who formed this world into its sensual existence, and now seem to live in it in chains, are in truth the causes of its life & the sources of all activity; but the chains are the cunning of weak and tame minds which have power to resist energy.' Pip's instinctive life is put in chains by his pursuit of gentility, and these chains only start to loosen when he recognises and accepts Magwitch, and comes to work for his benefactor's escape. In the burst of activity which this involves, some of the buried energies within Pip are released and – significantly – the mists which have dominated the atmosphere of the novel start to clear:

> Wednesday morning was dawning when I looked out of [the] window. The winking lights upon the bridges were already pale, the

coming sun was like a marsh of fire on the horizon. The river, still dark and mysterious, was spanned by bridges that were turning coldly grey, with here and there at top a warm touch from the burning in the sky. As I looked along the clustered roofs, with church towers and spires shooting into the unusually clear air, the sun rose up, and a veil seemed to be drawn from the river, and millions of sparkles burst out upon its waters. From me too, a veil seemed to be drawn, and I felt strong and well.

(ch. 53)

With the unveiling of illusion Pip overcomes his revulsion from Magwitch; the blacksmith's boy and the gentleman are integrated in the physical gesture of holding the old convict's hand in the boat and later, publicly, at his trial: 'For now, my repugnance to him had all melted away, and in the hunted wounded shackled creature who held my hand in his, I only saw a man who had meant to be my benefactor, and who had felt affectionately, gratefully, and generously, towards me with great constancy through a series of years. I only saw in him a much better man than I had been to Joe' (ch. 54). And it is appropriate that in the illness which follows Magwitch's death Pip should be nursed back to health by Joe in an episode which returns him, briefly and poignantly, to the old physical intimacy and dependence of childhood. Pip cannot be a child again, or preserve the old companionship once he has recovered; but Joe can heal him out of the 'wealth of his great nature' (ch. 57), his physical tenderness can penetrate the crust of genteel inhibition and release the flow of feeling which has for so long been trapped beneath. Again, this release and reintegration is signalled in the holding of hands:

> At last, one day, I took courage, and said, 'Is it Joe?'
> And the dear old home-voice answered. 'Which it air, old chap.'
> 'O Joe, you break my heart! Look angry at me, Joe. Strike me, Joe. Tell me of my ingratitude. Don't be so good to me!'
> For Joe had actually laid his head down on the pillow at my side, and put his arm round my neck, in his joy that I knew him.
> 'Which dear old Pip, old chap,' said Joe, 'you and me was ever friends. And when you're well enough to go out for a ride – what larks!'
> After which, Joe withdrew to the window, and stood with his back towards me, wiping his eyes. And as my extreme weakness prevented me from getting up and going to him, I lay there, penitently whispering, 'O God bless him! O God bless this gentle Christian man!'

Joe's eyes were red when I next found him beside me; but I was holding his hand and we both felt happy.

(ch. 57)

'O God bless this gentle Christian man!' Pip (and Dickens) separate the word 'gentleman' into its classless elements, the gentle man who, living by the Christian ideals of love and forgiveness, is the one type of gentlemanliness which the novel at the end un-equivocally affirms.

In its historical depth, social range and psychological penetration, *Great Expectations* is the most complex and satisfying fictional examination of the idea of the gentleman in the Victorian period. The truth of a novel is of course something different from social and historical truth, but one cannot read Dickens's book sympath-etically without feeling it taps a deep source of uneasiness in the Victorian cult of the gentleman. In the figure of Pip, this gentle man whose instinctive warmth and tenderness have been thwarted by his sterile passion for Estella and by the inhibitions involved in becoming Magwitch's 'brought-up London gentleman' (ch. 39), one senses a haunting knowledge of the social exclusions and psycholo-gical repressions that make gentility possible.

From Robin Gilmour, *The Idea of the Gentleman in the Victorian Novel* (London, 1981), pp. 105–48.

NOTES

[Robin Gilmour's eloquent account of *Great Expectations* forms the cen-tral chapter in his book *The Idea of the Gentleman in the Victorian Novel* and belongs to the same scholarly-critical tradition as commentaries by Humprey House and Q. D. Leavis (see Introduction, pp. 7–11). Such work pleads for a full consideration of Dickens's sociocultural context and is less hostile than some psychoanalytical criticism towards Dickens's own Victorianism, offering a firm reminder of what was actually expected and possible in the Victorian period. Though not assuming a rigid social deter-minism like that of some structuralist critics, this tradition of Dickens studies regards any resistance to the pressures of society as an arduous and painful business calling for scrupulous self-knowledge.

Essay 5 is made up of two extracts from Gilmour's long and richly detailed account. His starting point is that, whereas David Copperfield was worried that his gentility of birth might pass unrecognised, Pip is a black-smith's boy struggling to achieve gentility despite his secret complicity with a convict. Dickens dated the action of the novel to the first three decades of the nineteenth century so as to emphasise how far the urban society of his own day had come from the cultural poverty of that earlier more rural society, and the young Pip hopes that the development of his own sensibility places him well above his lowly origins. The truth is, however, that both Pip and Estella are inextricably linked with the criminal Magwitch, and that civilisation is for ever being undermined by brutality. An obvious case is the figure of Bentley Drummle, the upper-class thug. Yet even Estella flushes excitedly as she watches the blacksmith's arm of Pip deliver a drubbing to the pale gentility of Herbert. Pip is just as unwilling to see the streak of unrefined animality in Estella as he is to accept Magwitch as the sponsor of his own fashionable veneer. But eventually he resigns himself to the mutual dependencies of a class-divided society, so curing the division in himself between the guilt-ridden gentleman and the blacksmith's apprentice.

Gilmour's quotations are taken from *Great Expectations*, Oxford Illustrated Dickens Edition (London, 1953). Ed]

1. Lionel Trilling, 'Manners, Morals, and the Novel', in *The Liberal Imagination* (London, 1951), p. 211.

2. Julian Moynahan, 'The Hero's Guilt: the Case of *Great Expectations*', *Essays in Criticism*, 10 (1960), 60.

3. F. Harrison, 'A Few Words about the Nineteenth Century', *Fortnightly Review*, n. s. 30 (1882), 12.

4. Samuel Smiles, *Self-Help* (London, 1859), p. 262.

5. J. S. Mill, 'Civilisation', *Westminster Review*, 35 (1836), 12.

6. G. R. Porter, *The Progress of the Nation* (London, 1851), p. 681.

7. W. R. Greg, 'England as It Is', *Edinburgh Review*, 93 (1851), 330.

8. G. K. Clark, *The Making of Victorian England* (London, 1962), p. 64.

6

Prison-Bound: Dickens and Foucault

JEREMY TAMBLING

Great Expectations has been called an analysis of 'Newgate London',[1] suggesting that the prison is everywhere implicitly dominant in the book, and it has been a commonplace of Dickens criticism, since Edmund Wilson's essay in *The Wound and the Bow* and Lionel Trilling's introduction to *Little Dorrit*, to see the prison as a metaphor throughout the novels. Not just a metaphor, of course: the interest that Dickens had in prisons themselves was real and lasting, and the one kind of concern leads to the other, the literal to the metaphorical. Some earlier Dickens criticism, particularly that associated with the 1960s, and Trilling's 'liberal imagination', stressed the second at the expense of the first, and Dickens became the novelist of the 'mind forg'd manacles' of Blake, where Mrs Clennam can stand in the Marshalsea 'looking down into this prison as it were out of her own different prison' (*Little Dorrit*, pt. 2, ch. 31). This Romantic criticism became a way of attacking the historical critics who emphasised the reformist Dickens, interested in specific social questions: Humphry House and Philip Collins, the last in *Dickens and Crime* and *Dickens and Education* (1962 and 1964). With Foucault's work on the 'birth of the prison' – the subtitle of his book *Discipline and Punish* (1976) – it may be possible to see how the physical growth of the modern prison is also the beginning of its entering into discourse and forming structures of thought, so that the literal and the metaphorical do indeed combine, and produce the Dickens whose interest is so clearly in both ways of thinking about the prison.

Discipline and Punish is the first of Foucault's books about modes of power operating in western societies, and it succeeds his inaugural address at the Collège de France in 1970, the 'Discourse on Language', where his interest is in showing the way that knowledge is a form of manipulation, and must be thought of in the same breath as the word 'power'. Power in the absolutist state takes its bearings on the body, illustrated in the first part of the book, but the 'gentle way in punishment', associated with late eighteenth-century enlightenment thought, leads to a change in the way power is exercised – from 'a right to take life or let live to a form of power that fosters life, the latter being described as a power over life, in contrast to the former sovereign power, which has been described as a power over death'.[2] At the end of the eighteenth century, penal codes were drawn up which addressed themselves to the mind of the criminal, not defined as such, nor as an offender, but as a 'delinquent' (p. 251).[3] A personality type is thus created: the change Foucault marks is one towards the creation of an entity: a mind to be characterised in certain ways (whereas earlier the body was directly marked), to produce the 'docile body' – 'one that may be subjected, used, transformed and improved' – and thus fitted for new modes of industrial production. A 'technology of subjection' comes into use: Foucault refers to Marx's discussion of the division of labour in this context (p. 221). The arrangement of the bodies of individuals for productive and training purposes is facilitated by the renewed attention given to the mind, to the prisoner as personality.

Foucault's subject is thus the 'disciplinary technology' engineered in western societies, but perhaps the most compelling image in the book is the very utopist idea of the Panopticon – that which would have been the appearance of the superego in time, if it had been realised, not merely been left on paper by Bentham. The Panopticon, with its central tower where the unseen warders may or may not be looking at the several storeys of individually divided-off prisoners, who can see neither their controlling agency, nor the others in the cells, but are arranged in a circle around this surveillance tower, presents the possibility of total and complete control being exercised over the prison's inmates. Philip Collins discusses it in *Dickens and Crime* – a book still useful for its donkey work, though very undertheorised, and not able to question the role of the prison in western society – and Collins stresses that the Panopticon, while it was itself not to be recognised as a project, was to provide the model for all other types of institution: the birth of the prison means the birth of all kinds of normalising procedures, carried out in buildings still very familiar today, that all look exactly like the exterior of the nineteenth-century prison. Collins quotes Bentham: 'Morals reformed, health preserved, industry invigorated, instruction diffused, public burdens lightened, economy seated, as it were, upon a rock, the Gordian knot of the Poor Laws not cut but untied – all by a simple idea of Architecture!' Something of the Panoptical method is at work in *Hard Times* too: the idea being thought suitable for schools and factories. In Gradgrind's school, the pupils are so raked that each can be seen at a glance, and each individuated, though with a number, not a name. Leavis's influential account of this book stresses how Benthamism in Coketown stifles individuality, and life and emotions, but Foucault's argument implies that the Panopticon idea stressed individuality, though not in the idealist manner that the Romantic poets, themselves contemporary with this 'birth of the prison', saw that concept of the individual. The Panopticon's rationale was the sense that each subject of care was to be seen as an individual mind. Alongside this creation of separate sentinces, goes a discourse to sustain it – in the formation of the 'sciences of man ... these sciences which have so delighted our "humanity" for over a century ... (which) ... have their technical matrix in the petty, malicious minutiae of the disciplines and their investigations' (p. 226). The social sciences emerge out of what Foucault calls the 'constitution' of this individual with an individual mind, as 'a describable, analysable object' (p. 190); the sciences of man may have their origin, Foucault suggests, in the files of prisons and institutions, 'these ignoble archives, where the modern play of coercion over bodies, gestures and behaviour has its beginnings' (p. 191). This new carceral framework 'constituted one of the armatures of power-knowledge that has made the human sciences historically possible. Knowable man (soul, individuality, consciousness, conduct, whatever it is called) is the object-effect of this analytical investment, of this domination-observation' (p. 305). It is a retreat from this positivist conception that stresses 'man's unconquerable mind' – the conclusion to a poem significantly written to a man in prison – and that invests the mind with unknowable, unfathomable qualities – as both Dickens and Leavis-like criticism do. The two stresses run together.

Bentham, more than just the inspirer of Mr Gradgrind, is a voice behind a whole new 'disciplinary technology', then, and the Panopticon becomes a metaphor, or, to quote Foucault, the diagram of a mechanism of power reduced to its ideal form; its functioning, abstracted from any obstacle, resistance or friction, must be represented as a pure architectural and optical system: it is, in fact, a figure of political technology that may and must be detached from any specific use. It is polyvalent in its applications; it serves to reform prisoners, but also to treat patients, to instruct school children, to confine the insane, to supervise workers, to put beggars and idlers to work. It is a type of location of bodies in space, of distribution of individuals in relation to one another, of hierarchical organisation, of disposition of centres and channels of power, which can be implemented in hospitals, workshops, schools, prisons.

(p. 205)

As a metaphor, what is implied is that the prison will enter, as both reality and as a 'type' that will form the discourse of society. Trilling's discussion of the prevalence of the prison motif in nineteenth-century literature finds its explanation here: the sense that metaphysically the prison is inescapable – reaching even to a person's whole mode of discourse, and creating even Nietzsche's 'prison-house of language', so that nothing escapes the limitations of the carceral – is objectively true in the domination of the prison in other nineteenth-century forms of discourse.

What is in question is normalising delinquent mentalities and preserving them as abnormal, for Foucault makes it clear that normalising powers succeed best when they are only partially successful, when there can be a marginalisation of certain types of personality, and the creation of a stubborn mentality that resists educative and disciplinary processes. 'The prison, and no doubt punishment in general, is not intended to eliminate offences, but rather to distinguish them, to distribute them, to use them ...' (p. 272). On such bases, the vocabulary of power is sited, where, for additional prop, not the law, but the norm is the standard, and where not acts, but identities are named. The law was however involved as well: police surveillance grew especially in the 1850s, with as a result the nearly inevitable criminalising of so many sections of the population, due to the growth of number of penal laws.[4] In the Panopticon, that 'mill grinding rogues honest and idle men industrious',[5] identity is created and named: while the model prison (i.e. solitary confinement, either partial, and belonging merely to the prisoner's leisure time, or total, as in Philadelphia) is discussed by Foucault in terms of the way isolation becomes a means of bringing prisoners to a state where they will carry on the reform work of the prison in their own person, where the language of the dominating discourse is accepted and internalised.

To come with these insights of Foucault to *Great Expectations* is to discover two things. It is to see how far a nineteenth-century text is aware of this creation of power and of oppression that Foucault has charted so interestingly: to examine the text's relation to this dominant ideology as Foucault has described it. It is also to read the book, as having itself to do with 'the power of normalisation and the formation of knowledge in modern society', which is how Foucault describes what *Discipline and Punish* is concerned with (p. 308). The issue of seeing the prison as an essential condition of Victorian society, as also of the generation that was pre-Victorian, turns on the libertarian notion of the prison as inherently oppressive; that much is clear in the novel, with its Hulks, Newgate, and transportation, and prisonous houses, such as Satis House and even Wemmick's castle. It also has to do with Dickens's registering of the prison being bound up with questions of language and the control of language – which, of course, entails ways of thinking, a whole discourse. In other words, the book shows an awareness of the fact that to learn a language is connected with the control of knowledge. In the Panopticon, the knowledge of a person is both coloured and colouring, and to acquire knowledge, by entering into the dominant discourse, is to learn the language of oppression.

In Dickens there is a move from literal treatment of the prison from *Sketches by Boz* onwards, including the visits to the isolation penitentiaries in the United States in 1842, where he saw the 'Auburn system' at work – based on the prison at Gloucester (which Foucault refers to, p. 123) – at both Boston and Connecticut;[6] his accounts of both appear in *American Notes*, chapters 3 and 5. The 'silent association' system there – partial solitary confinement only – he preferred to the Eastern Penitentiary at Philadelphia. It is not hard to see both systems as relations of the Panopticon dream.[7] Dickens found what he saw distasteful. He questioned, in a letter to Forster, whether the controllers 'were sufficiently acquainted with the human mind to know what it is they are doing': while *American Notes* finds 'this slow and daily tampering with the mysteries of the brain to be immeasurably worse than any torture of the body'. The person must be returned from this state 'morally unhealthy and diseased'. It is halfway to Foucault's gathering of criticisms of the prison that were made in France between 1820 and 1845: indeed, Dickens's comments are sited within those criticisms, commented on in *Discipline and Punish* (pp. 265–8).

But, as criticism, it isn't free from the point that the thinking about the nature of the prison has not gone far enough to question its rationale, as a social fact, as the product of a type of thinking. The point may be made from *Great Expectations* (ch. 32), at a moment where Pip (the moment is almost gratuitous – Dickens is moving away from treatment of literal prisons) is invited by Wemmick to visit Newgate:

> At that time, jails were much neglected, and the period of exaggerated reaction consequent on all public wrongdoing – and which is always its heaviest and longest punishment – was still far off. So, felons were not lodged and fed better than the soldiers (to say nothing of paupers) and seldom set fire to their prisons with the excusable object of improving the flavour of their soup.

Collins links this observation to the riots that took place at Chatham Convict prison early in 1861,[8] and makes it clear that Chatham represented a heavily reactionary kind of discipline, certainly no 'better' than the Newgate Pip is describing. I put 'better' in quotation marks to suggest that the concept of progress in prison discipline and order cannot be assumed: in Foucault's terms, the more enlightened the prison, the more subtle its means of control, that is all. Can much be said in favour of this passage? Many readers of Dickens will assume it to be part of the dominant mode to be noted in Dickens's speeches and letters: the voice of the liberal consensus, wanting prisons as simply neither too hard nor too easy. But the quotation also gives the register of Pip, who is historically at the moment when he is furthest away from his knowledge about the criminal basis of society; most alienated from his own associations with criminality – hence, of course, the irony that the chapter closes with the facial resemblance that Estella has to Molly. In terms of writing, he is looking back ('at that time') and seems to have learned nothing: at least he still wishes to place prisoners as below soldiers and paupers, not seeing that both these groups endure the same oppression that makes people prisoners – a conclusion that the novel often comes to, not least in giving Magwitch the significant name of Abel and so making him the original innocent and hunted down figure. Pip's language, then, is still part of that of a 'brought-up London gentleman' (p. 339): it belongs to a Victorian dominant discourse. (And 'brought-up' also suggests 'bought-up' and goes along with the equations of property and personality that go on throughout; compare Havisham – Have-is-sham, even Have-is-am; the last the latest development of the Cartesian cogito. The dominators, no less than the dominated, receive their individuality from their position in the carceral network.)

Those who identify Pip's attitude with Dickens's assume there is nothing in the text to qualify what is said here, or else that a plurality in the text allows Dickens to engage in a journalistic point in the middle of Pip's narration. Either may be right, but I would rather regard the utterance as being ironic rather than sincere – a disavowal, in this most confessional and disavowing of books, of a way of thinking once held. Pip's mode is autobiographical and confessional almost in the Catholic sense of that last word: the book reveals Dickens's autobiography and self-revelation of disgust in the same way. The reader of *Great Expectations* is able to reject the opinions expressed at the start of chapter 32 in the light of the reading of the rest of the book. Behind the narrator, the author asks for a similar dismissal. Behind Pip's confession, lies Dickens's own: or Dickens's as the representative of a precisely positioned class, of the liberal petit-bourgeoisie. The novel distances itself from Pip's confessions perhaps in order to listen to Dickens's. But then that one – Dickens's – may itself be refused, be shown to be as relative as the one that it shadows.   .

What is clear is the prevailing confessional note of *Great Expectations*. TO BE READ IN MY CELL (p. 132) is apt meta-linguistically. That is to say, it comments on the text's sense of the way it should be read, and what Pip thinks it is about. This is not the fictional Augustinian mode of confession, though a 'cell' would well suit the Catholic form of confession: the point is rather that the mode of autobiography fits with Protestant thought. Trilling comments on the late eighteenth-century 'impulse to write autobiography' and says that 'the new kind of personality which emerges ... is what we call an individual: at a certain point in history men become individuals'.[9] The ability to confess in autobiography is constitutive of the subject for him-herself – but as Foucault would add, it would be 'subject "in both senses of the word"',[10] for confession would be the means whereby the dominant discourse is internalised. Foucault continues: 'The obligation to confess is now relayed through so many different points, is so deeply ingrained in us, that we no longer perceive it as the effect of a power which constrains us; on the contrary, it seems to us that truth, lodged in our most secret nature, "demands" only to surface.' *The History of Sexuality* is the continuation of that theme of power as constitutive of knowledge that runs through *Discipline and Punish* and it is a keypoint of the novel that Pip is ready always to confess: such is his autobiography, a disavowal. The interest in the prison and the interest in autobiographical confession: these two things converge.

For *Great Expectations* certainly recognises itself to be about the creation of identities, imposed from higher to lower, from oppressor to oppressed. From the first page there is the 'first most vivid and broad impression of the identity of things', where a considerable amount of naming goes on – 'I called myself Pip and came to be called Pip'; where the 7-year-old child names 'this bleak place overgrown with nettles' as 'the churchyard' and similarly characterises the marshes, the river, the sea, and himself as 'that small bundle of shivers growing afraid of it all and beginning to cry' who 'was Pip'. The phrasing of the last part suggests that the act of naming the self and nature is a rationalisation, an incomplete and unsatisfactory way of labelling what resists formulation. It fits with that pejorative way of describing the self just quoted: that too fits the confessional position. The self is mis-named from the beginning, minimised; and gross acts of naming take place thenceforth, from Mrs Hubble's belief that the young are never grateful, not to say 'naterally wicious' (p. 57) to Jaggers saying that boys are 'a bad set of fellows' (p. 111). Wopsle and company identify an accused with the criminal (ch. 18), Pip sees himself as George Barnwell, and receives a number of descriptions and names – Pip, Handel, 'the prowling boy' (p. 199), 'you young dog' (p. 36), 'my boy' (p. 50), 'you boy' (p. 91), 'you visionary boy' (p. 377). Anonymity, though not the absence of naming, hangs over Mrs Joe (defined, absurdly, through the husband), Orlick, whose name Dolge is 'a clear impossibility' (p. 139), Magwitch – Provis at all times to Jaggers, Trabb's boy, Dummle – the Spider –, the Aged P. and Mr Waldengarver. The power of naming confers identity: Q. D. Leavis's analysis sees the power as one that implants guilt.[11] That guilt-fixing belongs to Foucault's Panopticon society, and indeed the sense of being looked at is pervasive – whether by the young man who hears the words Pip and Magwitch speak, by the hare hanging up in the larder – an early execution image – or by the cow that watches Pip take the wittles on Christmas Day. Pip expects a constable to be waiting for him on his return; has the sensation of being watched by relatives at Satis House, has his house watched on the night of Magwitch's return, has Compeyson sit behind him in the theatre (where he himself is watching), and is watched by the coastguard and the river police in the attempt to take off Magwitch (none of the friendship here with the police implied in the 1853 article 'Down with the Tide': the Dickensian hero is shown here as in flight from the agents of law). Where such spying is an integral part of the book, the sense of being someone constituted as having a secret to hide is not far away. Pip feels himself a criminal, early and late; and Orlick tells him he is: 'It was you as did for your shrew sister' (p. 437) – this coming from the man who has tracked Pip constantly, and shadowed Biddy, too. Reflecting the first chapter's growth of self-awareness – where the child is crying over his parents' grave, as though not just feeling himself inadequate, but as already guilty, already needing to make some form of reparation – Magwitch says that he 'first became aware of himself down in Essex a thieving turnips for his living' (p. 360). Jaggers identifies Drummle as criminal – 'the true sport' (p. 239) – and encourages him in his boorishness and readiness to brain Startop. His method of cross-examination is to criminalise everyone, himself resisting classification, no language being appropriate for one as 'deep' as he. 'You know what I am, don't you?' is the last comment he makes after the dinner party where he has hinted that Molly (whom he seems to own) is a criminal type. The question is to be answered negatively, for he is like the unseen watcher in the central tower of the Panopticon, naming others, but not named himself (his centrality is implied in the address of his office), in the position, as criminal lawyer, of power, conferring identities, controlling destinies – not for nothing are those criminals in Newgate compared to plants in the greenhouse, and regarded with the scientific detachment that for Foucault is part of the 'discourse of truth' of nineteenth-century positivism.

Identities all become a matter of social control and naming: Estella might have turned out one way as one of the 'fish' to come to Jaggers's net, yet she is constituted differently (though almost as nihilistically) by the identity she receives from Miss Havisham's hands. Pip remains the passive victim whose reaction is to blame himself for every action he is in: his willingness to see himself as his sister's murderer (ch. 16) is of a piece with his final ability to see himself as characteristically unjust to Joe. Q. D. Leavis's account works against those which see the book as 'a snob's progress'; her emphases are useful in suggesting that it is *Pip* who sees himself thus; and that now he is 'telling us dispassionately how he came to be the man who can now write thus about his former self'.[12] The 'us', by eliding the 1860s readers of the text with these who come a century later, implies that there is a central ahistorical way of taking the text: a strong liberal-humanist ideology underwrites this assumption which also implies that there is some decent norm Pip could approximate to, which would untie all his problems. It thus assimilates all historical differences, at the least, to the notion of the free subject, who is at all times accessible to decent human feelings – and capable of reaching a central normality.

If what Q. D. Leavis said were the case, it would mean Pip had reached some degree of 'normality' by the end of what has happened to him, before he starts narrating. He is not a central human presence, but a writer whose text needs inspection for its weakness of self-analysis; for he never dissociates himself from the accusations he piles on himself at the time of the events happening, and afterwards. In Wemmick's and Jaggers's character-formulations of people as either 'beaters or cringers' he remains a cringer, and unable to recognise himself in Herbert's genial view – 'a good fellow, with impetuosity and hesitation, boldness and diffidence, action and dreaming, curiously mixed in him' (p. 269). That positive evaluation, binary nonetheless in its terms, in the same way as the Panopticon system lends itself to an extreme form of binary division, is beyond him: his self-perception makes him oppressor, while, more accurately, he is victim. Foucault stresses how the healthy individual is defined in relation to that which has been labelled as delinquent, degenerate or perverse; and his studies of madness, of the birth of the clinic and of the prison all meet in this: 'when one wants to individualise the healthy normal and law-abiding adult, it is always by asking him how much of the child he. has in him, what secret madness lies within him, what fundamental crime he has dreamed of committing' (*Discipline and Punish*, p. 193). On this basis, Pip might be said to be the creation of three discourses that intersect: he remains something of the child – his name, a diminutive, establishes that; he is never in a position, he feels, of equality with anyone else; his dreams of the file, of Miss Havisham hanging from the beam, of playing Hamlet without knowing more than five words of the play, his nightmarish sense of phantasmagoric shapes perceived in the rushlight in the Hummuns, and his sense of being a brick in a house-wall, or part of a machine, 'wanting to have the engine stopped, and my part in it hammered off' (p. 472) – all proclaim his 'secret madness'. His sense of criminality is fed by virtually each act and its consequences that he undertakes.

A victim of the language system, only on one or two occasions does he reverse the role and become implicitly the accuser; one is where he prays over the head of the dead Magwitch: 'Lord be merciful to him a sinner' (p. 470) where commentators such as Moynahan have found something false. It is inappropriate, but it seems to belong to the Pip whose sense of himself is not free enough to allow himself to deconstruct the language system he is in. The odd thing is not that he fails to see himself as the sinner, as in the parable (Luke ch. xviii), but that he should want to name Magwitch as such. But that act of naming is a reflection of the way the dominated have no choice but to take over the language of their domination – to continue to beat, as they have been beaten, to continue to name disparagingly, as they have been named. That act in itself continues to name Pip – implicitly, as the Pharisee, of course. The question the novel asks is what else he might do: he seems caught. The self can only retreat from that dominant discourse through schizoid behaviour, as happens with Wemmick and his dual lifestyles, yet does not the 'Castle's' existence betray the prison's presence still in Wemmick's thinking? He, too, has not got away.

A second time when the language of Pip's oppression becomes one to oppress another is at the end of the book where he meets the younger Pip and suggests to Biddy that she should 'give Pip to him, one of these days, or lend him, at all events' (p. 490). To this Biddy responds 'gently' 'no', but her answer might well have been a horrified one in the light of what surrogate parents do to their children in the book: Pip is offering to play Magwitch to Biddy's child. He has learned nothing: is indeed a recidivist, unaware of how much he has been made himself a subject of other people's power and knowledge. Magwitch, similarly, 'owns' Pip (p. 339) as he says with pride: it is well-meaning as a statement, but with Foucault's aid it may be seen that Magwitch as a member of the class marginalised and set apart by the Panopticon society, has had to take on those dominant oppressive values, and talks the same language of property. His attitude is not inherently selfish, but it is a mark of his social formation which conditions him to speak as he does. In this most sociologically interactionist of novels, it is recognised that the self can use no other language than that given to it. What liberty there is is suggested by Orlick, who cringes after Joe beats him, beats Mrs Joe and secures her cringing – which, indeed, as 'a child towards a hard master' (p. 151) she seems to enjoy, as she continues to draw the sign of his power over her: such is the token of her self-oppression. (The contrast with Rosa Dartle, also the victim of a hammer-blow, is worth attention: Rosa's whole position as poor relation is self-oppressive.) Orlick, through a certain upward mobility, derived from his association with Compeyson, changes from the cringer himself (paid off by Jaggers from service at Satis House) to the accuser of Pip in the sluice-house. He perceives he has been marginalised, in some ways defined as delinquent, but it is an insight that could not be the source of social action or improvement, for it never extends beyond himself: as he says to Pip, 'you was favoured and he (Orlick) was bullied and beat' (p. 437). Out of that crazed imperception, he lashes out at Pip: the reverse action to Magwitch's, who almost equally arbitrarily identifies Pip with himself. (The novel wishes to close the gap between the convict and Pip, so Herbert says that Pip reminded Magwitch of the daughter he had lost.) Orlick and Magwitch go in opposite directions: what unites them (as it links them with Pip) is their sense that they are the watched, the ones under surveillance. Orlick's reactions to Pip look like Nietzsche's *ressentiment*,[13] that quality that Foucault has made much use of in discussing the origins of the impulse towards power. Dickens's 'cringer' is like Nietzsche's 'reactive personality': for Nietzsche, it is characteristically this type that, fired by resentment, tries to move into the legislative position. Orlick's rancour is born out of the inability that those watched in the Panopticon society have (since they have been put in individual cells, they cannot see each other) to read their situation as akin to that of other marginalised figures.

Thus the production, and reproduction, of oppression is what the book charts. Orlick attempts to move over to the other side in the Panopticon, and from the attempted assumption of that position, turns against Pip. Magwitch's acquisition of money is his attempt to move to the other side, to create a Pip, whom he surveys. In fact, he remains the criminal in the way he is named. Nor can Orlick change, and though he is in the country jail at the end, the replication of the book's past events seems safe with him when he is released: he really has no alternative, and as such he remains an apt commentary on the course an oppressed class must follow. Pip, in terms of status, moves over to the other side, in Panopticon terms, but his social formation is already firm, and basically he cannot change either: the events in the second part of his 'expectations' are an aberration from what he is in the first and third parts. Ironically, since he is cast there as guilty, what he is at those points is preferable to what he becomes in the second part.

As the recidivist, he wishes to be given Biddy's child, which would start again the whole cycle of oppression; and self-oppressive to the end, he writes out his autobiography – one that remains remarkably terse as to its intentions and its status as writing and which rolls out as though automatically, the product of a consciousness that remains fixed. Comparisons with the modes of David Copperfield's, or Esther Summerson's, or George Silverman's narratives would bear out this frozen, and at times almost perfunctory, manner. Miss Wade begins her account of herself sharply with the statement that she is 'not a fool'. Pip says nothing about himself as he is at the time of writing. He remains as someone who seems not to have gone beyond the emotional state documented in the writing, so that there is nothing cathartic about the confession, and no release is gained, just as Dickens's revised ending remains as ambivalent as the former, much more telegraphic one. For 'I saw no shadow of another parting from her' (p. 493) allows the ambiguity that they did or did not separate, and the narrator shows how his mind is closed now: what follows is not known. Writing about himself and his childhood experience, Dickens said 'I know how all these things have worked together to make me what I am'[14] in a confidence belonging to the *Copperfield* period and akin to that expressed so often in Wordsworth's *Prelude* of 1850. The distance from *Great Expectations* is pronounced: the very dryness of the narrative is an ironic comment on the book's title. The more buoyant, earlier statement may have its optimism unfounded as far as its belief in development goes, but the mode of writing in Pip's case may be seen as carceral: it belongs to the prison in its sense of giving an automatic, unstopping confession, which pauses not at all in its recounting of events and its self-accusation.

Foucault's 'birth of the prison', the concept of the individual, the privileging of the autobiographical mode – these related ideas are intrinsic to the novel, and while there is the creation of the human subject through a relaying of oppression and through a dominant discourse that he/she is within, there is also, in *Great Expectations*, implicit commentary about the mode of autobiography. Autobiography defines the subject confessionally; it puts upon it the onus of 'explanation', makes it prison-bound: a state that proves naturally acceptable to so much Romantic writing, where the tragic intensity of those who have to inhabit alienating spaces or constrictions can be defined as the source and inspiration of their reality. 'We think of the prison' – Eliot's reading of F. H. Bradley in *The Waste Land* proves comforting as it suggests that the essence of humanity is that it is confined, this is its common condition. In contrast, Foucault's analysis is precisely useful in its stress on the prison as the mode that gives the person the sense of uniqueness, the sense of difference from the others. In that sense, autobiography becomes a mode that assists in the reproduction of the discourse that the Panopticon society promotes. And in Pip's case, subjugated as he is by these discourses, the mode becomes a vehicle for 'self-reflection' – and for nothing else. Not, that is, the self thinking and moving from there into an area of thought where it can question the terms of its language, but the self continuing to reify its own status, to see it as an isolated thing. It continues a divisive trend. Not only is Pip's autobiography one that is markedly end-stopped in the sense that there is no feeling for a future, no way in which there can be a further development of the self, so that experience seems to avail nothing; but that cut-offness exists too in Pip's relations with others, in his inability to see others' complicity in the events surrounding him, save perhaps with Pumblechook, and there it is hardly difficult to see. It is appropriate that Miss Havisham should say to him 'You made your own snares. *I* never made them' (p. 374). It is manifestly untrue as a statement; and especially as far as the second sentence goes, as Miss Havisham's own confession suggests, finishing as it does with her self-condemnatory immolation and her entreaty, 'take the pencil and write under my name, I forgive her' (p. 414) – Miss Havisham is the 'cringer' here, as so often. What is interesting is that Pip seems to receive this analysis and can't see that to individualise the issue in this way won't do. *Great Expectations* comes close to suggesting that in an understanding of a society, the concept of the individual is unhelpful, that what is important are the total manipulations of power and language by whatever group has the power of definition and control. Autobiography provides an inadequate paradigm.

Is that the final irony of *Great Expectations*, that it displays the bankruptcy of Pip's efforts to understand what has happened to him? That he speaks throughout in a language that has been given to him, and that includes the language of his perception of himself as a particular kind of being? If that is so, discussion might move at this point from what Pip might do with regard to his own inarticulateness in face of the dominant discourse, to what the text might do. The poststructuralist in Foucault displaces human consciousnesses for larger historical processes: Dickens as a nineteenth-century novelist is marked by more confidence in individual sentience. It might be possible to find in *Great Expectations* a modernity of attitude which means that its parabolic kind of narrative is open-ended; that the title hints at the space within it for the reader to construct his/her own sense of how to take it; that, unlike the warder at the heart of the Panopticon, the author is not felt to be directing and encouraging a labelling; that the text resists single meaning. The ambiguity of the ending, already discussed, is relevant here, and so too is the sense that the reader has only Pip's text to work upon, and that this is certainly not final or necessarily authoritative. At the same time, however, the bourgeois Dickens has been located often enough within the book: for example, what do we make of Herbert's reporting of his father's principle of belief that 'no man who ever was a true gentleman at heart ever was, since the world began, a true gentleman in manner ... no varnish can hide the grain of the wood, and ... the more varnish you put on, the more the grain will express itself' (p. 204)? Is not this like the voice of the conscious novelist, and if so does it not express a different, more essentialist view of humanity than the very relative one formed throughout the whole pattern of the book with its insistence on the social construction of identities? Herbert's decent liberalism of attitude, which is intended to cut through class distinctions, both in relation to the upwardly mobile and the aristocratic-snobbish, is tactfully put, but it represents a trans-historicalism, in its view of human nature 'since the world began', an 'essentialist' view of humanity.

I give this example as one of the many that might be cited to suggest that the novel resists the irony of its form – which, in its radicalness, is where Raymond Williams finds 'Dickens's morality, his social criticism';[15] and that it might allow for a basic human nature, which would stand against Foucault's account, since for the latter there can be no cutting through a statement which is not framed within the limits of a particular discourse. The passage quoted from the opening of chapter 32 has been similarly seen – as the authorial voice, as part of the classic realist text, as that where 'bourgeois norms are experienced as the evident laws of a natural order'.[16] But in response to this view that the novel does invest time and space in a 'decent' common-sense attitude, several points might be urged. The first would be that it was no more necessary to take the comment in chapter 32 as authorial than to assume that Herbert's views are purely normative. And even if they were, and Mr Pocket's views about what constituted a gentleman coincided with Dickens's, the statement might still be situation-specific, having to do with what a gentleman might be in a society that laid so much stress on this bourgeois title. But in any case, Mr Pocket's views themselves are not beyond criticism: chapter 23 where he appears presents him wittily as the liberal whose 'decent' attitudes are themselves subverted by his wife's tyrannies – he is nearly as helpless as Joe, and that ineffectuality itself invites criticism, is indeed even part of a self-oppression. Moreover, although the concept of a true gentleman may be a mirage pursued through the book (compare Pip's uttering 'penitently' at the end about Joe – often seen as the ideal – 'God bless this gentle Christian man' (p. 472), as though here at last disinterested, decent qualities were being displayed), as a term it is itself not allowed to stand by the novel.

Joe again drops out of the London scene after Pip has recuperated: Pip's terms for him are part of the vocabulary he has learned to deploy from Satis House – and from exposure to Estella's power, which makes him tell Biddy that he wants to be a gentleman (p. 154). The term – even in Mr Pocket's oppositional formulation about it – is not one that fits Joe, even in Pip's modified way of putting it. Joe needs to be seen in another set of relations, and what Pip says about him is inappropriate because it bears more on Pip's sense of his own deficiency; Joe is what *he* is not; he has not succeeded in living up to the terms of his cultural formation that have been dictated to him, so he believes. What Joe is in rescuing Pip requires a set of terms that do not involve assimilation of him into the power relations and language of middle-class society, from which he is nearly totally excluded, save when he has to wear holiday clothes, and which are supremely irrelevant to him.

It is the cruellest irony for Pip that he must disparage himself and praise Joe so constantly in his narration. Joe does not require any setting down, but Pip has no means of assessing the forge and the village life independent of his own given language: under the influence of Satis House and its language he feels ashamed of home (p. 134). Nothing more is given of the forge in the novel apart from Pip's perception of it, and the absence of such a thing makes the torture for Pip, the prisoner in the Panopticon societal prison, the more refined. For it remains as a deceptive escape for him, although one that he cannot endorse (so that his intention to go back and marry Biddy has something masochistic and self-oppressive within it), and any step that he takes, either of accepting or rejoicing in it, remains a compromise. The split is caught finely in the scenes leading to his going to London in the first instance, and a compromise is dictated to him by the dividing nature of the society as prison. For Foucault argues that there is no 'knowledge that does not presuppose and constitute at the same time power relations' (*Discipline and Punish*, p. 27). That is, the birth of the prison – that most divisive of institutions – is an instrument not only to create Man as individual, to be known thus, but also ensures that there is no common language – no means of making a value-judgement which is outside the terms of a particular set of power-relations. Foucault is opposed to totalising interpretations of society precisely because of the way they ignore the endless replication of modes of oppression, of imposition of languages. The methods of deployment of power are various, as are the social groupings; indeed *Great Expectations* displays something of that variousness. What Pip finds to be true of himself is the result of the way he has been set up; at the same time, he does not possess a set of terms to think about a different way of life – the forge – that are not themselves instrumental for control over that way of thinking. Difference is not allowed for. Pip is bought up completely. The illusion he is given is of seeing things whole, but to the very end he cannot see the forge way of life as something different from his, and one that his own language formation cannot accommodate, from the moment he got to Satis House.

The modernity of the novel lies in this area: Dickens commits himself to no view about Joe or Biddy, or Pip, but writes rather a *Bildungsroman* where the expectation that the hero will learn through experience is belied, and not only by the title. Readerly assumptions generated through the lure of the narrative are set aside, for the central figure can only proceed on the language assumptions given to him. *David Copperfield* was the standard kind of *éducation sentimentale*; *Great Expectations* questions the ideological assumptions inherent in the earlier book, by presenting (with the earlier novel consciously in mind, re-read just before embarking on it) a development that can be no development. If the hero learns at all, it is only within his terms of reference, so there is no breaking out from the obsession with the self. The mode of the novel is ironic (it is noticeable how Dickens emphasises what is 'comic' about it to Forster, as Forster relates in the *Life*, IX.3): 'comic', in spite of the comedy within it, seems inappropriate, but perhaps it may draw attention to what is subversive about the book. And Dickens's absence of explanation about it only emphasises the extent to which he as author has receded: the novel stands alone, open-ended, marked out by the lack of 'closure' within it supplied by the moralist Dickens.

Whatever liberalism affects the book – as in the 'poor dreams' that nearly save Mr Jaggers in spite of himself, or in the way that Pip seems to enjoy a reasonable bourgeois existence in the Eastern Branch of Herbert's firm, or in its casualness about dates and historical positioning – is not central: the book has little faith in human nature considered as a Romantic, spontaneous and creative thing; no sense that the issues it addresses may be met by the middle-class values that commonly sustain the nineteenth-century novel. The interest in character here – which still so often forms the basis of Dickensian criticism – does not sanction belief in the individual as ultimately irrepressible. Rather, the idea of the Panopticon as the chief model for the formation of any individuality in nineteenth-century Britain makes for something much more complex and gives rise to the sense that the formation of individuality is itself delusory as a hope. It is itself the problem it seeks to solve – through its way of dividing a society and separating it. The prison is not the 'human condition' in a transhistorical sense, as Denmark was also a prison for Hamlet, but is the apt symbol for enforcing models of helplessness: the more aware the self is of its position, the more it confirms the prison, and thus cuts itself off further. To that diagnosis, which demands a consideration of power structures in society such as Foucault gives, and which draws attention to language as a way of making the person prison-bound, the autobiographical mode of *Great Expectations* bears witness. In itself the mode works to keep the narrator in the prison. Just as Wemmick's father and his pleasant and playful ways, and the possibility that Jaggers himself might one day want a pleasant home, also ensure that the prison's durability is not in question: these individual escapes, simply by staying within the limits of the individual idea, address, effectively, no problem at all.

From *Essays in Criticism*, 36 (1986), 11–31.

NOTES

[Jeremy Tambling's provocative essay shares Robin Gilmour's concern (in essay 5) with Pip's historical environment. But Tambling is far less concerned with explicit socio-cultural notation or habits of conscious thought and, in striking contrast to both Gilmour and Jack Rawlins (in essay 3), espouses a very strong form of social determinism. For him, the human subject, unconsciously and willy-nilly, acquires a psychological formation that is an exclusively ideological product. One of the few exceptions to this rule is Dickens himself: as in the accounts of psychologising critics, Dickens, despite his Victorian liberalism and respectability, is said to be reluctantly privy to the processes of psychic formation at work. The essay argues that in certain insights Dickens even anticipates the French philosopher-historian Michel Foucault (1926–1984).

As the Introduction explains at greater length (pp. 14–15), the starting point for Tambling's structuralist critique of nineteenth-century ideology is Foucault's diagnosis of 'Panopticon thinking'. The Panopticon itself was a design for a prison which would regulate the minds of prisoners by carefully classifying them and keeping them under constant surveillance. Dickens, for his part, had already shown a strong interest in prisons in his documentary writings, and Tambling suggests that *Great Expectations* went on to make just the same connection as Foucault between supervisory prison regimes and structures of power in society as a whole.

Among other things, Tambling attaches particular significance to the novel's form as a first-person-singular autobiographical narration. He argues that autobiography tends to define the writer-subject confessionally, as different from other people and calling for special attention. But such confession is far from spontaneous and liberating. On the contrary, the subject's self-revelation is coerced, and feeds directly into the regulatory social processes whereby 'delinquency' is classified and rendered harmless. (For a further development of this idea, see Tambling's book, *Confession: Sexuality, Sin, the Subject* [Manchester University Press, 1990].) If Jaggers seems to be exempt from such pigeon-holing, this is because he is like the unseen supervisor in the Panopticon's central observation tower. As for Joe, he remains completely separate from the processes of social discourse and formation. On Tambling's view of things, if we try to place ourselves outside particular configurations of power relations we cannot even participate in a shared language. And once we opt for such participation, the relentlessly insidious processes of discoursal regulation quite undermine any liberal dream of human freedom and individuality.

Tambling's quotations are from *Great Expectations*, ed. Angus Calder, Penguin English Library (Harmondsworth, 1965). Ed.]

1. F. R. and Q. D. Leavis, *Dickens the Novelist* (1970), p. 331.

2. Barry Smart, *Foucault, Marxism and Critique* (1983), p. 90.

3. Michel Foucault, *Discipline and Punish*, trans. Alan Sheridan (Harmondsworth, 1979). All textual references are to this edition.

4. The theme is dealt with in Michael Ignatieff, *A Just Measure of Pain: the Penitentiary in the Industrial Revolution, 1750–1850* (1978).

5. Jeremy Bentham, quoted in *Dickens and Crime* (1962), p. 18.

6. See the *Letters of Charles Dickens*, vol. 3, 1842–3, ed. Madeline House and Graham Storey (Oxford, 1974), pp. 105, 436, 110, for details on these prisons.

7. See *Michel Foucault* by Mark Cousins and Athar Hussain (1984), pp. 183, 192, for further details about these prisons.

8. Philip Collins, *Dickens and Crime* (1962), pp. 20, 21.

9. Lionel Trilling, *Sincerity and Authenticity* (1972), p. 24.

10. Michel Foucault, *The History of Sexuality*, vol. 1 (Harmondsworth, 1981), p. 60.

11. F. R. and Q. D. Leavis, *Dickens the Novelist,* p. 288. Apart from this account of the novel, I am greatly in debt to Julian Moynahan, 'The Hero's Guilt: the Case of *Great Expectations*', *Essays in Criticism*, 10 (1960), 60–79, and A. L. French, 'Beating and Cringing: *Great Expectations*', *Essays in Criticism*, 24 (1974), 147–68. [French's article is reprinted as essay 1 above. Ed.]

12. *Dickens the Novelist*, p. 291.

13. '*Ressentiment*' is translated as 'rancour' and discussed in detail in the first essay of *The Genealogy of Morals*, trans. Francis Golffing (New York, 1956), see especially p. 170.

14. Forster, *Life of Dickens* I, ch. 2.

15. Raymond Williams, *The English Novel from Dickens to Lawrence* (1970), p. 48.

16. Roland Barthes, *Mythologies*, trans. Annette Lavers (1982), p. 140.

7

Stories Present and Absent in *Great Expectations*

EIICHI HARA

I

In the plethora of criticism on *Great Expectations* one central issue, although it has been recognised and referred to implicitly by many critics, has not yet been discussed substantially: the problem of authorship. By author I mean not the actual writer of the novel but the one 'implied' in the text, an entity quite different from the real author.[1] For Pip, as for David Copperfield, the novel is a kind of autobiography or memoir. But when the peculiar narrative situation in *Great Expectations* is considered the other way round, from the side of the narrated story, it seems to present Pip's 'authorship' as something hollow and void. If one takes the enigma of Pip's secret benefactor to be the central axis of the novel, as it indeed is, it is clear that the author of the story is not Pip but Magwitch, who has been devising, plotting and writing Pip's story. Magwitch is a character representing the double meaning of 'author': the writer and the father.[2] He is both the author of Pip's story and the father who has secretly adopted him as his son, begetter of the text and its hero at the same time. Thus the central axis of the novel poses the problem of authorship, providing a clue to other layers of the novel where story and its authors stand in ambiguous and sometimes quite incompatible relationships with each other. When Pip, urged by some inner compulsion, strives to write the story of his own life, just as David had done before him, his pen constantly fails him; for, as he writes, the written text slips out of his hand and is instantly transformed into stories written by strange authors. The problem of authorship is in fact the problem of writing or the failure of writing.[3] Pip fails to write his life story; the novel is never to be written by this 'author'. As Magwitch's writing of Pip's story suggests, Pip can never be the writer nor the independent hero of his own story; rather, the novel is structured around the central story of Pip as written by Magwitch, with other stories, also of Pip, encircling this central axis. Just as the Magwitch story destroys all Pip's false hopes, decomposes itself, the structure of these stories in the novel is to be seen as a self-destroying process, an unwriting, a structure that is non-structure. Because the stories of Pip are always written by other authors, they collapse by their alienation from the hero. Pip, always a passive object to be written, fails to be the 'hero of my own life': unlike David Copperfield, he fails to be the novelist, the writer of his own life story. But when presence of stories gives way to absence of stories, a story that is absent in *Great Expectations* emerges whose absence will guide us to the innermost depth of Pip's failed narrative. It is this structure of presence and absence, of author and story, that I would like to elucidate in the following argument.

II

Poetics of narrative fiction is perhaps the facet of literary studies that has profited most from the structuralist enterprise. Although such rigorously structuralist systems as Genette's *Narrative Discourse* or Todorov's *Poetics of Prose* will come to be seen with some misgivings in the wake of deconstruction, there is no doubt that they have clarified the workings of a fictional text and supplied useful terms and concepts for the discussions of narrative fiction. Among the most fundamental and useful of concepts is the distinction between 'story' and 'plot' bequeathed by the Russian Formalists. Here story means 'the story in its most neutral, objective, chronological form – the story as it might have been enacted in real time and space, a seamless continuum of innumerable contiguous events' and plot is 'the actual text in which this story is imitated, with all its inevitable (but motivated) gaps, elisions, emphases and distortions'.[4] As this definition indicates, story is the hypothetical construct that could be reassembled and arranged in chronological order from the often confused texture of actual narrative, with a beginning, a middle and an end neatly arranged as a completed whole. It is an assumed primal text or metatext that the reading process recovers and reconstructs, though the paradox is that it is to be recuperated *a posteriori*, only after the plot is worked out in narrative fiction. Of the two aspects that comprise narrative it is plot that has generally been the object of aesthetic studies since plot is what a novelist actually writes and is primarily present to the reader. Thus studies of the basic structure of *Great Expectations* have been concerned mainly with its plot.[5] In a recent and important essay, for example, Peter Brooks describes the novel as 'concerned with finding a plot and losing it, with the precipitation of plottedness around its hero, and his eventual "cure" from plot' (Brooks uses the word 'plot' in a somewhat different sense from the one defined above as he considers it 'not only design but intentionality as well').[6] Without questioning the validity of studies of plot, however, I would like to call attention to the presence – indeed the predominance – of *story* in the novel. Story, normally reconstructed almost as an afterthought from the actual narrative text, is in *Great Expectations* a presence *a priori*. It is already there, written by some writer other than the hero-narrator Pip, with its beginning, middle and end all complete even before the plot begins. My description of the novel would be that Pip does not find any plot but that story finds and traps him, plot as intentionality remaining always outside him. He is not 'cured' from plot; story or stories collapse and become absent, leaving him in the vacuum created by this absence.

That intentionality is outside Pip, that he is not the writer of his own story, is indicated in the novel's opening scene, in which he is a being poised in the space of ontogenetic ambiguity with an insignificant monosyllable for a name. His actual name is given in the text only as an appellation designated his by some alien agency: 'I give Pirrip as my father's family name on the authority of his tombstone.' Here the double meaning of author as father and writer as well as the pure textuality of Pip's existence come to the fore. Pip's father is dead, he has become a text, the inscription on the tombstone that locates Pip in a fixed space-time; and the contours of Pip's being begin to flesh out only after this textual location. He takes his being from the text of his absent father, whose authority is symbolically represented by Magwitch who starts up, like an apparition of the real father, 'from among the graves at the side of the church porch' (p. 2). Magwitch establishes complete control over the terrified child immediately; he turns him upside down, threatens him with cannibalism ('what fat cheeks you ha'got...Darn Me if I couldn't eat em'), orders him to bring a file and 'wittles', and extracts a pledge of strict silence. Thus, from the very beginning, Pip becomes involved in the world of criminality where crime, guilt and bad faith torment him. Though this criminality is to be the primal text in which he is caught, we would be mistaken to regard Pip as a guilty being who carries the burden of some transcendental original sin. The guilt here does not belong to him; it is something that is imposed upon him by outside authority. The helpless orphan boy is placed in an atmosphere of criminality by a force over which he has no control.

The otherness of the taint of criminality in Pip, the alienation of essence from being, is manifest in the fact that he is always regarded as a boy with criminal propensities by the adults around him who, like Magwitch, have incontestable authority over him. These adults are possessed with the idea that the young are 'naterally wicious', Pip especially so. With this preconception they treat him as if his life were already written and finished as a story, the plot of which Pip is going to follow as a predestined, assigned path. As authors of the story of Pip's criminal career, Wopsle and Pumblechook are more adept in writing stories than Mrs Joe, who uses only her hand and occasional applications of the Tickler. For example, at the Christmas dinner at Joe's house, they are quite aware of the nature of the novel's semiotic universe, in which one can write a story even in a word:

> Mr Pumblechook added, after a short interval of reflection, 'Look at Pork alone. There's a subject! If you want a subject, look at Pork!'
> 'True, sir. Many a moral for the young,' returned Mr Wopsle; and I knew he was going to lug me in, before he said it; 'might be deduced from that text.'
> ('You listen to this,' said my sister to me, in a severe parenthesis.)
> Joe gave me some more gravy.
> 'Swine,' pursued Mr Wopsle, in his deepest voice, and pointing his fork at my blushes, as if he were mentioning my christian name; 'Swine were the companions of the prodigal. The gluttony of Swine is put before us, as an example to the young.' (I thought this pretty well in him who had been praising up the pork for being so plump and juicy.) 'What is detestable in a pig, is more detestable in a boy.'
> (pp. 57–8)

Here a seemingly innocent word 'pork' undergoes radical transformations with an ever increasing semantic density. What is merely a thing to be eaten becomes a 'text' and the biblical reference brings forth 'swine', with its connotations of gluttony and sensuality, and 'prodigal', inevitably associated with the story of the Prodigal Son.[7]

Thus a sign, a word, is transformed into a story, a finished tale with a beginning, a middle and an end, which becomes a story of Pip as Pumblechook immediately transforms Pip into Swine with his pompous authority: 'If you'd been born a Squeaker ... would you have been here now? Not you ... You would have been disposed of for so many shillings according to the market price of the article, and Dunstable the butcher would have come up to you as you lay in your straw, and he would have whipped you under his left arm, and with his right he would have tucked up his frock to get a penknife from out of his waistcoat pocket, and he would have shed your blood and had your life' (p. 58). The story of Pip the Prodigal Son is thus present, written by these authors, even before any plot development could be introduced.

The story written by Wopsle and Pumblechook may seem an incomplete realisation of the story of Pip the Criminal since the story of the Prodigal Son does not include any criminal act, though, of course, the son is guilty of a moral crime against his father. Pumblechook's reference to the butchering of Pip the Swine, however, recalls the gallows and the execution of criminals. In the popular tradition, a story depicting the life of a criminal ends in his execution or suicide. Dickens, who had an avowed interest in crime and criminals, faithfully follows this tradition. Bill Sykes, Ralph Nickleby, Jonas Chuzzlewit and Mr Merdle all meet violent deaths at the end of their careers of crime. Pip's story as written by Pumblechook and Wopsle must also include the hero's death in total misery and wretchedness as the morally plausible outcome of a criminal life. The story will become complete when a plot that will realise it in a particular circumstantial context is established. For Wopsle and Pumblechook, there is no need to work out the story in all its squalid details since they have only to choose a text that fits into the prescribed pattern from the stock-in-trade of the popular criminal literature. Wopsle discovers a pertinent text in a bookshop: 'the affecting tragedy of George Barnwell', Lillo's *The London Merchant*. As it is his inevitable fate to come across authoritarian figures, Pip is seized by Wopsle in the street and made to listen to the recitation of the drama in the Pumblechookian parlour. The story of George Barnwell who, seduced by a harlot called Millwood, robbed his master and murdered his uncle, so alien to the innocent child, is turned into the story of Pip the Criminal. The transformation is so complete that Pip speaks of Barnwell as himself:

What stung me, was the identification of the whole affair with my unoffending self. When Barnwell began to go wrong, I declare that I felt positively apologetic, Pumblechook's indignant stare so taxed me with it. Wopsle, too, took pains to present me in the worst light. At once ferocious and maudlin, I was made to murder my uncle with no extenuating circumstances whatever; Millwood put me down in argument, on every occasion; it became sheer monomania in my master's daughter to care a button for me; and all I can say for my gasping and procrastinating conduct on the fatal morning, is, that it was worthy of the general feebleness of my character. Even after I was happily hanged and Wopsle had closed the book, Pumblechook sat staring at me, and shaking his head, and saying, 'Take warning, boy, take warning!' as if it were a well-known fact that I contemplated murdering a near relation, provided I could only induce one to have the weakness to become my benefactor.

(p. 145)

Identified with Barnwell, it is only natural that Pip believes he 'must have had some hand in the attack upon my sister' that happened just at the time. Orlick is wrong, however, to see Pip's guiltiness here as metaphysical ('It was you as did for your shrew sister'),[8] because the Pip who feels guilt is the Pip defined by Pumblechook and Wopsle and written into the story of Pip the Criminal, not the actual Pip who is perfectly innocent. As he is not the author of the story of Barnwell, begetter of the criminal Pip, he has no authority even over the feelings he has or the narrator says that he has. He feels guilt only because subjectivity, the 'I', has become unstable, because the story of Barnwell, which actually can never be the story of Pip, envelops him.

III

But George Barnwell, for all his difference from Pip, shares a significant factor with him. When criminality is removed from the story of Barnwell, it comes nearer to Pip's story: they are both apprentices torn by agonising desire for a worthless woman. Here again, as in the case of 'pork', the word 'apprentice' contains in it a complete story (or stories) that is present *a priori*, before plot is conceived and actualised. Moreover, the Barnwell story is only one aspect of a dualistic structure. There is another side, a positive story paired with the dark, negative story of the criminal apprentice. The duality of the apprentice story is best exemplified in William

Hogarth's series of engravings *Industry and Idleness*, by which Dickens was no doubt greatly influenced.[9] Hogarth presents two apprentices whose contrasting careers have almost exact parallels in the apprentice stories in *Great Expectations*. The story of the Industrious Apprentice, modelled on the legend of Dick Whittington, presents Francis Goodchild, who gains his master's confidence through his industry and honesty. He becomes partner in his master's business, marries his master's daughter, and finally attains the highest rung of the middle-class social ladder by becoming the Lord Mayor of London. The Idle Apprentice, Tom Idle, modelled apparently on George Barnwell (who had been a subject of popular ballads as early as the second half of the seventeenth century[10]) goes astray through his idleness and association with bad companions. Committing one crime after another, he is betrayed by his whore, arrested and brought before Goodchild who as magistrate must condemn him. Tom Idle is finally executed at Tyburn. For Dickens the dual story of the apprentice was the source of many characters and stories. The good apprentice appears as such heroes as Oliver Twist, Walter Gay, and in the references to Dick Whittington in *Dombey and Son* and *Barnaby Rudge* that indicate their origin.[11] The idle apprentice is presented in those villains who obstruct the hero's progress in life; Noah Claypole in *Oliver Twist*, Simon Tappertit in *Barnaby Rudge*, Uriah Heep in *David Copperfield* and Dolge Orlick in *Great Expectations* are typical examples. Again the explicit references to George Barnwell in *Barnaby Rudge* and *Great Expectations* reveal the origin of this recurring type.[12] For Dickens, to be an apprentice is to choose between the two poles of a story, each of which will lead to a course of life fundamentally incompatible with the other. But the uniqueness of *Great Expectations* among Dickens's novels consists in the fact that these two poles have been combined into one. For, if we follow the argument of critics like Julian Moynahan, the bad apprentice, Orlick, might be a psychological double, an alter ego, of Pip the good apprentice.[13] But, in Orlick's view at least, the disparity between the two is very marked because, as he tells Pip in the lime-kiln, Pip was the favoured, petted one who was always in Orlick's way; Pip, according to him, even came between him and 'a young woman' he liked (p. 435). Pip will succeed Joe some day in his profession and marry Biddy, frustrating all the expectations of the other apprentice. While the story of the criminal apprentice has been written by other authors, the story of the good apprentice Orlick describes might be the one that Pip can virtually be author and hero of. However much he deviates from the path of honesty, no one can deny his innate goodness, and as a Dickens hero he has qualifications enough to be another Francis Goodchild.

In fact, to pursue the course of the Industrious Apprentice, to live the story of Goodchild, is undoubtedly the life most natural to Pip. He is accustomed to the life at the forge and to his master Joe, who is both a father and best friend to him. With his unfailing goodness and kindness Joe will be an ideal master and companion to the orphan boy. Joe himself looks forward with genuine delight and expectation to the day when Pip will be his apprentice; he tells Pip that when Pip is apprentice to him, 'regularly bound', they will 'have such Larks!' (p. 48). For Pip, however, this natural state of life, the life of an apprentice to Joe, is suddenly transformed into something strange and unnatural, a story written by an alien hand, in Satis House.

The encounter with Miss Havisham is of great importance in Pip's life because she is expected to be the donor of both wealth and the beautiful maiden. But the encounter with Estella carries far greater weight, not only for the hero but for the overall structure of the novel. Estella is not only – and melodramatically – Magwitch's daughter, but she also plays a role essentially identical with her father's, the role of an author with dictatorial authority over his subject. Magwitch, as we know, is the anonymous author of Pip's fortunes; Estella also drastically changes the meaning of life for Pip when, with queenly disdain and cruelty, she ridicules his low birth and commonness. Pip, who has lived (albeit not very happily) with serenity and modest hopes, is compelled by Estella to look at his existence from an entirely new angle. Playing 'beggar my neigh-bour' with her, he is called 'a common labouring-boy'; his lan-guage, his limbs and his attire all become the objects of her spiteful attacks:

> 'He calls the knaves, Jacks, this boy!' said Estella with disdain, before our first game was out. 'And what coarse hands he has! And what thick boots!'
>
> I had never thought of being ashamed of my hands before; but I began to consider them a very indifferent pair. Her contempt for me was so strong, that it became infectious, and I caught it.
>
> She won the game, and I dealt. I misdealt, as was only natural, when I knew she was lying in wait for me to do wrong; and she denounced me for a stupid, clumsy, labouring-boy.
>
> (p. 90)

As Pip cannot be anything other than a future blacksmith, Estella's ridicule is directed against that state of existence which is most natural to him. A blacksmith's hands are coarse and black from work, the thickness of his boots is proper in the forge, and his language, as Joe demonstrates, is often capable of sustained dignity. There is no need for Pip to be ashamed of himself in front of this spoilt and proud girl. But he smarts, smarts terribly, because Estella, who is the erotic symbol of the great expectations, is not only proud but very beautiful; by virtue of her beauty she has power, irresistible authority over him. Pip is caught less in the magic web of Miss Havisham than in the text of an apprentice story that becomes thralldom not because of the class system but because Estella has rewritten the natural state of Pip's existence into a story alienated from himself. Suddenly his hands and boots, which have 'never troubled' him before, do trouble him; now he is 'much more ignorant than' he has considered himself so far and is 'in a low-lived bad way' (p. 94). Thus Estella becomes the author of the story of Pip the Apprentice which, though a presence from the beginning of the novel, becomes a hollowness, an absence when Pip, trapped in Estella's authority, becomes aware of his alienation from it. It is a story written and imposed upon him by others, by the social system or by Estella, a story he himself can never be the author of. But Pip has been caught in this story from the beginning. There is no way out; he is tightly 'bound' there by society and its institutions. Here the contrasting stories of Tom Idle and Francis Goodchild are synthesised through the catalyst of the hero's alienation; he is alienated from both aspects of the dualism. When the time comes for Pip to be apprenticed to Joe, it is no longer the moment of fulfilment, the moment of 'larks', but the moment of execution in which to be bound apprentice is tantamount to being bound in the halter:

> The Justices were sitting in the Town Hall near at hand, and we at once went over to have me bound apprentice to Joe in the Magisterial presence. I say, we went over, but I was pushed over by Pumblechook, exactly as if I had that moment picked a pocket or fired a rick; indeed, it was the general impression in Court that I had been taken red-handed, for, as Pumblechook shoved me before him through the crowd, I heard some people say, 'What's he done?' and others, 'He's a young 'un, too, but looks bad, don't he?' One person of mild and benevolent aspect even gave me a tract ornamented with a woodcut of a malevolent young man fitted up with a perfect sausage-shop of fetters, and entitled, TO BE READ IN MY CELL.

> The Hall was a queer place, I thought, with higher pews in it than a church ... Here, in a corner, my indentures were duly signed and attested, and I was 'bound'; Mr Pumblechook holding me all the while as if we had looked in on our way to the scaffold, to have those little preliminaries disposed of.
>
> (pp. 132–3)

It is quite fitting that Pumblechook, the prime author of the story of Pip the Criminal, is present as custodian in the scene where Pip is 'bound' in the story of Pip the Apprentice, a story now no more his own than the story of George Barnwell. Pip reflects: 'I ... had a strong conviction on me that I should never like Joe's trade. I had liked it once, but once was not now' (p. 134).

IV

After three years of apprenticeship to Joe, during which Pip works at the forge with forced industry much 'against the grain', nursing deep dissatisfaction, anguish and burning passion for Estella in his bosom, Jaggers, the dark lawyer, comes to him with the 'great expectations', the gift from an anonymous benefactor. The gift lifts Pip out of the apprentice story and, this time with his willing acceptance, places him in another story, the story of Great Expectations. Harry Stone and Shirley Grob, among others, have pointed out the strong presence of the fairy tale in *Great Expectations*. Viewed as a structuring principle, the fairy tale provides the basic materials of this new story in which Pip is henceforth to live.[14] Miss Havisham may be regarded as the fairy godmother, Estella as the beautiful princess, and Jaggers as the wizard who looks sinister at first but will prove, perhaps, benevolent in the end. The hero is Pip, of course, the knight errant who will rescue the princess caught in the magic castle, Satis House. As this arrangement of basic elements suggests, the story of Great Expectations has its origin in and follows, or seems to follow, the pivotal plot of a fairy tale that could be identified with one from the stock of traditional tales. Shirley Grob mentions 'The Golden Goose' as the typical example of the primitive form of fairy tale that Dickens uses with pointed irony. However, with regard to Satis House and its inhabitants, 'Sleeping Beauty', as Harry Stone suggests, is the fundamental text for the story of Great Expectations. Because of some fatal incident that occurred long ago Satis House set itself outside the flow of time and, making barriers to protect itself from the intrusion of outside forces, has slumbered in a timeless world. As Pip noticed when he first visited this strange place, the house 'had a great many iron bars to it'; windows were walled up or rustily barred, and even the courtyard was barred (pp. 84–5). There in the darkness Miss Havisham lives in the wedding dress she has worn since the fatal wedding day, stopping all the clocks at twenty minutes to nine, forever living in that moment when her heart was broken, but also perhaps sleeping forever in full outfit to receive the bridegroom who will never come. Time, with cruel disregard for her determination, has ravaged her body and dress but the decayed Sleeping Beauty is now replaced by a budding new one, Estella, whose coldness and remoteness suggest to Pip that she also is in a state of slumber, from which he as her knight hopes one day to arouse her. Pip imagines himself to be the hero of this romance of expectations – a significant departure from the apprentice stories. George Barnwell and Dick Whittington were roles Pip was made to play; their stories were grounded in a void that was to bring about their own undoing. In the fairy tale, however, Pip feels comfortably at home because the tale not only offers salvation from alien stories but also promises to fill the void engendered in Satis House, to satisfy the want, the horrible sense of deprivation he experienced at Estella's taunts. It is a story that he constructs for himself, building his groundless dreams about Miss Havisham and Estella. Circumstances, full of 'attractive mystery', have eloquently contributed to this false construction. But even in this fairy tale world, can Pip actually be the hero? Is his construction of this story wholly independent of those outside forces that have kept him, 'bound' him in the written text from the start?

The author of a story, the author in the sense we have been using it, is someone who maintains definitive authority over his creation, who determines and directs the course of action or plot of the story. The author of the fairy tale 'Sleeping Beauty' can be identified with a character who, though no hero nor heroine, is in complete possession of the destinies of heroes and heroines: the witch or fairy godmother. The fairy godmother is decisively important in the construction of the hero's or heroine's story, as is evident in 'Sleeping Beauty'. She is a prophetess, a visionary who foresees and determines the future. The hero or heroine, perfectly under her control, has virtually no freedom in choosing his course of action in the story. Despite all the precautions taken to keep her away from any spindle, the princess wounds herself on one, falling into a sleep of a hundred years and her sleep, however long and profound it may be, is instantly broken by a kiss from the prince. In Pip's version of 'Sleeping Beauty', Miss Havisham, the fairy godmother, has decided and prescribed the destiny of the hero Pip in a way that is absolute and unchangeable. Neither wealth nor beauty is in Pip's power to achieve; they are things given, bestowed by the fairy godmother whose will functions as the inevitable logic in the fairy tale structure. Thus Pip is deluded; since he has no power to create his life story, he can never be its real hero, the hero as author. Although he believes that in this dream world he has finally found a place congenial to his needs, he is still caught in a text written by a hand other than his. Pip remains a reader of texts. Max Byrd identifies 'reading' as the crucial, pervading theme in the novel and points out that Pip, through his unreasonable, incorrect reading of texts, creates a fiction that tends to enclose him, 'to transform him into a monomaniac: he begins to believe the fiction to be truth, indeed, the whole truth'.[15] The story of Great Expectations is the most inclusive of those fictions Pip has built by reading others' texts and in which he finds himself enclosed.

However, this fiction proves to be fictional in a double sense: it is, as we know, a fiction that Pip constructs with the aid of a heavy reliance on circumstances rather than on concrete evidence, and it is a fiction whose author turns out to be the wrong one. The abnormality, timelessness and madness associated with Miss Havisham has made Pip believe that the fairy godmother cannot possibly be any other person in his book of fairies. Yet Mr Jaggers's initial announcement to him that the name of his 'liberal benefactor remains a profound secret, until the person chooses to reveal it' (p. 165), indicates that the 'expectations' of this unfinished story are pointed expressly toward the future revelation of authorship. In the awaited denouement the fairy godmother reveals herself to be not Miss Havisham, not even a female, but the convict Abel Magwitch, who declares himself to be Pip's 'second father' (p. 337). The unmasking of the author/father instantly undoes the fairy tale, destroys its mirage, and transforms it into a hollowness, an absence: 'Miss Havisham's intentions towards me, all a mere dream; Estella not designed for me; I only suffered in Satis House as a convenience, a sting for the greedy relations, a model with a mechanical heart to practise on when no other practice was at hand' (p. 341). After the destruction of his dream Pip cannot attain wealth and gentleman's status with Magwitch's money, though it has been honestly earned by the transported convict, because the book Magwitch has written is utterly incompatible with his inner needs and desires, and also, because in the world of sober realities Pip regains his natural goodness of heart.

V

When the novel's central axis breaks down and the pivotal story of Great Expectations becomes absent, what are we left with? Is it only 'the impression of a life that has outlived plot, renounced plot, been cured of it'[16] that we have here? But neither plot nor stories have yet been exhausted. Before arriving at the sense of a life 'that is left over' we have to consider the moral framework in which Pip seems to remain even after the breakdown of the central story.

If the final meaning of the novel, the sum total of all its processes and plot workings, is the moral theme and the wisdom gained by the hero in his life story, *Great Expectations* manifests the moral orientation of the 'great tradition' rather starkly, as a simple moral of the sort appended to fables and 'moral tales'. For the novel might be taken to be, as Edgar Rosenberg suggests, 'a cautionary tale about an engaging, slightly contaminated young man whose head has been turned by his unwarranted expectations, who, confronted by the actualities of his situation, experiences a change of heart, and in the end gets more or less what he deserves.'[17] Rosenberg's summary seems an exact description of the kind of moral tale the novel is, an amalgamation of the dual story of Hogarth's apprentices. Pip discards the simple life of apprenticeship because of his infatuation with a foolish dream and, becoming morally degenerate as a result, finally loses everything. Bewitched by a worthless woman, he throws away his true friend Joe and his sweetheart Biddy, and incurs just punishment. When he goes back to Joe's forge to propose to Biddy, having finally recognised his own folly after the deaths of Miss Havisham and Magwitch, he finds that Joe has just married her. Thus Pip, the penitent Idle Apprentice, exiles himself from England to work as an industrious clerk at Clarriker and Co. for eleven years.

If we were to take this moral fable, the cautionary tale, as it is, Pip's return to the forge and his marriage to Biddy would be his return to and recovery of the story in which he can truly be the hero, the story to be reinstated after the breakdown of all the other, false, stories. Surely the moral framework of the novel seems to call for this as the norm from which Pip has deviated. Accepting the moral theme unreservedly, Forster and Bernard Shaw, and many critics following their lead, have voiced objections to the altered ending of the novel.[18] The hero who has gone astray from the path of honesty should be justly punished, whereas the happy (if equally sad) ending allows him to be united with Estella, the evil and worthless *femme fatale*. The critics claim that the revision is a falsification of the moral meaning of the story that does less than justice to the total moral framework that has been so carefully and expertly constructed. But is the cautionary tale really Pip's true story if he withdraws from it with a feeling not of despair but of relief and gratitude? Upon recovering from the first shock of the news of Biddy's marriage to Joe, Pip feels 'great thankfulness that' he has 'never breathed this last baffled hope to Joe'. Thanking his good fortune in not disclosing his intention, thanking Joe and Biddy for all they have done for him and all he has 'so ill repaid', asking forgiveness of both, he leaves them to go abroad (pp. 487–8). Why is the feeling of relief and gratitude predominant in the final crisis of Pip's life? It may be explained, as Milton Millhauser suggests, in terms of the insurmountable disparity between the state of the village blacksmith and that of the urban gentleman Pip has now become; for Pip, it is both impossible and actually impracticable to return again to Joe's class after his experiences in the upper sphere.[19] However, his feeling of relief and gratitude may also be explained in terms of the fundamental structure of the novel we have been discussing, the structure of stories constructed and destroyed, of presence made into absence. Pip feels relief because, the place of hero being justly occupied by Joe, he does not have to go back again to a story that is not his own. The story of Pip the Apprentice is alien to him, written by a hand other than his; it is quite unnatural for him to return to it. Or to put it otherwise, it is only too natural for an apprentice gone astray to go back with a penitent heart, after wandering and hardship, to the place where he naturally belongs. This would be to follow the moral pattern too neatly, to conform to the logical sequence of artificial moral fables. Instead, the final moral meaning that the novel offers suggests its own hollowness and falsity by being too neat and logical a construction. Moreover, according to the other forces at work in the novel, it is quite likely to be destroyed by its own artificiality. Why is this so? Why are natural outcome and logical sequence denied

here? When even the moral fable that seemed to be the ultimate
story present in *Great Expectations* is undone by the hero's
withdrawal from it at the last moment, we are directed to the
novel's deepest stratum.

VI

If Pip had been a character who acts and behaves according to the
dictates of reason, the ending neatly and logically ordered would
have been naturally his. But it is precisely at this point that logic
fails because if he had been such a character, he would not have
deviated from the path of the Industrious Apprentice in the first
place; it would have been simply impossible for him to err so
flagrantly in his choices. Actually Pip has always been a character
motivated and compelled by a force to which reason, logic and
morality are utter strangers. Because of this, the logical and moral
outcome finally eludes him; the teleological drive in the text rejects
him at the last moment. The character who symbolises this demonic
impulse in Pip is Estella. It is a strange neglect among the criticism
and commentary on the novel that Estella has not received the
critical attention she deserves as a character who controls Pip's life
in a more profound way than even Miss Havisham or Magwitch. It
is true that Estella is the novel's least realised character; her frigidity
and remoteness throughout give an impression of unreality and
when her heart melts at the last meeting with Pip, it is unconvincing. She appears infrequently, providing the reader with few
chances of penetrating into her inner self even to find the void there.
However, Estella's influence on Pip is inordinately great compared
with the scarcity of her characterisation. As I indicated earlier,
Estella transforms Pip's natural state of existence into a story
alienated from him. Because of her strong sexual attraction a 'poor
dream', the desire of becoming a gentleman, is engendered in him.
If apprenticeship is the norm, the moral standard, to which Pip
should finally return, Estella must be regarded as the character of
decisive importance because she first disrupts that standard.

While the critical censure of Pip's infatuation with Estella is valid,
before making judgements too facile to be worth making, we must
notice that Pip himself has been quite aware of the madness and
foolishness of his passion for Estella from the start. He has already
passed a forcible verdict on his own conduct when, as a young boy,

he confesses to Biddy his desperate passion for another girl. Biddy
asks him who it was that told him he was coarse and common and
Pip, compelled by uncontrollable impulse, replies:

> 'The beautiful young lady at Miss Havisham's, and she's more
> beautiful than anybody ever was, and I admire her dreadfully, and I
> want to be a gentleman on her account.' Having made this lunatic
> confession, I began to throw my torn-up grass into the river, as if I
> had some thoughts of following it.
>   'Do you want to be a gentleman, to spite her or to gain her over?'
> Biddy quietly asked me, after a pause.
>   'I don't know,' I moodily answered.
>   'Because, if it is to spite her,' Biddy pursued, 'I should think – but
> you know best – that might be better and more independently done
> by caring nothing for her words. And if it is to gain her over, I
> should think – but you know best – she was not worth gaining over.'
>   Exactly what I myself had thought, many times. Exactly what was
> perfectly manifest to me at the moment. But how could I, a poor
> dazed village lad, avoid that wonderful inconsistency into which the
> best and wisest of men fall every day?
>   'It may be all quite true,' said I to Biddy, 'but I admire her
> dreadfully.'
>   In short, I turned over on my face when I came to that, and got a
> good grasp on the hair on each side of my head, and wrenched it
> well. All the while knowing the madness of my heart to be so very
> mad and misplaced, that I was quite conscious it would have served
> my face right, if I had lifted it up by my hair, and knocked it against
> the pebbles as a punishment for belonging to such an idiot.

(p. 156)

Here Biddy's is the voice of the moral guide, the teacher she has
always been to Pip, the voice of reason and common sense. Her
judgement of Estella is absolutely and impeccably right. Pip cannot
by any means contradict her since he himself has seen the truth
already. But what we hear as the truth transcending the truth of
reason and common sense is Pip's, or rather the narrator's voice
remembering that hopeless passion which seized the boy, 'that
wonderful inconsistency into which the best and wisest of men fall
every day'. What reason and common sense tell him 'may be all
quite true', it is 'exactly what was perfectly manifest' to him at the
moment; yet, all these manifest truths notwithstanding, he loves her
'dreadfully'. Moreover, in the desolation of his heart, Pip is quite
aware of his folly, of how 'mad and misplaced' his passion for
Estella is. Yet he loves her simply because he 'found her irresistible'.

He knew he 'loved her against reason, against promise, against peace, against hope, against happiness, against all discouragement that could be' even when he was misled into believing that Miss Havisham had reserved Estella for him (pp. 253–4). In spite of the voice of reason, which is also his inner voice, in spite of Estella's warnings to him, in spite of Herbert's friendly admonition, he goes on loving her. His passion has already gone beyond the pale of rationality; Biddy admits, while teaching him, that Pip has 'got beyond her' and her lesson is 'of no use now' (p. 157). When passion has taken such complete hold, it is no longer possible for either outside or inside voices to have any influence, since the passion has already become a part of the essential being. Pip's mad passion is his life: 'it was impossible for me to separate her, in the past or in the present, from the innermost life of my life' (p. 257). He declares to her, not in a high-flown romantic confession of love but in a painful farewell: 'You are part of my existence, part of myself ... Estella, to the last hour of my life, you cannot choose but remain part of my character, part of the little good in me, part of the evil' (p. 378). For better or worse, Estella has been, in a sense, Pip himself. Thus the rational outcome, the logical ending of the moral fable, eludes him simply because of its rationality, naturalness and morality. The system of the fable as a completed whole entailing ordered chronology and an overriding logos or reason is alien to Pip because his true identity lies where such systems or stories are disrupted by impulses springing from the innermost depth of his psyche. After the destruction of all the stories, Pip's unquenchable passion remains impermeable to that dissociating force at work in the novel.

Pip fails, however, to write his own story, the one faithfully following his irrational love for Estella. He fails because Pip and Estella have been enclosed in the texts and stories written by others. Pip has been a subject to be written by Pumblechook, Magwitch and others, Estella a subject in Miss Havisham's writing of the story of revenge upon men in general. Or to advance our argument a step further, they have been enclosed in the text of *Great Expectations*, in Dickens's novels, which are enclosed again in the context of the nineteenth-century English novel. It was imperative for Dickens's novels to conform to the traditional framework, a plot structure dependent on moral teleology and the closed system of the novel. The disturbing, irrational depths of human beings had to be tamed and explained away in the unfolding of the moral plot so that the reading public and the dominant social order would not be offended. Yet the self-destroying structure of *Great Expectations* finally reveals the centrality of Pip's irrational passion for Estella, an instance of the irrationality, of the nonconformity to any systematising, persistently felt in Dickens's novels. Dickens often presented irrational passion, madness and violence capable of breaking through the closure of the novel system, beginning with some of the interpolated tales in *The Pickwick Papers* and pursued in the murderous impulses of Sykes and Jonas Chuzzlewit in *Oliver Twist* and *Martin Chuzzlewit*, in the perverted sensuality of Quilp in *The Old Curiosity Shop*, in the lunacy and wild violence of *Barnaby Rudge* and *The Tale of Two Cities*. Though these passions are treated always in the melodramatic mode, they often go beyond the merely sensational as is evident in the mob violence in the two historical novels and in the psychological agony of Bill Sykes that was Dickens's own nemesis. This irrationality is profoundly dangerous as it tends to destroy the traditional story on which Dickens's plot is always modelled and, at the same time, puts the concepts of fiction and its closure into doubt. Writing can be a dangerous act when it is influenced by this subversive force. The writing of *Great Expectations* accomplishes just that dangerous act, an act of unwriting in which the stories present at all levels in the novel are continuously vacated by the very act of writing.

Thus Dickens's novels are fundamentally different from other multiplot novels of the Victorian era. In Dickens the multiplicity of plots may be replaced by multiplicity of stories, yet this multistoried structure is always threatened with disintegration. The formula of the polyphonic novel, which Mikhail Bakhtin presents as the fundamental principle in Dostoevsky's poetics, can be applied with little modification to describe the basic structure of Dickens's novels. A Dostoevsky novel is 'dialogic', 'constructed not as the whole of a single consciousness, absorbing other consciousnesses as objects into itself, but as a whole formed by the interaction of several consciousnesses, none of which entirely becomes an object for the other'.[20] This dialogical principle is at work in Dickens's novels: the stories of the Idle Apprentice and the Industrious Apprentice are vying with each other to dominate the novel, each failing to absorb the other to create a single unified consciousness or story. Yet submerged under this dialogue is another dialogue that is not the dialogue between two stories, between two different kinds of logic (*dialogos*), but the more radical struggle between story as logical and moral system and the suppressed yet primordial force of subversion. This force, which continually undermines the system of the novel, should be identified with Bakhtin's carnival. During carnival the 'laws, prohibitions, and restrictions that determine the structure and order of ordinary, that is noncarnival, life are suspended ... what is suspended first of all is hierarchical structure and all the forms of terror, reverence, piety, and etiquette connected with it.'[21] Carnivalistic life is 'life drawn out of its *usual* rut, it is to some extent "life turned inside out", "the reverse side of the world"'.[22] Dickens's early novels are brimming with carnivalistic life linked essentially with the irrational, the comic and the nonserious. *Pickwick*, *Nickleby* and *The Old Curiosity Shop* are typical carnival literature full of animal vitality and disorder where the most fundamental rite of carnival, of decrowning (of Mr Pickwick, Squeers and Quilp, who are all to some extent Lords of Misrule), is repeatedly staged. But Dickens, being a novelist, had to curb his wild imagination to bring his work to a more or less orderly conclusion. Because carnivalistic life is essentially incompatible with closure (the public square is the centre of carnival), it has to be suppressed in a final working-out of the plot; otherwise it would be simply impossible to complete a novel. As Dickens 'matured' into a prestigious novelist this repression of carnival is more and more successfully undertaken in his writing. But in his most 'serious' and 'mature' novel the system of stories is shattered and now the absent, subversive force of carnival finally succeeds in making its irrepressible presence felt. The ending of the novel is actually the beginning of the absent story, the beginning of the greater dialogue between logos and passion, between story and carnival.

Though Pip has failed to write the true story of his life, failed to live his madness, his irrational passion, rooted in the core of his nature, asserts itself even in the final hour of the story's ordered chronology. Right after his declaration to Biddy that his poor dream 'has all gone by' he visits the site of the old Satis House, the ruins of texts and stories, to meet Estella, a being whose potential for a passion as warm as Pip's has failed to be actualised. Dickens has been very careful in suggesting this potential: when her identity is revealed Estella is found to be the daughter of a woman who 'had some gipsy blood in her' (p. 405). This woman had not only acted according to the traditional ideas of gipsy women in literature by murdering another for jealousy, but proves to be a descendant of the fiery witch of Colchis, Medea, who killed her own child by

Jason in revenge for his betrayal; Estella's mother 'was under strong suspicion of having, at about the time of the murder, frantically destroyed her child by this man – some three years old – to revenge herself upon him' (p. 406). When we are faced with the essential similarity between Pip and Magwitch – they are orphans manipulated by authoritarian figures – it is hard not to see that the story of Magwitch and Molly might easily have been one in which Pip and Estella figure as hero and heroine. Yet this story of two passionate human beings capable of ignoring morality and hierarchy or any interdiction society might impose upon them is absent in *Great Expectations*.[23] Pip's story as written by others has already come to an end; the system of the novel has closed itself. Yet Dickens had to write again the ending that is really a beginning; Pip and Estella, the two with more fundamental characteristics in common than they are aware of, must meet again to begin to write the story of their love just as Pip and Magwitch had encountered each other at the beginning to begin their entirely different love story. In a final paradox, however, this absent story has already been written. If the ultimate message of the novel may be seen as the disclosure and destruction of alienating stories and the revelation of irrationality that transcends textuality, the story Pip will write cannot be anything other than the text that has been *Great Expectations*.

From *English Literary History*, 53 (1986), 593–614

NOTES

[Eiichi Hara's fine essay challenges Peter Brooks's Freudian narratology (essay 4) with a Bakhtinian one. This disagreement, which illustrates major differences of approach between Freudian critics and poststructuralist critics, is discussed in the Introduction (pp. 17–19). Basically Hara feels that Brooks makes Pip's destiny seem too simple and too much a matter of his own choosing. By drawing on the work of Mikhail Bakhtin (1895–1975), Hara is able to speak about Pip as caught up in a number of different story-lines, none of which is peculiar to him since they all pre-exist within Victorian culture, reflecting different zones of the socio-ideological spectrum.

These different story-lines are largely applied to Pip by other people. In the opening pages, for instance, a combination of accident and 'atmosphere' casts him in the role of a criminal who will come to a sticky end, a stereotype confirmed by certain remarks of Pumblechook and Wopsle. It is *their* story about Pip. Wopsle also starts a second familiar story-line, viewing Pip as a bad apprentice: he associates Pip with the main character in George Lillo's popular play, *The London Merchant* (1731), which tells of George Barnwell, an apprentice who robs his employer and murders his uncle for the love of a wicked woman. One of the conclusions Hara draws is that, since Pip does not actually find or make plots for himself, he cannot really – *pace* Brooks – be 'cured' of plotting either. Rather, what happens at the end is that the various stories simply collapse, leaving a vacuum which could only be filled by the sheer irrationality of Pip's desperate passion for Estella. The dialogism of the competing plot-lines could only climax as a carnival of very un-Victorian misrule.

Hara's quotations are from *Great Expectations*, ed. Angus Calder, Penguin English Library (Harmondsworth, 1965). Ed.]

1. Wayne C. Booth, *The Rhetoric of Fiction* (Chicago, 1961), pp. 71–3. See also Seymour Chatman, *Story and Discourse: Narrative Structure in Fiction and Film* (Ithaca, New York, 1978), pp. 148–9.

2. For the discussion of various meanings of author and authority, see Edward Said's influential book, *Beginnings: Intention and Method* (New York, 1975). The problem of the father figure in *Great Expectations* has been given attention by many critics; the fullest consideration so far is: Lawrence Jay Dessner, '*Great Expectations*: "the Ghost of a Man's Own Father"', *PMLA*, 91 (1976), 436–49. See also Dianne F. Sadoff, 'Storytelling and the Figure of the Father in *Little Dorrit*', *PMLA*, 95 (1980), 234–45.

3. The problem of writing in *Great Expectations* has been discussed recently by Robert Tracy and Murray Baumgarten. Tracy is concerned with the tension between writing and speaking in the novel, the former, according to him, being constantly put into doubt; and Baumgarten's focus is on calligraphy as 'writing that bridges hieroglyphic and phonetic systems'. See Robert Tracy, 'Reading Dickens's Writing', and Murray Baumgarten, 'Calligraphy and Code: Writing in *Great Expectations*', *Dickens Studies Annual*, 11 (1983), 37–72.

4. David Lodge, *Working with Structuralism: Essays and Reviews on Nineteenth and Twentieth-Century Literature* (London, 1981), p. 20. This, I find, is the fullest and most succinct definition of *fabula* and *sjuzet* of the Russian Formalists. See also Tzvetan Todorov. *The Poetics of Prose*, trans. Richard Howard (Ithaca, New York, 1977), pp. 45–6.

5. See, for example, Dorothy Van Ghent. *The English Novel: Form and Function* (New York, 1967) pp. 154–70: John H. Hagan Jr, 'Structural Patterns in Dickens's *Great Expectations*', *ELH*, 21 (1954), 54–66; and E. Pearlman, 'Inversion in *Great Expectations*', *Dickens Studies Annual*, 7 (1978), 190–202.

6. Peter Brooks, 'Repetition, Repression, and Return: The Plotting of *Great Expectations*', in *Reading for the Plot: Design and Intention in Narrative* (Oxford, 1984), pp. 113–42. Brooks's essay was originally published as 'Repetition, Repression, and Return: *Great Expectations* and the Study of Plot', *New Literary History*, 11 (1980), pp. 503–26. [Brooks's essay is partly reprinted as essay 4 above. Ed.]

7. See ibid., pp. 131–2. Brooks asserts that 'all texts eventually speak of Pip himself as an unjustified presence, a presence demanding interpretations'. Yet the point of this scene is that interpretation is always *a priori*, already completed when Wopsle and Pumblechook trap Pip in an established story which does not allow any further designing or plotting.

8. Some critics have followed suit, notably Van Ghent, *The English Novel*. See p. 168.

9. See Ronald Paulson, *Emblem and Expression: Meaning in English Art of the Eighteenth Century* (Cambridge, Mass:, 1975), pp. 58–78, for a detailed discussion of Hogarth's work. Paul B. Davis points out that perhaps Dickens 'had the series in mind as he wrote *Great Expectations*; the account of Pip's apprenticeship seems to be one point where Dickens's general indebtedness to Hogarth becomes specific': 'Dickens, Hogarth, and the Illustrated *Great Expectations*', *The Dickensian*, 80 (1984), 131–43.

10. See *The London Merchant*, ed. William H. McBurney (London, 1965), p. xv.

11. See *Dombey and Son*, ed. Peter Fairclough (Harmondsworth: Penguin Books, 1970), pp. 98–9; and *Barnaby Rudge*, ed. Gordon Spence (Harmondsworth: Penguin Books, 1973), p. 302.

12. See *Barnaby Rudge*, p. 80.

13. Julian Moynahan, 'The Hero's Guilt: the Case of *Great Expectations*', *Essays in Criticism*, 10 (1960), p. 69–70.

14. Shirley Grob, 'Dickens and Some Motifs of the Fairy Tale', *Texas Studies in Literature and Language*, 5 (1964), 567–79; Harry Stone, '*Great Expectations*: The Fairy-Tale Transformation', *Dickens and the Invisible World: Fairy Tales, Fantasy, and Novel-Making* (London, 1980), pp. 298–339.

15. Max Byrd, '"Reading" in *Great Expectations*', *PMLA*, 91 (1976), 259–65.

16. Brooks, 'Repetition, Repression, and Return', p. 138.

17. Edgar Rosenberg, 'A Preface to *Great Expectations*', *Dickens Studies Annual*, 2 (1972), 333. Rosenberg borrowed the term 'cautionary tale' from the German scholar Ludwig Borinski.

18. John Forster, *The Life of Charles Dickens*, ed. A. J. Hoppé (London, 1966), 2: 289; George Bernard Shaw, 'Foreword to the Edinburgh limited edition of *Great Expectations* 1937', rpt. in Stephen Wall (ed.), *Charles Dickens: A Critical Anthology* (Harmondsworth, 1970), p. 294. For the problem of the novel's ending see, among numerous others: Marshall W. Gregory, 'Values and Meaning in *Great Expectations*: The Two Endings Revisited', *Essays in Criticism*, 19 (1969), 402–9; Martin Meisel, 'The Ending of *Great Expectations*', *Essays in Criticism*, 15 (1965), 326–31; Milton Millhauser, '*Great Expectations*: The Three Endings', *Dickens Studies Annual*, 2 (1972), 267–77; Edgar Rosenberg, 'Last Words on *Great Expectations*: A Textual Brief on the Six Endings', *Dickens Studies Annual*, 9 (1981), 87–115.

19. Millhauser, '*Great Expectations:* The Three Endings, p. 271.

20. Mikhail Bakhtin, *Problems of Dostoevsky's Poetics*, trans. Caryl Emerson (Minneapolis, 1984), p. 18. Dickens's influence on Dostoevsky has been studied by Donald Fanger, *Dostoevsky and Romantic Realism: A Study of Dostoevsky in Relation to Balzac, Dickens, and Gogol* (Chicago, 1967); N. M. Lary, *Dostoevsky and Dickens: A Study of Literary Influence* (London, 1973); and Loralee MacPike, *Dostoevsky's Dickens: A Study of Literary Influence* (London, 1981).

   Peter K. Garrett has found it feasible to consider the multi-plot baggy monsters of the Victorian age from the new point of view offered by Bakhtin. *The Victorian Multiplot Novel: Studies in Dialogical Form* (New Haven, 1980), p. 8.

21. Bakhtin, *Problems of Dostoevsky's Poetics*, pp. 122–3.

22. Ibid., p. 122. Ronald Paulson in his study of eighteenth-century sub-culture revealed the ambiguities involved in Hogarth's *Industry and Idleness*. Ronald Paulson, *Popular and Polite Art in the Age of Hogarth and Fielding* (Notre Dame, Indiana, 1979), pp. 21–2.

23. The absence may be explained also in terms of the paramount inter-diction imposed upon their relationship. As Magwitch is Estella's real father and also Pip's 'second father', their love could not be anything but incestuous. The possible perversity in Pip's love for Estella was pointed out by A. L. French, 'Beating and Cringing: *Great Expectations*', *Essays in Criticism*, 24 (1974), 151–8. [French's article is reprinted as essay 1 above. Ed.] See also Pearlman, 'Inversion in *Great Expectations*', p. 201; and Brooks, 'Repetition, Repression and Return', p. 128, for similar points.

8

The Imaginary and the Symbolic in *Great Expectations*

STEVEN CONNOR

As almost every critic and reader notices, the point of view of *Great Expectations* is interestingly split, between the older, mature Pip who 'tells' the story and the younger Pip who 'sees' and participates in its events. In the notable first paragraph of the novel, for example, there is a clear distinction between the point of view, or quality of perception, which seems to be that of an uninformed infant, and the actual language of the narrative, which has the amused and knowing condescension of an adult. It is not always easy to keep these two dimensions, and the separated selves or versions of Pip's self that they embody, completely distinct. When, a little later on in the opening pages, the language takes on the wide-eyed awe of the fairy tale – 'A fearful man, all in coarse grey, with a great iron on his leg. A man with no hat, and with broken shoes, and with an old rag tied round his head. A man who had been soaked in water, and smothered in mud' (ch. I, p. 2) – it is difficult to know whether this should be classified as 'free indirect style', that is, the narrative imitating the sort of account that the younger Pip might himself have given of the man, and therefore moving us closer to the texture of the child's thoughts and reactions, or whether the older Pip is still to be observed here wryly parodying this imagined childish style.

In fact *Great Expectations* does more than just shift its point of view around for the novel puts into question in various ways the very notion of personality as stable and coherent. One of the ways in which this is done is precisely by upsetting ordinary notions of point of view. The tenacity of the metaphor of the point of view in literary studies is probably due to our sense of the domination of sight in human experience, and our natural sense that the 'I' exists in some sense at the origin of our line of sight – 'I' marks the place from which I speak and from which I look out at the world. But consciousness is not just a matter of looking out on the world, and it takes only a moment's thought to confirm this. It is quite possible, and, indeed, necessary in consciousness to occupy different positions within imaginary visual fields. We can think of ourselves as looking (without being seen) for example, or we can imagine ourselves in the place of the person or object being looked at, therefore being looked at in our turn, or we can imagine ourselves looking and being looked at at the same time. These different positions are not real but rather a matter of how we individually and collectively conceive of physical space and our occupation of it. They are in fact positions established relative to one another and as such are differential signs. This means that looking itself can be considered to be organised into a system or 'text'.[1]

Great Expectations opens up the structure of looking to scrutiny in various interesting and important ways. If we return to the beginning of the novel we can see immediately how crucial looking is to consciousness. Pip looks at the inscriptions on the gravestones in order to try to form some sense of what his parents and brothers were like, and looks intently round at his surroundings. For Pip the coming to consciousness involves a sudden opening or raising of the eyes to take in the whole landscape at once and to compare and distinguish different elements within it. At the end of that panoramic sweep Pip's gaze lights upon himself, so that there are the peculiar sensations for Pip and for the reader of being in two places at once, as the gazer and as the object of the gaze. Similarly, it is the terrifying gaze of Magwitch when he seizes Pip that the narrative fixes upon:

> After darkly looking at his leg and at me several times, he came closer to my tombstone, took me by both arms, and tilted me back as far as he could hold me; so that his eyes looked most powerfully down into mine, and mine looked most helplessly up into his.
>
> (ch. I, p. 3)

By disturbing Pip's own focus, Magwitch is able to reduce him to a mere object, for all that Pip can see in Magwitch's eyes is the fact of his own being seen.

Throughout the novel, and perhaps particularly in the early part of it, Pip suffers in the position of one who is watched, without the privilege of sight himself. During his guilty journey across the marshes to take Magwitch's food to him he imagines himself fixed by the stares of the cattle; when summoned by Miss Havisham he is forced to play cards with Estella under Miss Havisham's gaze; and at the end of the novel, when Pip has been captured by Orlick, it is the fact that he is watched so intensely that is emphasised, as Orlick fixes him 'with a deadly look', gloating at 'the spectacle I furnished' (ch. LIII, p. 402). And, throughout the novel, Pip's progress is watched by Magwitch in the person of Jaggers.

Of course, Pip himself does look at things and people as well, and his growth into maturity can be seen partly in terms of his move to the position of spectator rather than that of spectacle. The conflict between the two conditions is dramatised extremely well in the passage which describes Pip's first sight of Miss Havisham. Time seems to be suspended as Pip's gaze moves across the details of the room and of Miss Havisham's dress. In fact Pip seems to go over the details twice, once to register them and then again to reinterpret them, and the effect given, with the relentless repetition of 'I saw', is of a slow, Imaginary possession of the scene by Pip:

> It was not in the first few moments that I saw all these things, though I saw more of them in the first moments than might be supposed. But, I saw that everything within my view which ought to be white, had been white long ago, and had lost its lustre, and was faded and yellow. I saw that the bride within the bridal dress had withered like the dress, and like the flowers, and had no brightness left but the brightness of her sunken eyes. I saw that the dress had been put upon the rounded figure of a young woman, and that the figure upon which it now hung loose, had shrunk to skin and bone
> (ch. VIII, p. 53)

At the end of the passage there is a shocking reversal, for suddenly Pip realises that all the time he has been watched by the figure that he is watching:

> Once, I had been taken to see some ghastly waxwork at the Fair, representing I know not what impossible personage lying in state. Once, I had been taken to one of our old marsh churches to see a

skeleton in the ashes of a rich dress, that had been dug out of a vault under the church pavement. Now, waxwork and skeleton seemed to have dark eyes that moved and looked at me. I should have cried out, if I could.

(ch. VIII, p. 53)

This sudden exchange of seeing and being seen recalls the passage at the beginning of the novel in which Pip sees himself in the landscape and then realises that he has been watched by Magwitch. The switch of conditions seems to be about to result in a cry, which is stifled (by Magwitch in the first passage, apparently by Pip himself in the second), and is followed up by the demand that Pip give his name, twice on both occasions (ch. VIII, p. 53). Like Magwitch, Miss Havisham fixes Pip in her stare, trying to envelop his gaze. In fact Pip seems to remember the encounter on the marsh when Miss Havisham asks him to look at her heart, for this makes him think of the murderous young man invented by Magwitch (ch. VIII, p. 53).

These moments of intense mutual observation suggest the enactment of some Imaginary relationship between Pip and the Other that he sees. In both cases, Pip begins by trying to capture the Other in vision, but ends up himself captured in the Other's stare. This resembles of course the double movement of recognition and aggression in the mirror stage as Lacan describes it. Like the child beholding its own image, Pip looks out at the world as a subject, to see himself reflected there as an object, and the result is a collision and conflict of looks.

Miss Havisham herself seems clearly to be locked into an Imaginary relationship with her own image. Her masochistic self-immurement is, like most masochism, an attempt to close off in advance and master pain and humiliation imposed from the outside – in her case the pain of her rejection by her swindling lover. Her deliberate neglect of herself means that she can reduce herself to an object which she can then possess and control. The looking-glass is therefore extremely important to her, because it is the guarantee of the sado-masochistic bond between the seer and the image. This illustrates very well Lacan's idea that the mirror stage gives a totality which is actually based upon a splitting of consciousness. The more Miss Havisham exhibits herself (to herself and to others) the greater the degree of voyeuristic satisfaction she obtains from being in two places at once, as both humiliated victim and humiliating controller of the situation.

Fear and aggression are also apparent in the way Pip perceptually constructs his world in the narrative. They are to be found, for example, in the encounter in the garden of Satis House when, looking up at a window, he finds himself 'exchanging a broad stare with a pale young gentleman with red eyelids and light hair' (ch. XI, p. 84). Before he knows what is happening he is fighting with him. Interestingly, the next, rather friendlier occasion on which they meet provokes the sense of an encounter with a mirror opposite:

> As I stood opposite to Mr Pocket, Junior, delivering him the bags, One, Two, I saw the starting appearance come into his own eyes that I knew to be in mine, and he said, falling back:
> 'Lord bless me, you're the prowling boy!'
> 'And you,' said I, 'are the pale young gentleman!'
> (ch. XXI, p. 265)

A similar, more threatening image of himself is offered to Pip by Trabb's boy in his very funny mimicry of Pip's airs and graces. Pip rejects rather than embracing this mirror image, and indeed contemplates physically attacking him (ch. XXX, pp. 232–3).

As Pip grows older, he becomes firmly settled into his position of spectator rather than spectacle. He is able to watch relatively unmoved the mayhem at the Pockets' house and to record it with precision and detachment (ch. XXIII), as he is to observe the details of Wemmick's courting of Miss Skiffins (ch. XXXVII). Perhaps the most striking example of Pip's increasing sense of detachment and security of being is his account of Wopsle's performance in *Hamlet*; though extremely funny, this can also be seen as a ruthless revenge on the unfortunate Wopsle (ch. XXXI). For Pip, to see others comes increasingly to be a sign of his own mastery of them, his tendency to subordinate them imaginatively – and the position of spectator in a theatre, all-seeing and appraising and yet unseen oneself, is a very good one from which to exercise this sort of mastery.

But the promotion of seeing over being seen is also often, in the middle sections of the novel, a sign of Pip's self-deluding independence which, in its bullying fixation upon himself, belongs to the Imaginary. In avoiding the look of reproach that he catches in Joe's eyes when he is visiting him in London, Pip is making of Joe an object to be seen and described without himself being allowed to see or look (ch. XXVII, pp. 210–11). It is a refusal of interchange or contact and an Imaginary reaction on Pip's part. The power of sight to fix and master an otherwise unpleasant or threatening reality is evidenced again in the account of Pip's and Herbert's attempts to get their affairs in order:

> 'Be firm, Herbert,' I would retort, plying my own pen with great assiduity. 'Look the thing in the face. Look into your affairs. Stare them out of countenance.'
>
> (ch. XXXIV, p. 262)

It is the Imaginary line of sight which produces Pip's crucial and extended mistake, the belief that Miss Havisham is his benefactress, and that he is chosen to be the fairy tale knight who will redeem the sterility of Satis House. Pip convinces himself that he *sees* the truth about Miss Havisham, as night after night she sits, 'her wan bright eyes glaring at me ... I saw in this, that Estella was set to wreak Miss Havisham's revenge ... I saw in this, a reason for her being beforehand assigned to me ... I saw in this, that I, too, was tormented by a perversion of ingenuity (ch. XXXVIII, p. 288). Lest we miss his purpose and take 'seeing' to refer here merely to realisation, Dickens stresses the physical fact of sight, and restates the mirroring relationship between Pip and Miss Havisham:

> In a word, I saw in this, Miss Havisham as I had her then and there before my eyes, and always had had her before my eyes; and I saw in this, the distinct shadow of the darkened and unhealthy house in which her life was hidden from the sun ... As I looked round at them [the candles in the room], and at the pale gloom they made, and at the stopped clock, and at the withered articles of bridal dress upon the table and the ground, and at her own awful figure with its ghostly reflection thrown large by the fire upon the ceiling and the wall, I saw in everything the construction that my mind had come to, repeated and thrown back at me.
>
> (ch. XXXVIII, pp. 288–9)

There are also examples to be found in *Great Expectations* of relationships of characters which involve more than the Imaginary gaze. A good example to begin with is the look exchanged between Pip and Magwitch on the marshes, just before he is led away. The look is one of complicity and understanding, and from it, we are to assume, dates Magwitch's continuing interest in Pip. But the look that passes between them is not one of equal and symmetrical exchange:

> I looked at him eagerly when he looked at me, and slightly moved my hands and shook my head. I had been waiting for him to see me, that I might try to assure him of my innocence. It was not at all expressed

> to me that he even comprehended my intention, for he gave me a look that I did not understand, and it all passed in a moment. But if he had looked at me for an hour or for a day, I could not have remembered his face ever afterwards, as having been more attentive.
>
> (ch. V, p. 34)

In fact, the look that passes between them is incomplete, Pip not knowing whether he has been understood and equally not understanding Magwitch. Looking here initiates a gap of understanding; the meaning of the look is not contained in itself, but can only emerge in the course of the narrative, and this opens up and makes more indefinite the closed reciprocity of the mirror relationship between Pip and Magwitch.

In addition to this, the look is one exchanged in public, in a confidential space, as it were, hollowed out from the public gaze, and it derives some of its meaning from this relative position. These private looks exchanged obliquely in public are very common in *Great Expectations* – Pip and Joe communicate in this way in Mrs Joe's kitchen (ch. II), the stranger in the bar looks privately at Pip even as he addresses Joe (ch. X), while Joe himself looks at and speaks to Pip all the way through his interrogation by Miss Havisham (ch. XIII).

So apparently simple exchanges of looks can turn out to be not quite so simple as they appear, and can involve more complex shiftings of position within a structure of looking. When Pip first sees Miss Havisham, for example, there are, as we have seen, two distinct stages to his observation. His first gaze registers the scene in its intended signification, while the second goes over and re-reads the first gaze, recognising the failure of interpretation of the first. So the second look observes, among other things, the first look. The passage ends with Pip's recognition that he is being looked at in his turn. But there is more than this, for Miss Havisham is also looking at Pip looking at her, and assessing the effect that she is having, as seems to be made clear a few moments later:

> I stopped, fearing I might say too much, or had already said it, and we took another look at each other.
>
> Before she spoke again, she turned her eyes from me, and looked at the dress she wore, and at the dressing-table, and finally at herself in the looking-glass.
>
> 'So new to him,' she muttered, 'so old to me; so strange to him, so familiar to me; so melancholy to both of us! Call Estella.'
>
> As she was still looking at the reflection of herself, I thought she was still talking to herself, and kept quiet.

'Call Estella,' she repeated, flashing a look at me.
'You can do that. Call Estella. At the door.'

(ch. VIII, p. 54)

Here we see first another exchange of looks, then Miss Havisham looking away from Pip at herself in the mirror, in order to remind herself of what Pip sees. She seems also to be looking in the mirror at Pip looking at her looking at herself in the mirror. No wonder that Pip doesn't know whether he has been addressed or not, for these exchanges of looks move him out of a central, observing position so that he becomes a sign in the complicated system or 'text' of looks obtaining between the two of them.

This can be seen as a kind of delayed acquaintance with the Symbolic for Pip. The Symbolic look, we can say, differs from the Imaginary look in that it is only ever part of a positional system of viewpoints in which all the positions are relative to each other rather than being fixed lines of sight emanating from particular unified subjects.

The most powerful example of Pip's removal from the centre of the structure of looking actually occurs in the theatre where he is watching Mr Wopsle perform (ch. XLVII). Pip is alarmed to hear afterwards Mr Wopsle's account of the stranger whom he has seen sitting behind him. The intersection of the lines of sight produces a worrying complexity; Pip has been watching Wopsle, aware that he is seen by him, but unaware that Wopsle also sees that he (Pip) is being watched by another, Compeyson. There is a sense of a dynamic circulation of roles, as the reader, along with Pip, is moved from one position to another to encompass all the observation points in the ensemble of looks. Once again, this involves a transition from Imaginary looking to Symbolic looking, with Pip realising that he is not the originating centre of the scene but just an element in a kind of text which plays itself out through him.

Nor does the narration of looks even stop here with this triangle, because Wopsle adds to it another narration, that of the chase and arrest of the two convicts on the marshes. This too culminates in a dynamic of looks in which the theatrical metaphor is found purposefully repeated:

'[You remember] that the soldiers lighted torches, and put the two in the centre, and that we went on to see the last of them, over the black marshes, with the torchlight shining on their faces – I am particular about that; with the torchlight shining on their faces, when there was an outer ring of dark night all about us?'

(ch. XLVII, p. 365)

This narrative shifts Compeyson (and Magwitch) to the position of spectacle, there to be looked at as though in a theatre, and correspondingly moves Wopsle into the position of spectator alongside Pip. There is, however, an interesting ambiguity of position even in Wopsle's narrative. He says that there was 'an outer ring of dark night all about us'; this puts Wopsle and Pip inside the lurid glare of the torchlight, with the convicts, making of them too a spectacle to be watched by Compeyson and Magwitch.

There seems also to be an uncanny repetition in the theatre scene of an earlier episode in which Pip, on a stage-coach journey, suddenly recognises the convict whom Magwitch has sent to give him money. Pip sits in front of the convict just as he sits in front of Compeyson, so close, in fact, that he feels 'his breath on the hair of my head' (ch. XXVIII, p. 215). Though here the triangle of looking is not represented in full in the text, it is nevertheless acted out in imagination by Pip, who sees himself with the convict sitting behind him, even as he stares unseeing into the darkness. Indeed at one point, Pip moves imaginatively into another position in the triangle, that occupied by the convicts themselves, in the 'disagreeable and degraded spectacle' which they form – 'they both laughed, and began cracking nuts, and spitting the shells about. – As I really think I should have liked to do myself, if I had been in their place and so despised' (ch. XXVIII, p. 215).

These three scenes of looking, marsh, stage-coach and theatre, are not closed off from one another, but represent variations on a similar configuration of visual positions, around which Pip is moved. Despite these moments of awareness of the Symbolic however, Pip retains a view of the world which is Imaginary in its narcissism, and resists all the evidence of the splitting of identity which he encounters.

For the reader, though, this split is continually evidenced by the split in the narrative, with the older, wiser Pip all the time as it were at the shoulder of his younger self. And in fact the optical metaphor which is so important to the younger Pip in the book is also involved quite closely with the relationship of the two Pips of the book, the narrating and the narrated. The younger Pip is conceived of as a point of view, looking out at the world (or trying to) with the older

Pip standing back and looking at his younger self looking out. Of course, this narrated Pip can also on occasion look at himself, and as his path and that of his narrator come closer towards the end of the novel he is given more opportunity to do so. As Orlick is gloating sadistically over his prey, Pip in turn sees himself in the past and in the future. In this he seems to come close to the condition of the older narrating Pip that he is eventually to become.

From Steven Connor, *Charles Dickens* (London, 1985), pp. 126–37.

NOTES

[Steven Connor's brilliant poststructuralist account of *Great Expectations*, which is a chapter in his book on Dickens, shares Jeremy Tambling and Eiichi Hara's interest (essay 6 and 7) in the social conditioning of human subjects, but draws its explanatory model from the developmental psychology of the French psychoanalyst Jacques Lacan (1901–81). This involves an important distinction between the Imaginary and Symbolic orders, an explanation of which is given in the Introduction (pp. 19–21). Although the passionately straightforward likes and dislikes of the Imaginary mainly belong to an early and more 'selfish' stage of development, they are for ever re-emerging in adult life as well. They seductively challenge the socially acquired hesitations and uncertainties of the Symbolic, and this painful struggle between the two orders becomes the main focus of the Lacanian literary critic.

Connor begins by mapping the conflict onto three major tensions in *Great Expectations*: the (Imaginary) intensity of Pip's childhood experience versus the (Symbolic) detachment of Pip the middle-aged narrator; the unproblematic (Imaginary) way of interpreting words and things versus the more disconcerting (Symbolic) way; and, most fundamentally, characters' firm (Imaginary) sense of their own personal identity versus the (Symbolic) dissolving or reshaping of that identity within the structures of language and society. In the extract reprinted here as essay 8, Connor links the same Imaginary/Symbolic oscillation to the question of narrative point-of-view, i.e. to Dickens's way of getting the story told by manipulating 'the structures of looking'. Dickens realised that human beings not only look, but are looked at. Furthermore, they are looked at not only by others but by themselves, sometimes from a later point in their own psychological development. One of Connor's arguments is that the difference between Pip the child and Pip the narrator enables Dickens to highlight the typically human self-division between the closure of Imaginary desire and the socialised openness of Symbolic deferral.

Connor's references are to the Oxford Illustrated Dickens Edition of *Great Expectations* (Oxford, 1953). Ed.]

1. I have drawn in this section upon Freud's 'Instincts and their Viscissitudes' (*The Standard Edition of the Complete Psychological Works of Sigmund Freud* [London, 1953–74], vol. 14, pp. 117–40) and Lacan's idea of the function of the 'gaze' (in *The Four Fundamental Concepts of Psycho-Analysis* [London, 1977], pp. 67–179, and the 'Seminar on "The Purloined Letter"', *Yale French Studies*, 48 [1972], 39–72).

9

Reading for the Character and Reading for the Progression: John Wemmick and *Great Expectations*

JAMES PHELAN

If we do not begin with an obligation to thematise, we can respond more fully to the literal level of Dickens's first chapter. In the passage recounting his 'first most vivid and broad impression of the identity of things', Pip tells us, as Brooks points out, how in effect he has become certain of his own difference from and aloneness among everything else. He concludes his litany of what he knows ('this was the churchyard, there were the graves of my dead parents and brothers, that was the marshes, that over there was the river, and beyond that was the sea') with his conclusion that 'the small bundle of shivers growing afraid of it all and beginning to cry, was Pip'. Because Pip's acquisition of self-consciousness is accompanied by his fear and grief, the narrative identifies the initial instability as one involving Pip's own identity and place in the world. In this respect, the omission of Pip's situation as the adopted son of Joe and Mrs Joe is significant: that situation is less a part of his identity than his awareness of himself as orphan.

At the same time, Dickens's presentation of the instability induces the authorial audience[1] to adopt a set of attitudes toward Pip's situation that are crucial to our experience of the whole narrative. Dickens handles the style of the first-person narration to convey Pip's discovery of his own misery with a combination of wit and matter-of-factness that results in our responding to the discovery with full and deep sympathy rather than as a sign of Pip the narrator's own unattractive self-pity. In fact, the humour of Pip's misreading of his parents' tombstones and of the 'five little stone lozenges' (p. 1) marking the resting places of his brothers all but deflects our overt attention from Pip's situation as an orphan. As we have already seen, when Pip declares his own discovery of self-consciousness, it comes both matter-of-factly and wittily at the end of a series of discoveries (this place was the churchyard, etc. down to 'the small bundle of shivers growing afraid of it all and beginning to cry, was Pip' [p. 2]). With this arrangement and the shift to the third person, we register the narrator's own distance from the scene and so give our sympathy without reservation. Because Dickens establishes this initial sympathy at the time he establishes the initial instability, he has almost irrevocably established the authorial audience's positive attitude toward Pip. He then takes advantage of this firm foundation of sympathy later in the narrative when he shows how egregiously Pip wrongs Joe. At these points our foundational sympathy – as well as Dickens's recourse to letting the mature Pip comment on his former self – moves us to be pained not just for Joe but also – and perhaps even more – for Pip.

There is a lot more to say about the affective dimension of the opening pages, especially about the nuances of response Dickens builds into the representation of Pip's encounter with the convict, but allow me to turn my attention to the progression of the narrative as a whole. There are three distinguishable tracks along which the instabilities operate, all three of which are related to the initial instability of Pip's anxiety about identity. These three are what we might call the convict plot, the home plot, and the Satis House plot. In addition, the initiating moments of the convict plot and the Satis House plot establish some significant tensions that suggest an expansion of the scope of the narrative beyond Pip's struggle; the early moments of the convict plot establish a tension about the relationship between Pip's convict and his hated counterpart, and the introduction of Miss Havisham immediately introduces a tension about her past as well as about the presence of Estella in her house. Although the resolutions of these tensions, like the development of the instabilities along three different tracks, do place Pip's story in a much broader thematic context, those resolutions are also striking for the way in which Dickens skilfully links them to the pattern of instabilities surrounding Pip.

As we move into the middle of the narrative we see that the chief (though by no means only) source of the complication of the instabilities is Pip's resistance to the identity offered by his home: he can be an honest blacksmith like Joe. At the same time, we recognise that the way in which Dickens has intertwined the plots makes Pip's acceptance of that identity virtually impossible. Dickens begins with the convict plot, immediately interlaces it with the home plot, and then further entwines them both with the Satis House plot, first covertly, then overtly. More specifically, Pip's association with the convict not only complicates his life with Mrs Joe by making him steal from her, but for him it also increases his tendency to internalise her treatment of him as 'naterally wicious'. With this sense of his identity firmly established by the time he goes to Satis House, he is of course easily stung by being regarded as 'common' and his desire to escape the scenes of his identity as criminal is understandably strong. At the same time, however, the home plot shows us that another side of his identity, the one that develops in his relationship with Joe, has made him unfit for the role he tries to play when the Expectations arrive. He goes on miserably caught between these two sides of his identity until Magwitch makes himself known, a resolution of a tension that also brings a major shift in the development of the instabilities. In short, Magwitch's return sets in motion a chain of events in which Pip works through his anxiety and fear about his identity by working back through the instabilities of the now fully interconnected plots and coming finally to accept and appreciate first Magwitch, then Joe, and finally himself.

In the course of these events the main tensions of the Satis House plot and the convict plot are also resolved in a way that signals the success of Pip's working through. Magwitch gives Pip part of the story about Compeyson, Herbert gives him part of the story about Miss Havisham, and he – and the authorial audience – learn of the connection between Miss Havisham and Magwitch through Compeyson. Jaggers and Wemmick give Pip part of the story about Molly, he makes the connection between Molly and Estella, Magwitch tells Herbert about the woman in his past and Pip puts all the pieces together, even going so far as to startle Jaggers with his conclusions. When Pip is able to tell Magwitch on his deathbed that his daughter is alive and that he, Pip, loves her, the working through is essentially complete. It then remains for Pip to re-establish his relation with home, first through his reunion with Joe in London when Joe comes to nurse him through his illness and then through his being appropriately chastened for his dream of marrying Biddy by arriving home on the day of her wedding to Joe. Finally, Pip needs to get some closure on his relation with Estella.

This account of the progression, of course, is only a modest beginning: for it to have an appropriate middle and end, I would need to flesh it out with a discussion of the affective quality of our response to its various turns and with an explanation of the relation between the mimetic, thematic and synthetic spheres of the narrative. Since space is limited, however, I will just offer a very quick sketch of the relation of the three spheres and a more extended analysis of Wemmick's role in the narrative as a way to substantiate that sketch and to illustrate what a fuller account of the progression would entail.

Although the progression of the narrative has multiple turnings, including turnings back on itself, the principles governing the conversion of thematic dimensions into thematic functions are fairly straightforward. *Great Expectations* contains multiple characters with multiple thematic dimensions, many of which are converted by the turns of the progression into thematic functions without there being a single dominant function acting as the central point of the progression. At the same time, we can identify an especially significant group of functions developed from the actions of the main characters: both Magwitch and Miss Havisham function in part to exemplify the dangers of making others conform to our own images of what they should be; Joe functions as the exemplification of simple, honest dignity, while Estella exemplifies the absence of feeling. Pip has multiple thematic functions. His responses to his expectations exemplify the consequences of a false pride. His responses to Estella offer a picture of irrational love. His susceptibility to the convict, Mrs Joe, and Satis House all exemplify the difficulty of forging a strong identity in the world of this novel. This list is neither exhaustive nor impressive for the subtlety of its inferences about thematic functions. But lack of subtlety in the thematic sphere is, I think, a characteristic feature of Dickens's work. It is in the ingenious working out of those thematic elements on both the mimetic and synthetic level that his strength and distinctiveness are to be found.

Indeed, we are often led to pay attention to the thematic sphere of his works not only by the turns of the progression but also by his occasional foregrounding of the synthetic sphere. As a result, the reading of a Dickens novel typically involves a more fluid movement by the authorial audience among the spheres of meaning than occurs in the reading of a narrative by, say Austen or James where the synthetic remains covert. One of the features of *Great Expectations* that contributes to this fluidity of movement – and to the ingenious working out of thematic material – is Dickens's handling of Wemmick.

After even a quick consideration of Wemmick's function in the narrative, we ought not be surprised that Brooks does not discuss his character at any length. Not only does Wemmick not fit into the pattern of repetition and return that Brooks identifies as the central part of the narrative's middle, but he also plays no main role in the working out of the resolution. If he were not in the novel, Dickens would have to find another means to accomplish such tasks as informing Pip about the best time to make his escape, but I daresay that none of us would feel that there was a big hole in the narrative, that Dickens just ought to have invented a virtually schizophrenic character whose life was as sharply divided between home and office as Wemmick's. Our first question then is whether Wemmick actually makes a contribution to the progression that is consonant with the attention that the narrative gives to his character, and if so, what precisely the nature of that contribution is. Our second question will be about the relation of the components of his character and the influence of that relation on the progression as a whole.

Let's begin with the relation between Wemmick's peculiar mimetic status and the variety of synthetic functions that he performs in the novel. Wemmick is a character with multiple mimetic dimensions and a doubtful mimetic function. This mid-fortyish man has two distinct personalities – Walworth Wemmick and Little Britain Wemmick. The first is a gentle, caring, sensitive soul who takes devoted and patient care of his Aged Parent and who dotes on Miss Skiffins. He also exercises his imagination, as we see in the way he has done up Walworth like a fort. The fort motif is of course symbolic: his private self is hidden behind that fort – so much so in fact that even when he ventures outside of it in his private mode he hides his intentions, as we see in the appearance of serendipity he tries to put upon his marriage to Miss Skiffins. As a rule, once

Wemmick moves to the Little Britain side of the 'moat', his character gradually hardens until he becomes the man with a mouth like the slit in a post office box, and with dints instead of dimples on his chin. His values undergo a corresponding change: he is almost as hard as Jaggers himself and his raison d'être becomes the acquisition of portable property.[2]

In the Wemmick of Little Britain, Dickens gives us a character who is part of the convict plot, and he takes advantage of his mimetic dimensions to accomplish certain synthetic functions. Wemmick's showing Pip the importance of portable property in their tour through Newgate and at other times keeps Pip in contact with the 'soiling consciousness' of his own identification with the convict, a contact which encourages his repression of the connection between Estella and Molly until after he has worked through his own relation to Magwitch, and that also contributes to his neglect of Joe.[3] In Walworth Wemmick, Dickens gives us a character who invites reflection on the instabilities of the home plot. Wemmick performs the synthetic function there of providing a contrast between his treatment of his Aged P. and Pip's treatment of Joe. To that extent, the synthetic function reinforces the authorial audience's and the mature Pip's own judgements about Pip's treatment of Joe.

Yet the predominant effect of Wemmick's presence on the affective structure of the text is quite different from the function of either the Little Britain or the Walworth Wemmick alone. The very facts that foreground Wemmick's synthetic component – the sharp division and exaggeration of his two sides – give him a thematic function that in turn has consequences for our response to the mimetic function of Pip. Wemmick's extreme self-division exemplifies the difficulty of living satisfactorily in two different spheres, among two very different sets of people.

Consequently, Wemmick's very presence in the novel works to generalise Pip's difficulty in honouring his lower-class background as he embarks upon his expectations. The problems we see Pip face are not just ones of his own reactions but ones endemic to living in that society where social mobility is becoming more common and where the separation between public and private spheres is becoming more and more pronounced. At the same time, Wemmick's situation indicates one kind of solution to that difficulty. Although Wemmick is more successful than Pip in living in both spheres, the very division of his personality indicates that his solution is less than ideal. Despite the charm of the Walworth Wemmick, Dickens's point is clear: Pip needs to work through to an integration of his different spheres that Wemmick never attains.

In these ways, then, Dickens uses Wemmick to complicate our judgements about the instabilities of the home plot, especially Pip's relation to Joe. Even as the mature Pip is appropriately severe in his judgements of his earlier self's treatment of Joe, Dickens's elaboration of Wemmick's character puts his behaviour in a broader context, which allows a greater understanding of Pip's problem and a softer judgement of his failures to solve it until so late in the narrative. Dickens uses Wemmick in an analogous way in connection with the convict plot which of course is tightly wound together with the other plots in the latter stages of the narrative. Wemmick's self-division functions to deepen our sense of what it is that Pip must overcome as he slowly comes to accept Magwitch. If Wemmick shuts out his private self from his public life, if Pip experiences a difficulty acknowledging Joe once he comes into his Expectations, then how much more difficult is his task of acknowledging and accepting the fact that the source of those Expectations is the convict. Consequently, Wemmick's presence substantially increases our sense of what Pip eventually achieves in working through to that acceptance. Thus, despite being 'compartmentalised' in both Little Britain and Walworth, Wemmick functions to influence significantly the authorial audience's responses to the main narrative line. At the same time, the way in which his foregrounded synthetic component leads to an emphasis on his thematic function which in turn influences our response to the mimetic level of Pip's story illustrates my earlier claim about the fluidity of movement among the three spheres of meaning in Dickens. When Pip and Wemmick interact, the authorial audience has an overt awareness of all three components of their characters. In one sense, this simultaneous overt awareness makes *Great Expectations* less strictly realistic than, say, 'The Beast in the Jungle', but it does not lead to either a rejection or even a subordination of the mimetic level of reading.

There is still more that could be said about Wemmick and the progression, especially about how Dickens's elaboration of a mini-plot that ends with Wemmick's marriage has consequences for our ability, if not to prefer, then at least to accept the revised ending, of the novel,[4] but I would like to move toward my conclusion by reflecting first on this argument about Wemmick's functioning and second on the relation of my model to Brooks's. In effect, I am arguing that Wemmick functions on the thematic level to alter the way the authorial audience responds to the mimetic and thematic functions of Pip and thus to the whole narrative. Now if the connection between the main and the secondary characters is to be found on the thematic level, will one ever say that a character is extraneous to a progression? Can't one always find a thematic connection?

A thematic connection is not itself sufficient to justify the relevance or explain the contribution of the secondary character. The connection on the thematic level needs to be tied not only to an affective result but also to the specific narrative means for achieving that result. In *Great Expectations*, Dickens's use of Wemmick works wonderfully well with his decision to have the mature Pip tell his own story. Dickens can then guide his audience's response by having Pip judge his treatment of Joe in the harshest possible terms, while also directing that audience to see the difficulty of Pip's position in relation to both Joe and Magwitch through the presentation of Wemmick. In that sense, Dickens's handling of Wemmick can be seen as the consequence of his decision to write the novel as a retrospective first-person account.

Consider, by contrast, Dickens's handling of Matthew Pocket and his family. This material, which emphasises the way in which the Pocket children 'were not growing up or being brought up, but were tumbling up' (p. 178), can be seen as thematically related to Pip's own experience of being brought up by hand. To my mind, however, that thematic connection is not sufficient to justify these scenes because it does not materially alter our understanding or judgements of Pip or his actions. It does indicate some of the difficulties and ironies of his situation – with his great expectations comes this environment – and it does increase Pip's desire to help Herbert, but the extended focus on the family is much less integrated into the novel than the material on Wemmick, if in fact it is not altogether extraneous. Dickens's depiction of the Pocket family is funny in the way that Dickens is often funny, but the humour lacks the punch accompanying his depiction of Wemmick because the depiction itself is finally digressive.

In emphasising the differences between Brooks's model and my own, I have shied away from any claim that the trouble with his is its commitment to psychoanalysis, and located the trouble primarily in its failure to account for affective response. One consequence of this approach to Brooks is that he could come along and recast my whole rhetorical approach to progression in a ,psychoanalytical frame. That is, he could take my account of the sequential and affective structure of narrative and give it a psychoanalytical reading. I would have no great objection to such a procedure provided that no strong claims were being made about that recasting being a superior (rather than an alternative) form of explanation.

The reason I would object to any claim for superiority is connected to the one way in which I would fault Brooks for his turn to psychoanalysis. Such a move presupposes that to explain the surface structure of texts, to explain the experience of reading, we need to move away from that surface and that experience and propose a model of their deep structures. The consequence of that move is that it immediately causes one to work at some distance from the details of texts, as one tries to find a model that will be applicable to all texts. In my view, we need to do more work with the details of the surface structures before we are ready to consider different models of deep structures. My concept of progression commits its user to very little in the way of conclusions about the nature of any narrative to be read and interpreted. Instead, it seeks to posit principles of analysis that correspond to the experience of reading, principles that are specific enough to lead to worthwhile insights about particular narratives but flexible enough to be useful across the wide variety of surface structures that narratives offer us.

From *Journal of Narrative Technique*, 19 (1989), 70–84

NOTES

[James Phelan's account of *Great Expectations* appeared in 1989, both as a separate essay and as a chapter in his book *Reading People, Reading Plots* (Chicago). As explained in the Introduction (p. 26), the critical tradition within which he is working goes back to the Chicago critics of the 1950s, and has much to contribute to current research into readers' processing activities. Phelan is particularly concerned with the effects of plot, in which connection he seeks to give a new lease of life to character criticism.

Phelan says that characters are 'synthetic' (i.e. artificial) images of possible people and carry thematic features representative of a whole class or of some idea. But for him the most important thing about characters is that they have an affective function. The precise nature of this will depend on the relationship between particular mimetic or thematic features of the characterisation and the entire narrative progression, which in turn is a matter of instabilities among the characters or among the author, the narrator and the reader. The net result is that readers come to like or dislike particular characters, judging them as good or bad, and having hopes and fears about them. Phelan therefore criticises Peter Brooks, who (in essay 4) says a lot less about the thoughts and emotions of readers than about those of the characters in the story. In Phelan's view, Brooks makes readers' activity sound too exclusively cognitive, interpreting the novel at a level of abstraction far removed from the sheer human interest of the people and actions described in it. Brooks finds little to say about Wemmick, for instance, even though *Great Expectations* would be unimaginable without him. The section of Phelan's account reprinted here as essay 9 argues that Wemmick not only has a role in forwarding events, but acts as a focus for feelings and attitudes, both Pip's and the readers' own. By responding to the case of Wemmick, readers actually become clearer and firmer in their verdict on Pip, not least on Pip's behaviour towards Joe.

Phelan's quotations are from *Great Expectations* (Holt, Reinhart, & Winston: New York, 1972). Ed.]

1. [Where other critics might speak of an 'implied reader', Phelan uses the term 'authorial audience', which he takes from Peter J. Rabinowitz, 'Truth in Fiction: a Re-Examination of Audiences', *Critical Inquiry*, 4 (1977), 121–41. Phelan has in mind what he describes as the hypothetical audience Dickens is writing for. This audience not only knows that it is reading a novel and that Dickens, not Pip, is the author of the text. It also responds to the narrative's signals as Dickens intends. Real readers try to become this hypothetical audience. Ed.]

2. Lawrence Jay Dessner argues that the division between the two sides of Wemmick is not as great as first appears ('*Great Expectations*: The Tragic Comedy of John Wemmick', *Ariel*, 6 [1975], 65–79). But Dessner also says that his analysis 'does not often correspond with the aesthetic experience of the reader' (p. 78). I think that the authorial audience does see Wemmick as sharply divided but is able to accept the 'integration' of his character which I describe below.

3. For a fuller discussion of repression in the novel see James L. Spenko, 'The Return of the Repressed in *Great Expectations*', *Literature and Psychology*, 30 (1980), 133–46, and Michal Peled Ginsburg, 'Dickens and the Uncanny: Repression and Displacement in *Great Expectations*', *Dickens Studies Annual*, 13 (1984), 115–24.

4. I take up these issues in Chapter 4 of *Reading People, Reading Plots*.

10

Great Expectations as Romantic Irony

ANNY SADRIN

Such is the paradoxical nature of *Great Expectations* that it has all the outward signs of romance, and yet is not a romance. All the fairy tale motifs are there – the enchanted house, death-in-life, the captive Princess, the weird Witch-like lady – but the hero himself is not a fairy tale hero. He has in truth no right to be one: literary conventions forbid it because he is also the narrator of his own story.

A fairy tale hero must pay the price of overprotection that will ensure the happy ending: he has no say in what happens to him. Always a third person, he has to trust his fate entirely into the hands of the almighty narrating authorities. Comparing fairy tale heroes and the heroes of realistic short stories, André Jolles judiciously suggests that they might be defined according to the questions they arouse in the reader's mind: 'What is he going to do?' in the latter case, 'What is going to happen to him?'[1] in the former. Judged by these standards, Oliver Twist is a perfect fairy tale hero. He progresses through life guided 'by a stronger hand than chance',[2] and takes no active part in his own adventures. He has the passivity, says J. Hillis Miller, 'of waiting, of expectation, of "great expectations"'.[3] His one bold action, asking for more, is imposed upon him as the result of drawing lots: 'it fell to Oliver Twist',[4] a phrase that seals his destiny and is the true index of his election. But, apart from this memorable utterance, he hardly ever says a word; his retorts, in fact, are so few and so short – 'Yes, sir', 'No, sir', in most cases – that, placed on end, they would amount to little more than a hundredth of the whole book. He is even strikingly absent from twenty-one chapters in the fifty-three that make up the novel. Yet, he remains all the while the sole object of other people's preoccupations and activities. Without his having to interfere or even show up, his problems are settled for him by benevolent men and women whose main object is, in Mr Brownlow's own terms, 'the discovery of [his] parentage, and regaining *for him* the inheritance of which, if this story be true, he has been fraudulently deprived'.[5] There is no telling even how much he knows of what is going on in his absence when these good people are discussing and furthering what Mr Grimwig himself calls 'the life and adventures of Oliver Twist'[6] as if he were a hero of his own fiction, and, as far as we can judge, he has no awareness that his story is being recorded.

Oliver Twist and *Great Expectations* are often compared as exemplifying two diametrically opposed plot patterns, which they do, but the difference is also a matter of heroic status and narrative technique. Oliver might be described as a fairy tale hero placed in an ordinary setting that has even gained the novel a reputation for its realism. Pip, on the contrary, is an ordinary hero placed, at least for a time, in a fairy tale setting which, as story-teller, he himself contributes to making even more romantic than it is. Oliver plays no part in either forwarding the plot or relating his adventures. Pip is held responsible for all that happens and for the way it is told: a twofold responsibility whose two aspects are closely linked since Pip's chief difficulty as a character is to appreciate people and events at their fair value, whereas his main endeavour as a narrator is to show that he was in his youth a most incompetent reader of the book of his life.

'Reader' is not a far-fetched simile: from the moment he enters Satis House, Pip acts like someone who has inadvertently found his way into a work of fiction, which he improves, as he reads on, with his own marginal notes.

As long as he remains an outsider – the 'common labouring boy' who comes to play at Satis House for the day and goes back at night to the Forge, which he knows is his true home – his metaphorical embellishments are rather harmless and do not alter the meaning of the book. Neither, for that matter, does his fantastic account of how he 'got on up town' and 'what like' Miss Havisham is. He merely dyes black the ghastly white picture and gives back to the scene the true colour of 'melancholy' that so impressed him that he could not play. So true to the spirit of his experience is his dream-like version of it that he even condemns himself in his phantasmagoria to take his meal in banishment: 'And I got up behind the coach to eat mine, because she told me to' (ch. ix, p. 97), says the boy who was fed 'on the stones of the yard', like 'a dog in disgrace' (ch. viii, p. 92).

So far, Pip knows his place and his fibs are not untruths. Real misconstructions begin when he finds himself changed overnight into a young man with great, yet greatly unexpected, expectations and, urged by circumstances to take himself for a fairy tale hero, forces his way into the wrong book and the wrong literary genre.

He has the givens of the plot: his great expectations, a mysterious benefactor. His imagination provides at once the missing information, finds the setting, names the other actor: Satis House, Miss Havisham. Hasty as it may be, and mistaken as it will prove, his choice is admirably true to the workings of desire and its inner contradictions. 'What I wanted, who can say? How can *I* say, when I never knew?' (ch. xiv, pp. 135–6), he had confessed not so long ago, describing the discontent of his 'restlessly aspiring self', a perverted, yet common form of desire that feeds on its own frustration. And what place could better satisfy this insatiable need than Satis House itself, the official abode of wish fulfilment where wishes are never fulfilled:

> 'Enough House,' said I; 'that's a curious name, miss.'
> 'Yes,' she replied; 'but it meant more than it said. It meant, when it was given, that whoever had this house, could want nothing else. They must have been easily satisfied in those days, I should think'.
> (ch. viii, p. 86)

Satis House is a wicked place, as Pip has learnt to his cost, a place where he has been humiliated, made to play, made to weep, made to love, and beggared always, but there is 'a cruel attraction in the place', just as there was in Chancery, and this is where, 'against reason, against promise, against peace, against hope, against happiness, against all discouragement that could be' (ch. xxix, pp. 253–4), he chooses to belong and play the leading part.

This cannot be done unless he revises his text and suits his similes to the occasion, which he does without the slightest hesitation: the 'Witch of the place' is with no further delay promoted 'fairy godmother' to justify his own magic transformation:

> 'This is a gay figure, Pip,' said she, making her crutch stick play round me, as if she, the fairy godmother who had changed me, were bestowing the finishing gift.
> (ch. xix, p. 183)

When he leaves her, she has become '*my* fairy godmother' (p. 184, my emphasis), though she still has 'weird eyes' and her magic wand still is the witch's 'crutch stick'.

Such tricks, if they provide an interesting insight into the nature of the human heart and into the art of self-delusion, are totally out of place in a would-be fairy tale. A fairy tale hero has no business and no power to delude himself in that way. He lives surrounded by characters endowed with well-defined functions, 'helpers', 'donors', 'opponents',[7] and he is never mistaken for long as to which is which. Neither is the reader who tells good from evil with unerring intuition, no matter how hard villains try to deceive him, for the narrator himself has a firm hold on the text and leaves no room for incertitude. But a first-person narrative permits the double mystification and the shared uneasiness as to which 'as if' is the right one.

Through the agency of his narrator, Dickens actually compels us to read *Great Expectations* as we do 'mystery tales' or 'uncanny stories'. Contrary to 'fairy tales', such narratives are usually written in the first person precisely in order to create mixed feelings in the reader,[8] uneasily torn between suspicion about the tale and regard for the teller: the reported events sound unbelievable, but the reporting 'I' ought to be reliable as first-hand witness of the facts, and will be all the more so if he writes apologetically, which he often does, recording in particular his own past incredulity and astonishment on first experiencing the strange phenomena that he now feels impelled to relate without omitting to add as a saving clause: 'Was there ever such a fate!' (ch. xli, p. 357).

Reliable in this narrow sense, but never authoritative, Pip's narrative gives us imperfect and contradictory information: facts, hints, mere surmises from which we cannot fairly sort out *the* truth. We are *told* by Pip that Miss Havisham is his benefactress but given no proof of it; we are *shown* disturbing coincidences and made to suspect some connection between the hero's progress and his shameful past; and we have, of course, strong premonitions that the convict will reappear, for what would become of literature if characters were lost on the way? But it is not until we discover with the hero himself that Provis is the 'donor' (ch. xxxvi, p. 307) that we know the real story. Reading an ordinary ironic novel, we would have been taken long ago into the narrator's confidence. Reading a fairy tale, we would merely ascertain that our guesses were right or our wishes properly fulfilled.

Our surprise is assuredly nothing compared to Pip's astonishment on discovering the identity of his benefactor, but our forebodings were not foreknowledge properly speaking: when the moment of revelation comes, we know just as much and just as little as the hero does, we have received no side information from the homo-diegetic narrator, as we might have if he had been an outsider, and we have been placed in no superior position from which to 'look down' on the hero and wait for the catastrophe with amused anticipation, which is common practice in traditional third-person novels. When, for instance, in *Daniel Deronda*, Gwendolen Harleth eventually discovers the existence of her Jewish rival and of a world beyond her own, we have long been introduced to Mirah and to Jewish society, thanks to George Eliot's double plot, and we have been trained from the first to appreciate the heroine's moral shortcomings through the narrator's strictures and ironic portrayal. But in this novel, all the premonitory signs of plot reversal were perceived in time by the hero himself and are plainly reported as part of his own experience, not as narratorial exclusive knowledge. And our only superiority over Pip rests in our readiness to interpret these strange coincidences and recurrences, while the protagonist prefers to ignore them or rule them out of his memory. Thus, the unsolicited appearance at the Three Jolly Bargemen of the stranger who stirs his rum-and-water with Joe's file and bestows upon him the two one-pound notes leaves Pip 'stupefied by this turning up of [his] old misdeed and old acquaintance' (ch. x, p. 107) and he goes to bed overburdened with guilt for being 'on secret terms of conspiracy with convicts'; but then, to our surprise, he calls his 'old misdeed' 'a feature in my low career that I had previously forgotten' (how could he?) and he tries hard to forget it again, endeavouring at once to replace the nightmare by sweeter dreams: 'I coaxed myself to sleep by thinking of Miss Havisham's, next Wednesday' (ch. x, p. 108). It will never occur to him to interpret this visit as the harbinger of his own convict's return or, later, to associate his great expectations with this early instalment of money. Denegation is his usual reaction when the past haunts him too disturbingly, as the following two examples show:

> If I had often thought before, with something allied to shame, of my companionship with the fugitive whom I had once seen limping among those graves, what were my thoughts on this Sunday, when the place recalled the wretch, ragged and shivering, with his felon

iron and badge! My comfort was, that it happened a long time ago, and that he had doubtless been transported a long way off, and that he was dead to me, and might be veritably dead into the bargain.

(ch. xix, p. 173)

I consumed the whole time in thinking how strange it was that I should be encompassed by all this taint of prison and crime; that, in my childhood out on our lonely marshes on a winter evening I should have first encountered it; that, it should have reappeared on two occasions, starting out like a stain that was faded but not gone; that, it should in this new way pervade my fortune and advancement ... I beat the prison dust off my feet as I sauntered to and fro, and I shook it out of my dress, and I exhaled its air from my lungs.

(ch. xxxii, p. 284)

Our aloofness as readers leaves us much freer to face strange situations, dwell on the meaning of unexpected encounters and associations and put two and two together. As we are not personally involved in the story, we do not mind being caught in a web of connections and cross-references. We rather tend, on the contrary, to welcome them as possible clues to the mystery that we are trying to pierce, not unreasonably suspecting them to have been purposely sifted from a heap of recollections by the autobiographer as especially meaningful. In other words, we are not better informed than the hero but what information we get is better signposted and we are more receptive to it. So much so that, although we read the same story, we read quite a different book. The two books even belong to different fictional modes: in Northrop Frye's classification ours would come under the heading of 'low mimetic mode' since 'the hero is one of us' and 'we respond to a sense of his common humanity'; whereas the hero's should be affiliated to 'naïve romance', which is 'closer to the wish-fulfilment dream'.[9] The latter affiliation is explicitly propounded by the narrator himself who, after being long behindhand in grasping the meaning of his life-story, proves a sharper critic than might have been expected and audaciously steals a march on the structuralists:

Betimes in the morning I was up and out. It was too early yet to go to Miss Havisham's, so I loitered into the country on Miss Havisham's side of town – which was not Joe's side; I could go there to-morrow – thinking about my patroness, and painting brilliant pictures of her plans for me.

She had adopted Estella, she had as good as adopted me, and it could not fail to be her intention to bring us together. She reserved it for me to restore the desolate house, admit the sunshine into the dark rooms, set the clocks a going and the cold hearths a blazing, tear down the cobwebs, destroy the vermin – in short, do all the shining deeds of the young Knight of romance, and marry the Princess. I had stopped to look at the house as I passed; and its seared red brick walls, blocked windows, and strong green ivy clasping even the stacks of chimneys with its twigs and tendons, as if with sinewy old arms, had made up a rich attractive mystery, of which I was the hero.

(ch. xxix, p. 253)

The last and catastrophic stage of Pip's expectations is heralded by a new reference to literary fiction:

In the Eastern story, the heavy slab that was to fall on the bed of state in the flush of conquest was slowly wrought out of the quarry, the tunnel for the rope to hold it in its place was slowly carried through the leagues of rock, the slab was slowly raised and fitted in the roof, the rope was rove to it and slowly taken through the miles of hollow to the great iron ring. All being made ready with much labour, and the hour come, the sultan was aroused in the dead of the night, and the sharpened axe that was to sever the rope from the great iron ring was put into his hand, and he struck with it, and the rope parted and rushed away, and the ceiling fell. So, in my case; all the work, near and afar, that tended to the end, had been accomplished; and in an instant the blow was struck, and the roof of my stronghold dropped upon me.

(ch. xxxviii, p. 330)

The allusion is to one of James Ridley's *Tales of the Genii* (1776), 'The Tale of the Inchanters, or Misnar, the Sultan of the East'. Ridley's book had been a great favourite with young Dickens, as it was later to be with young David Copperfield, and the story of Misnar had even so appealed to his childish imagination that, when still at Chatham, he had made himself famous in the family circle for writing a tragedy founded on it and entitled 'Misnar, the Sultan of India'.[10] All his life, the novelist retained a nostalgic fondness for the fabulous heroes and friends of his youth who had so often 'kept [him] company' and whose adventures had 'kept alive [his] fancy';[11] and it is significant that, after a long lapse of years, when, in his own fiction, he came to depict the predicament of a young man suddenly driven out of the world of romance, the subject should have triggered off an associative process that took him back to those early days of escapism into romantic illusion, suggesting to him this comparison with the very story from which he had derived his first notion of tragedy.

As Ridley's were popular tales, widely read among Dickens's contemporaries, there was no need for the novelist to press the analogy, but as they have gone out of fashion, it is not inappropriate today to offer a brief summary of the story in question. Misnar is a prosperous ruler, beloved by all except Abubal, his envious brother who, wishing most particularly to dispossess him of a recently built abode of unequalled magnificence, takes up arms against him and, with the help of two enchanters, finds himself 'in one Day ... Master of India; his Brother defeated; and his gaudy Pavilion wrested from him'. Having settled at once with his companions in the coveted pavilion, Abubal gives a banquet there in celebration of his victory during the night that follows. Meanwhile, Misnar has sought refuge in the mountains with Horam, his faithful vizier. In the middle of the night, Horam wakes up his master and takes him to a cave among the rocks; there, removing a stone, he uncovers a strong rope, one end of which runs through the rocks while the other is fastened to an enormous ring of iron. Placing an axe in the hands of his master, Horam enjoins him to strike and sever the rope. The Sultan obeys without in the least suspecting what the consequences of his gesture will be. But the next morning a messenger apprises him of the death of his enemies 'crushed to Atoms' by a ponderous stone artfully concealed in the roof of the pavilion and released from its confinement when the rope had been cut. Foreseeing rebellion, Horam, unbeknown to his master, had installed the apparatus to trap unwelcome visitors.

Seen in the light of this original context, the analogy does more than express the crumbling of Pip's hopes and castles in air; it implies no less than the well-deserved destruction of an impostor. The once 'Knight of romance' now identifies himself with the villain of a moral tale and, by so doing, invites us to reconsider our notion of heroism. Of course, we cannot deny him the right to remain 'the hero of [his] own life'[12] and we are bound to admit that if 'plot consists of somebody doing something', he remains that somebody; but, now that he is no longer 'superior in *degree*', we are faced with the difficulty pointed out by Frye 'in retaining the word "hero"'[13] to describe his new fictional status. Chesterton helps us out of this dilemma: '*Great Expectations*', he writes, 'may be called ... a novel without a hero ... I mean that it is a novel which aims chiefly at showing that the hero is unheroic'.[14]

Chesterton's expression 'aims at showing' is appropriate: Dickens's demonstration is achieved with almost pedagogical rigour. Aware that heroism, or the lack of it, is not just a matter of the hero's moral fortitude but of his 'power of action' and is strictly determined by 'the level of the postulates made about him'[15] as well as by environment, plot pattern, values at stake, forces at play, he simply sets two plots against each other, one supposedly real, the other supposedly imaginary, with the same character in the part of the hero. The result is that we get two heroic types in one person.

The following diagrams, based on Greimas's actantial pattern,[16] will help us visualise the discrepancy between these two plots and appreciate their respective and relative implications.

Pip's plot:

Sender	Object	Receiver
Miss Havisham	Money, gentility, Estella	One of society's arbitrarily chosen few
Helpers	Subject	Opponents
Jaggers (and Wemmick)	Pip	Sarah and Camilla Pocket Drummle

Magwitch's plot:

Sender	Object	Receiver
Magwitch	Money, gentility, 'bright eyes'	A working-class child rewarded for a good deed
Helpers	Subject	Opponents
Jaggers (and Wemmick)	Pip	The Law Compeyson and Orlick

Let us examine the second pattern and see how it differs from the first.

Pip, of course, retains his central position in the diagram, being as before the subject of the quest; but, as a receiver, he undergoes a drastic change owing to the change of sender. In his imaginary plot, Miss Havisham had acted arbitrarily, like the God of the puritans, whimsically electing him as, once upon a time, Oliver Twist had been elected. In Magwitch's plot, he merely gets his due: a perfect type of the modern receiver, he must now face the consequences of his fall from grace and accept his new condition as responsible

Victorian hero, far less prestigious and enviable than that of Hero by divine right.

The other major novelty is the almost entirely new cast of 'actants'. As Magwitch comes in, Miss Havisham has to go; and not only is she dislodged from the sender's square, but she disappears from the diagram altogether, having no part to play in the new plot either as helper or as opponent. It is quite clear that, had she never existed, or had he never met her, Pip's great expectations would have been just the same, and we have every reason to believe that he would have renounced them just the same on discovering his benefactor's identity. Only his bitterness would have been less acute.

The first consequence of Miss Havisham's departure, as Pip immediately perceives, is that Estella has no reason to stay as object of the quest: 'Miss Havisham's intentions towards me, all a mere dream; Estella not designed for me' (ch. xxxix, p. 341). And it is one of the most dramatic ironies of the new plot that the new sender, having been kept in total ignorance of his daughter's fate, should be denied the right to place her on his prize list. All he can offer is to buy Pip 'bright eyes ... if money can buy 'em' (ch. xxxix, p. 338).

With Estella no longer starring, *exit* Drummle, whose part as opponent belongs to another plot. *Exeunt* in their turn the ugly Pockets, who have nothing to fear from Pip's expectations because the prize-money is no property of their rich and much fawned-upon relative. And thus the world of Satis House entirely recedes into the background.

The real actants in the new drama, Magwitch, Jaggers, Wemmick, Compeyson, Orlick, belong either to the world of crime or to the world of the Law, two worlds at times so ambiguously connected as to seem but one and to justify Pip's impression that to be in the hands of lawyers is an experience strangely similar to that of being handled by a starving convict: 'As I sat down, and he preserved his attitude and bent his brows at his boots, I felt at a disadvantage, which reminded me of that old time when I had been put upon a tombstone' (ch. xxxvi, p. 305), he says, recording one of his visits to his enigmatic guardian. Jaggers and Wemmick are actually the only pawns that are not moved on the chessboard or out of it: significantly, the lawyer and his clerk can play helpers to any cause in any plot, work on behalf of a lady or of a convict alike, only provided they are commissioned to do the job and financially rewarded for it. And the Law, when it eventually forbids the happy outcome of Magwitch's scheme, fulfils the same function as the two villains of the book.

Thus, from a narrowly structural point of view, Pip is the hero of a novel that turns out to be much more of the Newgate than of the silver-fork type, however earnestly he had wished it to be so. The Satis House episodes now appear as little more than a digression through Wonderland, a place fit to harbour the dreams and fears of a child, but not those of a grown-up. We had sensed this, in fact, from the start; but, only too glad to be admitted, and not locked out like Pumblechook, we had entered this secluded world with no thought of sorting out child truth from child fiction. Pip's fairy tale associations had appealed to the child who survives in each of us and we had at once responded to the enchantment; but we had had no difficulty in facing adult truth again on returning to more ordinary places, whereas Pip's tragic flaw is precisely his inability to leave childhood well behind him on reaching the age of man. David Copperfield had believed at about the same age that life was 'like a great fairy story, which [he] was just about to begin to read';[17] but, for Pip, life is rather like a sequel to a tale which he has just finished reading and unreasonably wishes to read over and over again.

Admonition is not spared him, but remains of no avail. When he is removed from the enchanted house on getting apprenticed to Joe, he is clearly advised not to return there:

> 'Joe,' said I; 'don't you think I ought to make Miss Havisham a visit?'
> 'Well, Pip,' returned Joe, slowly considering. 'What for?'
> 'What for, Joe? What is any visit made for?'
> 'There is some wisits, p'r'aps,' said Joe, 'as for ever remains open to the question, Pip. But in regard of wisiting Miss Havisham. She might think you wanted something – expected something of her.'
> 'Don't you think I might say that I did not, Joe?'
> 'You might, old chap,' said Joe. 'And she might credit it. Similarly she mightn't.' ...
> 'You see, Pip,' Joe pursued ..., 'Miss Havisham done the handsome thing by you. When Miss Havisham done the handsome thing by you, she called me back to say to me as that were all.'
> 'Yes, Joe. I heard her.'
> 'ALL,' Joe repeated, very emphatically.
> 'Yes, Joe. I tell you, I heard her.'
> 'Which I meantersay, Pip, it might be that her meaning were – Make a end on it! – As you was! – Me to the North, and you to the South! – Keep in sunders!'
>
> (ch. xv, p. 138)

But he goes back all the same, enthralled by the place and its inhabitants, even at the risk of passing for a beggar: 'Everything was unchanged, and Miss Havisham was alone. "Well?" said she, fixing her eyes upon me. "I hope you want nothing? You'll get nothing"' (ch. xv, p. 143). He goes again on his birthday and again is suspected of wanting or 'expecting' something: 'she gave me a guinea when I was going ... I tried to decline taking the guinea ..., but with no better effect than causing her to ask me very angrily, If I expected more?' (ch. xvii, p. 152). Miss Havisham's contemptuous use of the word 'expect' should prevent all misconstructions when the expectations do come, but Pip has by then forgotten the message or chosen to ignore it.

Warned against misplacing his expectations, Pip is also warned against misplacing his affections: 'You ridiculous boy,' Estella says to him when they meet in London, 'will you never take warning?' (ch. xxxiii, p. 287). And later, at Richmond, the warning is reiterated almost literally:

> 'Pip, Pip,' she said one evening ... 'will you never take warning?'
> 'Of what?'
> 'Of me.'
> 'Warning not to be attracted by you, do you mean, Estella?'
> 'Do you mean! If you don't know what I mean, you are blind.'
> (ch. xxxviii, p. 319)

Not blind, but self-blinded, Pip confesses: 'Whatever her tone with me happened to be, I could put no trust in it, and build no hope on it; and yet I went on against trust and against hope. Why repeat it a thousand times? So it always was' (ch. xxxiii, p. 288). The impenitent dreamer, 'visionary boy – or man?' (ch. xliv, p. 377), goes on believing in the stories of his own making as indeed we all do when in our day-dreams we give credence to our falsehoods.

Felix culpa! Were it not for Pip's fictions and misconstructions, *Great Expectations* would be a straightforward novel amounting to no more than one of its plots. 'The Return of the Convict' – for such might be the title of this edifying, sentimental drama – would not be lacking in pathos and in romantic appeal, thanks to the mythical figure of the outcast in the part of provider; but with no other plot with which to mirror itself, it would be deprived of its ironic and nostalgic dimension and the novel as a whole would lose much aesthetically.

As things are, the 'real' plot, Dickens's, can never be read as a self-contained story and Pip's dream pattern remains to the end superimposed on Magwitch's, blurring the picture. Miss Havisham's shadow, in particular, hovers formidably over the sender's square, making her absence so conspicuous that she gains in charisma what she loses in power and becomes active as a 'non-actant'. 'You made your own snares', she tells Pip when he reproaches her with deceiving him, '*I* never made them' (ch. xliv, p. 374); and how could he gainsay it? And when he complains 'You led me on', she simply corrects him: 'I let you go on', she says. 'Was that kind?' he asks; but then all he gets by way of a reply is a question rhetorically addressed to both reader and character: 'Who am I, for God's sake, that I should be kind?' (ch. xliv, p. 373). The answer, which we feel allowed or requested to provide, might well be that she is the ironist of the book, the contemptuous outsider who watches things from a distance, takes pleasure in not interfering, asks questions and gives no answers, and never speaks 'straight'[18] the better to deceive her interlocutors.

Irony is a cruelly subversive game, which requires victims and victimisers and leaves little room indeed for kindness, even on the part of the lookers-on: what reader could boast that he never enjoyed Miss Havisham's equivocations or that he never played Trabb's boy to the hero, never took advantage like 'that unlimited miscreant' (ch. xxx, p. 266) of his position as someone 'whom no man could hurt; an invulnerable and dodging serpent who, when chased into a corner, flew out again between his captor's legs, scornfully yelping' (ch. xxx, p. 267)? Yet, even granting that Pip deserves moral castigation, that all his faults and shortcomings make him often ridiculous and occasionally truly despicable, who could deny that he is, by and large, more sinned against than sinning and has a right to feel 'vaguely convinced', as he puts it, of being 'very much ill-used by somebody, or by everybody', even though he 'can't say which' (ch. xvii, p. 157)?

'Vaguely convinced', 'somebody', 'everybody', 'I can't say which': this overdone understatement is rather puzzling, even suspicious. Surely, if he tried, Pip would have no difficulty in listing the names of all those who once wronged him, bullied him, misled him, told him what to expect or whom to love, and taught him to be dissatisfied with himself and his condition. But his reluctance to denounce certain people, Estella in particular, also leaves the sentence open to more general interpretations and allows us to exclude no one from the list of wrongdoers, least of all the hero's maker who engineered all the mischief. Might we not even read the remark as a disguised authorial intrusion and tongue-in-cheek *mea culpa*?

It will be argued, of course, that Dickens has nothing to reproach himself with, that the misfortunes and blemishes of fictitious characters cannot fairly be blamed on their creators and that such narrow-minded censorship would soon be the death of fiction-making. Sure enough. But Pip's case is rather special in that he is not just a character who happens to be good or bad or whatever: in his own endeavour to achieve his conversion from Romanticism to Victorianism, Dickens '*ill-*uses' him because he *uses* him and takes him for his whipping-boy. Pip thus finds himself ridiculed for sticking to Dickens's standards, which are in the process of being discarded, and gets severely punished for the unpardonable anachronism of taking himself for Oliver Twist!

This seems all the more unfair on the poor lad as Dickens's enterprise never really carries conviction. It is even quite remarkable that, under the pretext of destroying romance, the novelist should have allowed himself in this book, as in no other before, the right to build a most romantic story, which his very *coup de théâtre* destroys most romantically. So that, when romance is over and 'realism' has taken over, irony loses its edge and takes on a new quality: mellowed and melancholy, it becomes almost elegiac.

From Anny Sadrin, *Great Expectations* (London, 1988), pp. 146–64.

NOTES

[Anny Sadrin's magisterial guide to *Great Expectations* is one of the best books on Dickens there has ever been, and the section reprinted as essay 10 well illustrates the current interest in intertextuality and reader activity (see Introduction pp. 21–34). Sadrin is asking the question: How, as readers, do we relate *Great Expectations* to other things we have read? And how does this help us to assign it some kind of shape and *raison d'être?* She suggests that the novel's most distinctive feature is a restlessly unstable romantic irony, a diagnosis which corroborates Connor's Lacanian account (in essay 8) of the Imaginary/Symbolic oscillation, but in a purely literary terminology. Sadrin elucidates the structural implications of romantic irony with the aid of the actantial model of narrative described in the Introduction (pp. 11–13).

In *Oliver Twist* and much of Dickens's other work, there are strong elements of fairy tale wish-fulfilment. At the opposite extreme, novels such as *Martin Chuzzlewit* and *Bleak House* seem fully aware that a trust in providential rewards and other expectations can lead to bitter disappointment and even serious psychological damage. But in *Great Expectations* Dickens's more utopian and more realistic tendencies come paradoxically together, giving rise to a story in which dreams are both indulged and deconstructed. This is what Sadrin is describing as the 'subjective objectivity' of romantic irony, a concept which was first expounded by the German Romantic writer and critic Friedrich Schlegel (1772–1829).

Essay 10 is only an extract from Sadrin's discussion, but the romantic irony is at work in the novel from beginning to end. The opening chapters, originally serialised in *All the Year Round* during the month of December, have much in common with Dickens's Christmas stories, yet in a parodic form which suggests that any hopes of peace and goodwill are utterly unfounded. Conversely, just when chapters 6 and 7 have almost settled down into conventional realism, chapter 8 propels us into the wonderland of Satis House. And the middle-aged Pip's career in Egypt works in much the same way. On the one hand, it all reads like a no-frills story of sober hard work. On the other hand, there are overtones of the Arabian Nights; his kindness to Herbert is providentially rewarded; and the success of Clarriker and Co. represents a miraculous synergy between Miss Havisham's (a lady's) capital and Magwitch's (a convict's).

Sadrin's quotations are from *Great Expectations*, ed. Angus Calder, Penguin English Library (Harmondsworth, 1965). Ed.]

1. A. Jolles, *Einfache Formen* (1930), quoted by Tzvetan Todorov, 'Poétique', in *Qu'est-ce que le Structuralisme?* (Paris, 1968), p. 142.

2. *Oliver Twist*, Clarendon Dickens (Oxford, 1966), p. 335.

3. J. Hillis Miller, *Charles Dickens: The World of his Novels* (Cambridge, Mass, 1958), p. 43.

4. *Oliver Twist*, p. 11.

5. Ibid., p. 281.

6. Ibid., p. 89.

7. See Vladimir Propp, *Morphology of the Folktale* (Leningrad, 1928), translated by Lawrence Scott (University of Texas Press, 1958). On Propp's theory, see Terence Hawkes, *Structuralism and Semiotics* (London, 1985), pp. 67–9.

8. Cf. Tzvetan Todorov, *Introduction à la littérature fantastique* (Paris, 1970), pp. 87–91.

9. Northrop Frye, *Anatomy of Criticism* (Princeton, New Jersey, 1974), pp. 34, 37.

10. See Edgar Johnson, *Charles Dickens: His Tragedy and Triumph* (London, 1953), vol. 1, p. 23.

11. *David Copperfield*, Clarendon Dickens (Oxford, 1982), p. 48.

12. Ibid., p. 1.

13. See Frye, *Anatomy of Criticism*, pp. 33–4.

14. G. K. Chesterton, *Appreciations and Criticisms of the Works of Charles Dickens* (London, 1911), p. 199.

15. Frye, *Anatomy of Criticism*, p. 33.

16. See A. J. Greimas, *Sémantique Structurale* (Paris, 1966). For a summary of this theory, see Hawkes, *Structuralism and Semiotics*, pp. 87–95.

17. *David Copperfield*, p. 233.

18. Wayne C. Booth, *A Rhetoric of Irony* (Chicago, 1974), p. 1.

11

Gothic Plot in *Great Expectations*

THOMAS LOE

In spite of the enormous amount of critical attention the plot of *Great Expectations* has received in the last two decades, there has been a reluctance on the part of critics to identify its structure in terms of traditional genres. The novel's length, number of characters, and elaborate texture make plot identification a subtle issue, especially since the sense of progression of the story is skilfully interwoven with the development of Pip's character. With few exceptions, critics looking at structure tend to synthesise all these elements into one main plot. Such syntheses demonstrate that *Great Expectations* is probably the most unified of Dickens's novels, but in unravelling the elaborate tissue of its unifying elements they invariably fail to account for its diversity of action.

My thesis is that there are three main lines to the concrete experiences and literal actions of *Great Expectations*, and that these can be described by using traditional genre designations: the *Bildungsroman*, the novel of manners, and the Gothic novel. My primary concern is with the Gothic plot because its particular structural significance has been virtually ignored. One could argue that this is only because *Great Expectations* is such a successful work: its generally acknowledged superior plot construction conceals the overlapping patterns of its different genres in a way that one would expect in a work of deeply resonant unity. K. J. Fielding, for example, claims that in *Great Expectations* Dickens 'completely mastered the skill of construction',[1] and Lionel

Stevenson says that it 'was his masterpiece of form and structure'.[2] Yet Dickens's own ambivalence about the conclusion and the ongoing critical debate about the meaning and appropriateness of the two endings suggest that the various plots do not coalesce as neatly at the end of the novel as they are synthesised during its development. Examining the plot lines through the terms afforded by genre may not resolve interpretive debate, but it will allow insight into the structures that knit the book together, help reveal what the interpretive issues are, and establish parallels for comparing novels.

Viewing *Great Expectations* as *Bildungsroman* is the most popular approach through genre. George Worth's invaluable *Great Expectations: An Annotated Bibliography*, published in 1986, reveals about two dozen studies that employ the concept as a significant way of reading the novel. G. B. Tennyson, for example, writes 'To my mind the most complete expression of the Bildungsroman is *Great Expectations*'.[3] Critics who view the novel as *Bildungsroman* tend to find the same patterns and reveal that there is nothing particularly sequential to those patterns because they consist more of thematic elements than structural ones. G. Robert Strange's remark, '*Great Expectations* is not more profound than other development-novels, but it is more mysterious'[4] locates its chief distinction. The reason it is more mysterious is that the *Bildungsroman* plot in *Great Expectations*, unlike most other novels of the genre, is given a sense of sequential progression and heightened action through a combination with other plots. My contention is that the story of Pip's story of psychological and moral formation and his social progress is supported and directed by the simpler and more tightly knit plot derived from the Gothic novel.

The fictional biographical or autobiographical impulses of the nineteenth-century novel could easily become the 'large loose and baggy monsters' Henry James describes without a more definite shaping force.[5] Students of the *Bildungsroman* generally agree that it was left to Marcel Proust, James Joyce, and Virginia Woolf to perfect the techniques of point of view and patterned motifs necessary to structure that complex genre. In terms of his *Bildungsroman* plot, Pip's journey is the metaphor of his development, and Joe is emblematic of the standard which Pip has left and to which he must eventually return in order to make accurate judgements about himself. Joe does not change, although he progresses in time, and the *Bildungsroman* plot he represents is not so much static as circular for Pip, which Meyer Abrams suggests is typical of the genre which has a 'dialectical organisation – it must have reached the *Wissenschaft* at the end of its journey before it can set out upon that journey from its beginning'.[6] Any remaining questions about the suitability of the term as applied to *Great Expectations* are answered by Marianne Hirsch's conclusive 'The Novel of Formation as Genre: Between *Great Expectations* and Lost Illusions'.[7] Pip's maturation progress, which includes his mistakes, may be judged against that standard to which he repeatedly returns from London, a circling progress of the coming together of younger and older self,[8] 'ostensibly to make reparation to the neglected Joe, an intention never realised'.[9]

Most critics are naturally interested in describing the development of Pip's character, for it is in Pip's personality and the evolution of that personality that the salient literary merit of the book resides. The movement is a process in which Pip's ability to perceive his fall becomes an essential part of the discovery of self, as well as providing a venue for him to discover what he must do to redeem himself. In this way *Great Expectations* can move from rudimentary meanings to more complex ones in its powerfully harmonious fashion. But these are not systematic or casual movements, and they reflect meaning, not action; theme, not structure. Even with modern techniques for interior dramatisation, the shape of the *Bildungsroman* plot generally described by critics remains a loosely chronological one, a fluid movement of gradually increasing self-consciousness punctuated by epiphanies.

A sharper sense of progression is provided for *Great Expectations* by its novel of manners plot. An enormously popular genre in the latter part of the eighteenth century and the early part of the nineteenth century, the novel of manners had expended much of its raison d'être by mid-century. Although it had provided a guide for the newly emerging middle class into the mysteries of an increasingly complex bourgeois society, it was soon too limited by its subject to meet the demands of a better educated and more sophisticated audience. Distinguished by its focus on piloting an individual through the nuances of society's rituals, the novel of manners plot does have a more orderly structure than the *Bildungsroman*, but because its concern is primarily with social practice rather than with growth of an individual, it generally lacks any substantial development in depicting its protagonists. In fact, the novel of manners could be regarded as the obverse of the *Bildungsroman*:

instead of offering the teasing subtleties of growing self-knowledge, it offers situations where an individual must compromise or give up claims to individuality in order to succeed. Although many important *Bildungsromane* stop short of the protagonist's 'accommodation to the modern world',[10] this same 'accommodation' is one of the distinguishing features of the novel of manners.

The plot of this genre is best exemplified by the basic situation of Jane Austen's novels: a female protected by her unmarried domestic situation becomes involved in a romance which leads her away from her family and toward an integration with society. Part of the appeal of these actions has been that they are unremittingly realistic; its courtships were treated in the mimetic manner of the novel rather than that of the romance. Marriage, as a confirmation of society's values, usually takes place, but whether it does or not, marriage provides closure. The mainspring for the pacing of the events in the story, however, is the love story itself, a major difference between the novel of manners and the *Bildungsroman*. If Pip were female, the importance of the romance to his story and the effect it has on the development of his character would be much more evident since his situation is a typical one for many eighteenth- and nineteenth-century novel-of-manners heroines. The romance provides a reasonably casual sequence with a logical progressive series of developing successes and failures and separations and reunions. It has, then, a greater fixed pattern to its actions than the *Bildungsroman*.

The waning interest in the novel of manners had much to do with the evolution of a confidence by middle-class Victorians in their social practices. Yet the novel of manners still proved to be a powerful source for satire: by exposing the hypocrisy and self-interest of upwardly mobile aspirations, the novel of manners could offer an amusing corrective. This latent power is a potent force in all established genres. The generally acknowledged expectations of Pip consist of his aspirations to fulfil a superficial and limited notion of what it meant to become a 'gentleman': the novel of manners plot which structures these expectations inverts the progress of events and the obligatory romance included with them, so that they become a parody for revealing humbler expectations characterised by the work ethic so central to the Victorian middle class. Dickens thereby afforded his readers some luxury of seeing Pip's middle-class aspirations distinct from their own and disarmed much of the threat of an uncomfortable identification with Pip's aspirations. Yet, the plot of social progress orders events as it deconstructs and mocks them; like most parodies it depends upon the original plot of a work while mocking its theme.

Much of the vitality provided by the novel of manners plot derives from its familiar situations and simple casual progress; it is easy to trace the distinct logic of Pip's social movements even though they coalesce with formation of his character: Pip is motivated to leave his apprenticeship to Joe because of his infatuation with Estella. He accepts the opportunity to go to London in order to become a gentleman so that he might win her favour. In London he accepts the unsavoury lodgings, friendships, and cultural opportunities as those appropriate to the style of a gentleman when they are, in fact, parodies of real culture. His comic experiences with fashionable education at the hands of the Pockets or his travails with the Finches of the Grove provide only caricatures of what should be available to him, yet Pip feels these experiences promote his desirability. His feeling for Estella is ridiculed by her and by her eventual acceptance of his rival, Bentley Drummle, who possesses the veneer of social accomplishment Pip is striving to attain for himself. His increasing talent for wasting time and money, going 'from bad to worse' (ch. 36) is documented by the cycle of his visits to Jaggers and his returns to his marsh village. His lack of industry is countered by Herbert's energy when the latter eventually begins to plan for his own life. While we are shown that Pip is not 'naterally wicious' (ch. 4) by the parallel with Orlick who seems to be, we also know his accomplishments are limited to those superficial attainments that define a gentleman for Magwitch and Jaggers. We know that Pip reads, attends plays, and can speak foreign languages, but these never become dramatised as an integral part of his personality. His social attainments are, apparently, only for show. Eventually Pip's fashionable accomplishments are revealed to him in all their essential hollowness, and his actions turn to rebuilding his values on a secure personal basis. He realises he is as much a monster as Frankenstein's (ch. 40). 'Pip's acquired "culture" was an entirely bourgeois thing', writes Humphry House, 'it came to little more than accent, table manners, and clothes'.[11]

If Joe can be regarded as the emblem of the *Bildungsroman* plot, Estella can be regarded as the emblem of the novel of manners plot and marriage or the possibility of marriage as its metaphor. The romance involving Estella also gives an initial motivation and a continuing rationale for Pip's actions in the social world, even though the scenes from that social world often resemble parodies or exposés. Significant changes in Pip's social behaviour are demarcated by his reaction to Estella, like his decision to ask Biddy, who is in many ways Estella's counter, to marry him. At least partially because the novel of manners plot in *Great Expectations* is essentially a satiric inversion of the genre, Dickens is prevented from concluding the novel with Pip's unequivocal union with Estella, which would thereby appear to embrace the very mode of plot he has been caricaturing. Nevertheless, this frequently interrupted but uncomplicated plot provides a solid medium for carrying the novel's convincing social texture. Even so, compared to the plots of other popular mid-nineteenth-century novels that could be regarded as candidates for the novel of manners genre, *Great Expectations'* structural rhythms are much more logically tightened than simple romance and social situation allow, especially in its final stage. The plot that combines with the novel of manners plot and the *Bildungsroman* plot to accomplish this tightness derives from the Gothic novel.

The resurgence of critical interest in the Gothic novel and its influence on the English novel from the 1970s onward parallels the interest in the *Bildungsroman*. A connection between the two genres in *Great Expectations* has been observed by several literary historians such as Walter Reed who sees them as 'counterfictions': 'a novel of *Bildung* unable to free itself from Gothic *schauer*'.[12] Even though the presence of the general effect of the Gothic novel has been observed in Dickens's novel, little has been written about the Gothic plot of *Great Expectations*, perhaps because the greatest obvious effect of the Gothic novel is its affective atmosphere. Extended studies of such Gothic qualities range from Walter Phillips's early *Dickens, Reade, and Collins: Sensation Novelists* of 1917 (New York) to ones like A. C. Coolidge Jr's which have shown how Dickens utilised Gothic techniques to establish pacing and arouse heightened responses.[13] Above all else, it is a genre dominated by its setting. The major effect of this setting is to establish a sense of isolation for its protagonists and create situations beyond the social norms of generally accepted practices and behaviour. Since the Gothic novel offers experiences that call ordinary modes of perception into question, it seems ideal as a medium for developing the *Bildungsroman*'s emerging self-consciousness. Yet the Gothic novel also possesses an equally distinct plot. In *Great Expectations* this plot has usually been identified as its 'mystery' plot, and its presence has been described or praised by critics from the time of its publication to the present. The Gothic plot is the highest energy plot of all three plots. Its deliberate causal progress, excitement, and suspense are so evident, in fact, that it is usually seen only as another element of sensationalism. In the hands of a skilled novelist like Dickens, however, the clear-cut pacing and causality become a vehicle for structuring the much less energetic plots of character development and social progress in *Great Expectations*. Barbara Hardy writes that 'Pip's progress in *Great Expectations* is probably the only instance of a moral action where the events precipitate change and growth as they do in George Eliot or Henry James'.[14] *Great Expectations* need only be compared to the very similar 'biographical' story of *David Copperfield*, or to the dominance of melodrama and sensationalism in *Oliver Twist*, in order to recognise the thoroughly synergetic relationship of the plots that involve Pip.

What distinguishes the Gothic novel plot from a simple mystery plot and what are the dynamics of such a plot? The 'suspense' plots or plot sequences identified by Phillip Marcus appear to have strong Gothic plot characteristics.[15] Peter Wolfe also is surely writing about Gothic plot as well when he asserts that the 'melodrama ignores complexity and subtlety. It simplifies reality into ready categories of good and evil, and it aims at evoking a simple response – like horror, sympathy, or loathing'.[16] Yet the actual terms of the Gothic plot could be defined more specifically, and its relationship with the other plots clarified. It is perhaps best seen in terms of the structure perfected by Ann Radcliffe and still a puissant force for structuring types of popular narrative today. The essential ingredient of this plot derives from an element defined by Edmund Burke's *Philosophical Enquiry into the Origin of Our Ideas of the Sublime and Beautiful* published about 1757. Burke's *Enquiry* became a virtual handbook of narrative principles for novelists and painters trying to achieve the sublime effect. The pre-eminent quality Burke locates that can be successfully applied to plot is that of obscurity. In Anne Radcliffe's most accomplished novel, *The Italian*, and in many of the novels that follow it, this principle takes the form of 'layering' mystery upon mystery within a powerful affective atmosphere so that the original motivation for the novel's action is greatly obscured. The original motivation is most often a crime, frequently involving an inheritance and heir, and its effects are visited upon a subsequent generation – usually represented by the character of an innocent and passive young female – who must seek assistance from a more powerful and experienced donor in order to resolve the mysteries of her origin and thereby re-establish a sense of order. In this type of natural or 'explained' Gothic novel, what seem to be supernatural forces acting for a pervasive threatening evil always have some eventual rational explanation. A romance is present in such novels as well, but its story is made up of a series of separations and reunions which are distinctly secondary to the action precipitated by the persecutions of an unidentified villain, just as the romance plot is secondary in the *Bildungsroman*. Above all else, the Gothic plot provides a logic for the actions of the story which seem to have no apparent connections, and they need to be followed backwards in order to recreate the primal crime. In this regard the Gothic novel is the forerunner of the detective story; it is no accident that Dickens introduced the first detective, Inspector Bucket of *Bleak House*, to the English novel and that Dickens himself was a friend, colleague, and sometimes collaborator of Wilkie Collins, who wrote the first English detective novel, *The Moonstone*.

The Gothic novel plot of *The Italian* fits the literal circumstances of the action of *Great Expectations* very closely, and even though subdued by the *Bildungsroman* and novel of manners plots that dominate the first two stages of Pip's story, this plot initiates the action of the novel and emerges in the final stage to unify and conclude the novel. Some specific parallels could even be argued to exist between the two novels if not pressed too far: Pip resembles both the persecuted Ellena and Vivaldi in his passivity and innocence; Miss Havisham, in her dedication to revenge, resembles the plotting Marchesa; Magwitch and Schedoni have similar roles as accomplices to Compeyson and Nicola, and their ultimate exposures of one another and their deaths are also similar: both books have henchmen like Orlick and Spalatro, who figure in the final explanations about the suspicions of persecution that permeate the novels; and Estella's relationship as daughter to Magwitch is very much like the father–daughter relationship thought to exist between Ellena and Schedoni. The most important structural similarity, though, is the way crime and two shadowy criminals, Nicola and Compeyson, lurk in the backgrounds of the plots in both novels. In *Great Expectations* these archvillains function as they do for the Gothic novel in general: they provide memorable, smoothly coherent actions by allowing the malignant effect of an original evil to be traced through cliff-hanging interruptions. Crime, the manifestation of this evil, is the major metaphor of this plot for all Gothic novels. 'That evil genius' (ch. 50) Compeyson, despite his only occasional, furtive presence, is the emblematic character for crime and the prime mover of the Gothic plot which eventually ties together all the major lines of action in *Great Expectations*.

So, although Compeyson and his crimes have been taken to task by critics because they are obscure in the first two-thirds of the novel and then blatant and melodramatic, it is from their very obscurity that they derive their forcefulness and eventual dominance in the structure of the novel. Dickens begins the action with the intrusion of Magwitch and Compeyson into the formative starting point of Pip's life, his 'first most vivid and broad impression of the identity of things' (ch. 1), which becomes interwoven with the images of crime, convicts, guilt, and terror which characterise his narrative. Magwitch and Miss Havisham, as well as Estella, Pip, and Jaggers, are important participants in this hidden Gothic plot, and even Orlick's mysterious behind-the-scenes actions are enveloped in his associations of Compeyson. The effect of Pip's imagination working on the associations he has with Orlick, for example, heighten his reaction to the glimpses and reports of a 'lurker' he gets (ch. 40, ch. 43) prowling around his lodgings. This response parallels and presages the more awful 'terror' generated later by the presence of Compeyson, who is revealed by Mr Wopsle to have sat behind Pip in the theatre: 'I cannot exaggerate the enhanced disquiet into which this conversation threw me, or the special and peculiar terror I felt at Compeyson's having been behind me "like a ghost"' (ch. 47). The 'special and peculiar' effect is created largely because it is a secret and internalised one. It is an interior effect, a psychological one, created by an imaginative reaction to events, rather than the actual events themselves. Robert Heilman has shown how the similar Gothic accoutrements of *Jane Eyre* create an internalised heightened response in that novel.[17] This same principle of obscurity, so skilfully utilised by Ann Radcliffe, employs Pip's internalised fears to create links between the various plots in *Great Expectations*. Compeyson's crimes against Miss Havisham and Magwitch are created before the time that the novel opens,[18] and the consequences that are visited upon Pip and Estella by their distorted donors are greatly removed from the times and scenes of the crime itself. It is these removed actions that have to be sorted out retrospectively, making the Gothic plot resemble a detective plot.

From a retrospective perspective the Gothic plot appears straight-forward, like the evil behind it. It consists of Pip's initial help to Magwitch and Magwitch's subsequent attempt to play patron to Pip. Magwitch tries to revenge himself against the society he feels is responsible for his criminal fall and subsequent prosecution, linked in his mind with Compeyson. The parallel plot for Estella is created by Miss Havisham in revenge against men for being deserted by Compeyson. Both plot motivations are bound tightly with Com-peyson's evil. Although overlaid in the first two-thirds of the novel by the *Bildungsroman* plot and the novel of manners plot, the Gothic plot is kept active by interspersed, brief, but important, reminders of its presence, such as the man stirring his rum-and-water with a file (ch. 10) or the later indirect encounter with this same emissary on a stage-coach (ch. 28). Fear-inspiring Gothic imagery connected with death, decay, violence, and mental distor-tions support such actions, and foreshadow the eruption of the Gothic plot with Magwitch's appearance in chapter 39, in what Pip calls 'the turning point of my life' (ch. 37). Locating the stories and motivations and sorting out the connections between Compeyson, Magwitch, Miss Havisham, Arthur Havisham, and Jaggers make up the rest of the Gothic plot. These correspond generally with the separate plot lines that are played off against one another by creating expectations for the reader, and then interrupted with another story. Even though the plotting and actions leading up to the final river flight and its aftermath are often regarded as 'one of the highest achievements of the sensation novel',[19] they are integrally bound with the deliberate obscurity of the main Gothic plot that flows, subdued or dominant, throughout the novel. What has been deliberately concealed is finally revealed for maximum effect. This third type of plot is also bound closely with the change of heart that Pip has towards Magwitch, the last important development of his *Bildungsroman* plot, and with the concurrent collapse of his social aspirations inspired by his idealisation of Estella, the motivation behind the novel of manners plot.

Seeing the variety of plots that makes up the actions and series of intricate connections between characters in *Great Expectations* leads one to conclude with Peter Brooks that the novel's 'central meanings depend on the workings-out of its plot'.[20] With the revelations that come about through the manipulation of his life and the deliberate withholding of information that has let him misconstrue events so that he fails to plot his own life knowingly,

Pip does indeed seem 'cured' of plot, or very nearly so, as Brooks asserts.[21] The subdued Pip at the end of the novel accepts a plot option he unwittingly created for himself earlier in the action when he generously bought Herbert a partnership in Clarriker & Co., and he joins Herbert and Clara where, by dint of hard work over a long period, he moves from clerk to partner. Pip's secretly playing patron to Herbert was, as Dickens himself wrote, 'The one good thing he did in his prosperity: the only thing that endures and bears good fruit'.[22] Pip's eleven years' work in Cairo is recounted in two short paragraphs and seems far removed from his earlier energetic plots. The confirmation of the work ethic in this final plot would be endorsed by Victorians, but it does not make a story worth telling.

Yet the continuing appeal of the plots we do get in *Great Expectations* is in understanding the general truth of all their selfishness, guilt, misinterpretations, extravagent feelings, egotism, and violent actions. Sorting out the three main plots that carry these truths helps to do this, even though the net result of the mixture of plots in *Great Expectations* is clearly greater than the mere sum of its separate parts, and such sorting must necessarily ignore other essential ingredients. What the identification of various plots reveals especially well, however, is the authentic drama of nightmarish quality of an individual's life when others have manipulated it, and the consequent need for moral self-determination. The amalgam of plots in *Great Expectations* created by Dickens's mature, resourceful, and highly imaginative understanding of reality resembles the mixed texture of life itself, and the reader of *Great Expectations* must understand and actively reconstruct its plots and their relative importance, just as life's patterns must be understood and evaluated in the constant process of reappraising our own version of reality.

From *Dickens Quarterly*, 6 (1989), 102–10.

NOTES

[Thomas Loe's perspicuous essay represents several types of current critical interest. Like Sadrin (essay 10), he discusses questions of intertextuality. Like Sadrin, Brooks and Hara (essays 10, 4, and 7), he deals with plot. And like Phelan and Sadrin (essays 9 and 10), he pleads for a fidelity to the facts of reader response. His main emphasis falls on the intertextual 'work' to be carried out by readers as they try to distinguish a text's salient features and to place it on the larger map of literature. He implicitly recognises that part of his own task as a critic must be to supply present-day readers with a helpful historical perspective, a point whose importance is discussed in the Introduction (pp. 27–33).

So is *Great Expectations* a *Bildungsroman*, a novel of manners, or a Gothic mystery? Loe points out that it has elements of all three, but hints that the Gothic aspect has been greatly underplayed in modern criticism. While (in essay 4) Peter Brooks's theoretically sophisticated search for the 'repressed' only leads back as far as Magwitch, Loe reminds us that readers can actually read in a more primitive 'mystery-and-suspense' fashion. This way, they will trace the chain of cause and effect to the even more deeply submerged figure of Compeyson. It is in reaction to the evil doings of Compeyson that Magwitch and Miss Havisham set in motion their schemes for revenge against, respectively, society in general and men only.

Loe's quotations are from the Signet New American Library edition of *Great Expectations* (New York, 1963). Ed.]

1. K. J. Fielding, *Charles Dickens: A Critical Introduction* (London, 1965), p. 221.

2. Lionel Stevenson, *The English Novel: A Panorama* (Boston, 1960), p. 351.

3. G. B. Tennyson, 'The *Bildungsroman* in Nineteenth-Century English Literature', in *Medieval Epic to the 'Epic Theatre' of Brecht: Essays in Comparative Literature*, ed. Rosario P. Armato and John M. Spalek (Los Angeles, 1968), pp. 135–46, esp. p. 143.

4. G. Robert Strange, 'Expectations Well Lost: Dickens's Fable for His Time', in *The Victorian Novel: Modern Essays in Criticism*, ed. Ian Watt (London, 1971), pp. 110–22, esp. p. 111.

5. Henry James, 'Preface to *The Tragic Muse*', in *The Art of the Novel*, ed. R. P. Blackmur (New York, 1934), pp. 79–97, esp. p. 84.

6. M. H. Abrams, *Natural Supernaturalism* (London, 1971), p. 235.

7. Marianne Hirsch, 'The Novel of Formation as Genre: Between *Great Expectations* and Lost Illusions', *Genre*, 12 (1979), 293–311.

8. John Halperin, *Egoism and Self-Discovery in the Victorian Novel: Studies in the Ordeal of Knowledge in the Nineteenth Century* (New York, 1974), p. 110.

9. Peter Brooks, *Reading for the Plot: Design and Intention in Narrative* (New York, 1985), p. 125. [Partly reprinted in the present volume as essay 4. Ed.]

10. Jerome H. Buckley, *Season of Youth: The Bildungsroman from Dickens to Golding* (Cambridge, Mass., 1974), p. 18.

11. Humphrey House, *The Dickens World* (Oxford, 1942), p. 159.

12. Walter Reed, *An Exemplary History of the Novel: The Quixotic Versus the Picaresque* (Chicago, 1981), pp. 171–2.

13. A. C. Coolidge, *Charles Dickens as Serial Novelist* (Ames, Iowa: 1967).

14. Barbara Hardy, 'The Change of Heart in Dickens's Novels', in *Dickens: A Collection of Critical Essays*, ed. Martin Price (Englewood Cliffs, 1967), pp. 39–57, esp. p. 51.

15. Philip Marcus, 'Theme and Suspense in the Plot of *Great Expectations*', *Dickens Studies*, 2 (1966), 57–73.

16. Peter Wolfe, 'The Fictional Crux and the Double Structure of *Great Expectations*', *South Atlantic Quarterly*, 73 (1974), 335–47, esp. 337.

17. Robert B. Heilman, 'Charlotte Brontë's "New Gothic"', in *The Victorian Novel: Modern Essays in Criticism*, ed. Ian Watt (London, 1971), pp. 165–80.

18. *Dickens's Working Notes for His Novels*, ed. Harry Stone (Chicago, 1987), p. 321.

19. Lionel Stevenson, *The English Novel*, p. 352.

20. Peter Brooks, *Reading for the Plot*, p. 114.

21. Ibid., p. 138. [Reprinted in the present volume, p. 107. Ed.]

22. *Dickens's Working Notes*, p. 323.

12

A Re-vision of Miss Havisham: Her Expectations and Our Responses

LINDA RAPHAEL

Q. D. Leavis begins her essay 'How We Must Read *Great Expectations*' by asserting that 'it must have been very much easier to read *Great Expectations* adequately – that is, with a sympathetic and intelligent comprehension of the spirit in which it was written and of what it was actually about – in Dickens's own day, or in any time up to the present, than it evidently is now [1970]'. Leavis continues with a deprecation of her contemporary critics and general readers, who presumably 'have no real knowledge of the constitution and actuality of Dickens's society'.[1] The corrective Leavis provides for *Great Expectations* begins with a quotation from Lord Brain, who in a 1960 lecture to a medical association extolled what Leavis terms 'Dickens's intuitive apprehension of the relation between the inner and the outer life [and]... question[ing] as to the why of human conduct'. What seems curious is that Leavis later asserts the value of this novel over Dickens's other works because of its 'greater relevance outside its own age'.[2] Is not a part of that relevance determined by the response of late twentieth-century readers, who understand the novel differently than Dickens's contemporaries?

Since Leavis published her essay, a host of scholars – especially those whose work has been informed by Marxism, feminism, and psychoanalysis – have given us new insights into texts and the ways we as readers make sense of them. Much of this recent work challenges claims for the superiority of readings contemporary to a work by asserting the openness of the text to new interpretations. While Leavis's reading of *Great Expectations* illuminates many of its fine qualities, particularly those which require psychological interpretation, her argument that later readers are impaired suggests a stagnant location of the text in a precise time and place and a privileging of its contemporary readership that similarly ignores the dynamic nature of texts. Moreover, Leavis's thesis fails to take into account a central concern of novels, articulated succinctly by William Myers in his discussion of *Little Dorrit*: 'as a work of art, [the novel must] be against the reader in a certain sense: it must disconcert his aesthetic expectations; it must trap, surprise, and frustrate, as well as gratify, the literary appetites of the English bourgeoisie.'[3] The endurance of *Great Expectations* as a valuable work of art depends on its ability to continue to 'trap, surprise, and frustrate' us – to ask us to go further into and beyond the text to fully appreciate its accomplishments.

Perhaps one of the most significant figures in *Great Expectations* in terms of affective power is Miss Havisham. Dickens's contemporary readers probably understood, either consciously or subconsciously, that Miss Havisham's ill-fated marriage and her consequent behaviour made a peculiar sort of sense in their world. On the other hand, since stories like Miss Havisham's have been retold, from Dickens's day to ours, in the continuing narrative of western experience and have been articulated in theoretical conceptions as well as in other fictional works, this frustrated spinster may seem very familiar to present-day readers. Like Dickens's contemporaries, we respond to the codes that inform *Great Expectations* almost intuitively: the difference is that our intuitions are informed by a century of additional developments, both cultural and literary. The characterisation of Miss Havisham provides a model of the power of repressive forces, especially in their dual roles as agents of society at large acting on the individual and as internalised matter directing one to govern the conduct of self and others according to unstated principles. For the late twentieth-century reader, the richness of this novel may be enhanced by an analysis that pays attention to the cultural dynamics at work during Dickens's time with an emphasis on what more recent psychoanalytic, social, and literary narratives offer us for understanding.

Embodying the mythic horrors of countless cruel mothers, step-mothers, and witch-like figures, Miss Havisham has often been described by critics as one more instance of an irrational and vindictive female figure. For example, comparing her to other Dickensian women who are 'perverted by passion', Michael Slater asserts that 'Miss Havisham is the most compelling and the most haunting'.[4] In *The Providential Aesthetic in Victorian Fiction* Thomas Vargish has named her 'the most clearly culpable' when compared to Magwitch because 'her twisting of Estella's nature seems more consciously malevolent than his plan for Pip',[5] and H. P. Sucksmith refers to 'the extremely powerful effect and vision which the figure of Miss Havisham contributes to *Great Expectations*'.[6] Vargish's claim, which depends on his assertion that Miss Havisham 'was brought up as a lady, with a lady's advantages,' raises the question of what it meant to be brought up as a lady, in general, or in Miss Havisham's case, in particular. Dickens probably counted on his readers' ability to answer the 'in general', since he provides only a brief summary of her life, offered to Pip by Herbert Pocket. However, her significance in the novel may be positively linked to the brevity of details about her background rather than in spite of it. In other words, readers may have always responded to Miss Havisham with an almost automatic comprehension of her state of mind and her actions – and clearly this sort of reaction depends on the text's evocation of shared cultural, and often literary, concepts.

Miss Havisham – bedecked in her withered bridal gown and half-arranged veil, resembling grave-clothes and a shroud, one shoe on, one off – creates a vivid and lasting image for the reader, one which is made more grotesque because of its convolution of the symbolic import of a wedding scene. Since at least biblical times, depictions of betrothal and marriage scenes have functioned as literary devices.[7] However, rather than signifying the celebration of a joyous social and personal event in which private lives are endorsed by public ceremony, the remains of the aborted wedding – the table still laid for a feast and the jilted bride in her yellowed gown – visibly enact a gap between opportunity and desire which frequently occurred in the lives of Victorian women. The dismal scene mirrors Miss Havisham's failure to make her private dream a public reality and to create an identity outside her private sphere. In making the point that 'there is nothing that is not social and historical – indeed, that everything is in the last analysis political', Frederic Jameson defines the 'structural, experiental, and conceptual gap between the public and private [as] maim[ing] our existence as individual subjects and paralys[ing] our thinking about time and change'.[8] And surely Dickens depicts in Miss Havisham's experience a social, historical, and 'in the last analysis political' event. Few authors, with the notable exception of Faulkner, particularly in 'A Rose for Emily' and *The Sound and the Fury*, create characters so paralysed in thinking about time and change as Dickens does in the case of Miss Havisham.

Miss Havisham's choice – if we can call it a choice finally – to live reclusively in the inner space of Satis House, enduring in a fetid atmosphere which threatens also to engulf young Estella, repeats the fate of many Victorian women. As Elaine Showalter concludes in her analysis of 'The Rise of the Victorian Madwoman':

> the rise of the Victorian madwoman was one of history's self-fulfilling prophecies. In a society that not only perceived women as childlike, irrational, and sexually unstable but also rendered them legally powerless and economically marginal, it is not surprising that they should have formed the greater part of the residual categories of deviance from which doctors drew a lucrative practice and the asylums much of their population.[9]

Because of the macabre nature of Miss Havisham's environment – one which has resisted all but the most negative effects of the passage of time – we may not immediately connect her existence to those of other nineteenth-century fictional females, such as Jane Eyre, whose confinement to closed spaces is a metaphor for entrapment in a society whose functioning depends in part on females' complicity with their own imprisonment. Herbert Pocket's report to Pip of Miss Havisham's past – that she was a motherless young girl whose father, anxious about his newly-achieved financial status, doted on her and neglected his son, who in turn resented the child so clearly favoured over him – recounts, on one level, the history of a spoiled woman who, when her expectations are sorely disappointed by a jilting fiancé, will spend the rest of her life impotently raging at the forces that worked against her. Thus, readers have generally considered Miss Havisham's isolation as self-inflicted, but probing into the causes of her tortured manner of living reveals the workings of a complex system which has made her reclusiveness inevitable. While her financial independence has allowed her to escape confinement to an asylum, a fate we would imagine for a woman who behaved as she but did not have property or money, she lives as disconnected from the outside world as if she were institutionalised.

The 'madwoman' who spends her life thus has many fictional counterparts, whose thrashings in a world deaf to their cries symbolise the same sort of unsatiated female passion and desire that smoulder in Miss Havisham. It is instructive, for example, to connect Faulkner's Emily with Miss Haversham because of their similar roles as daughters who held a special place in their fathers' imaginations. The world of *Great Expectations*, like that of 'A Rose for Emily', refracts complex and changing social values. Each work concerns itself particularly with those changes which challenge the privileged status of a family as a source of identity but simultaneously frustrate individual identity. Ironically, they seem to say, the same system which esteems individual enterprise limits the ability of those not powerful or lucky enough to find a secure niche within a competitive system that renders all things, including human relationships, subordinate to their profit and exchange value. Miss Havisham and Emily remain within the privacy of their homes, perhaps initially filling a role like the one Davidoff and Hall describe in their social history, *Family Fortunes*, as common to a young motherless woman: she might serve as an emotional focus for her father, protecting him from an 'ill-considered' remarriage while gaining for herself 'responsibility, respect and affection without a break from familiar surroundings and the necessity to cope with a new, sexual relationship'.[10]

Set later in the century, *Great Expectations* interprets this sort of intimate familial arrangement negatively, if we judge by the consequences in Miss Havisham's case, and presages fictional works which reflect even more stultifying emotional consequences for women.[11] By the time Dickens was writing, upper and middle class family structures, which had previously offered security against an increasingly unfamiliar outside world, were threatened by the divisive forces of industrialism and capitalism. One consequence of the movement of the workplace away from the home was that women's direct participation in the productive aspects of work – other than child-bearing, of course – diminished. Davidoff and Hall describe the effect of changes in the economic structure on women in the following way:

> Women's identification with the domestic and moral sphere implied that they would only become active economic agents when forced by necessity. As the nineteenth century progressed, it was increasingly assumed that a woman engaged in business was a woman without either an income of her own or a man to support her.[12]

The protection a father offered his daughter from the world outside was sometimes an ironic gesture: the unfamiliar world outside the home might well have been the place where she could have established a sense of self-worth. Yet it was the place from which she was consistently shielded, a social reality Dickens reveals in the case of Bella Wilfer in *Our Mutual Friend*, who sees her father's place of work for the first time when she is a grown woman about to become married.[13] Since women's roles became more narrowly defined throughout the century, fictional depictions, increasingly sensitive to the inner lives of characters, plumb the depths of despair experienced by women whose growth is arrested at the stage of 'daughter'.

Although Miss Havisham has the privileges that Vargish associates with a 'lady', the prerogatives she enjoys essentially limit her exchange value to the small marketplace she has created in Satis House. Again like Emily, who could not function in her post-Civil War American southern town which no longer apprised the social status of her family, Miss Havisham's worth to Compeyson and then to her relatives, and even to some extent to Pip (he imagines that she is a means to attaining the love of Estella as well as a source of material wealth), is measured by the monetary gains they believe they can realise from her. What a surprise for a woman who had no dealings with the public world in her years of growing up and who had received preferential treatment at the hands of her father, who himself had stature in his community.

Indeed, Mr Havisham and his daughter are described by Herbert Pocket as 'very rich and very proud'.[14] However, in casting Mr Havisham in the role of a brewer, Dickens suggests that his pride may have been a compensation for feelings of inferiority in comparison with upper-class rich men. Herbert explains that one may not be a baker and be a gentleman, nor, he and Pip agree, may one keep a public house and be a gentleman. It seems that a brewer enjoyed only a marginal status in the gentleman class, and Mr Havisham risked this when, after Miss Havisham's mother's death, he privately married his cook.[15] For years he did not acknowledge the son born to him by this second wife, while he indulged his daughter, in keeping with both his class aspirations and her sex. She, in turn, learned to be proud and to expect to do little to earn her reward, and thus adopted the attitudes common to some upper-class Victorian women. She would be virtually useless – and unthreatening – in the marketplace, while she would support and embellish with her home-bound presence the role of the males in her life (first her father and then hopefully a husband) in the public sphere. The little that we learn of Miss Havisham's upbringing suggests at least that it intentionally disempowered her. This would not, of course, make her an unseemly bride for the greedy Compeyson.

As H. P. Sucksmith points out, Compeyson is one of Dickens's characters who is 'calculated to repel with a ... plain variety of evil'.[16] And it does not take much analysis on the reader's part for her to completely abhor him. Yet, as quick as our understanding may be of his actions, we are nevertheless responding to the complex machinery of a society in which individuals are dehumanised. By identifying Compeyson as a public-school educated gentleman, who has become a forger, Dickens asserts that treachery knows no class distinctions. Nor, considering Miss Havisham's original feelings for Compeyson, does the human condition of another deter the most cunning deceivers any more than it affects the less violent, but nonetheless crass, use of others depicted in the actions of Mrs Joe, Pumblechook, or Mrs Coiler. When Herbert Pocket speaks of Miss Havisham's response to Compeyson, he judges, with a degree of sympathy, that she 'passionately loved [Compeyson]' with 'all the susceptibility she possessed'. It is worth noting that she loved him not with a strength or energy of passion, but with a susceptibility. What she was susceptible to was her passion's potential to make her vulnerable to the plottings arranged by the members of what *was* strong and energetic: a homosocial alliance. As Eve Sedgewick has amply demonstrated in her study of British life and literature of the past few centuries, such alliances played significant and well-understood roles in social and economic intercourse.

In terms of Miss Havisham's marital plans, a brief history of traditional modes of arrangement helps to explain her special position vis-à-vis the male alliance between her step-brother and Compeyson. Until the eighteenth century, alliances between children of propertied families had been arranged by their families. Since the move toward arranging one's own courtship and marriage was in harmony with other social movements toward autonomy, Miss Havisham's choice to marry someone for whom she felt 'all the passion of which she was susceptible' may be interpreted as a response to new social possibilities. However, the self-determined woman, often associated in popular culture with witch-like old maids, would have good cause to feel vulnerable to social criticism and to potential rejection from her object of desire. Herbert reports that when his father warned Miss Havisham that she was placing herself too much in Compeyson's power, she responded in an angry rage – a response that we might interpret as a sign of her fear that he was right as well as a sign that she behaved explosively as a young woman. Thus, Miss Havisham's half-brother, while hardly an upstanding member of the family, ostensibly protects her in two ways. He provides a socially acceptable context by introducing a friend to marry his sister, since the custom of a male family member arranging a marriage when parents were deceased follows the pattern which was still somewhat in place at the time; and his intermediary status deflects somewhat the passion with which Miss Havisham approaches this relationship. Thus, the homosocial alliance finds its strength in norms which reflect women's subordination in legal, social, and emotional affairs.

Dickens has depicted the role of the patriarchy in making nuptial decisions, but at the same time, Miss Havisham emerges as a woman who attempted to take advantage of the new potential independence of a woman making a choice based on emotional intuition. Moreover, this reconstruction of the brief history of Miss Havisham's romance may explain why she would have desired to trust her half-brother and why she would have additional causes, besides the obvious one, for rage when this arrangement proves to have made her *more*, not less, vulnerable. Another insight Dickens has afforded with these quick strokes concerns the brother: collapsing the distinctions between psychological and social causes, Dickens has created a character who was treated so differently within his own nuclear family because of the lower status he shares with his mother that his development into a vengeful man is inextricable from both psychological and class-related factors.

No matter how tied to her spinster-status Miss Havisham's character may be, we would be mistaken to conclude that Dickens refracts social dynamics which affect only the single woman. The many female characters in nineteenth- and twentieth-century British and American fiction who fail to thrive within the confines of their privatised existences include not only single women living in frustration, but married women suffering as well the iniquities of a gender-biased society. Charlotte Perkins Gilman's 'The Yellow Wallpaper' and Kate Chopin's *The Awakening* recall the 'madwoman' image of Bertha in Charlotte Brontë's *Jane Eyre* and anticipate the chilling story of repression in a mid-twentieth-century British woman in Doris Lessing's 'To Room Nineteen'. Both

Gilman and Chopin refract ironically the social status and potential bankruptcy of luxurious spaces – 'a big airy room, the whole floor nearly, with windows that look all ways and air and sunshine galore' in 'The Yellow Wallpaper' or 'a large, double cottage, with a broad front veranda ... scrupulously neat ... rich and tasteful ... the envy of many women' in *The Awakening*. These opulent spaces may confine and eventually suffocate, drown, or set aflame a woman as effectively as the attic room where Rochester's wife spent her tortured days and nights. While we can look back on Miss Havisham as a paradigm for the female characters of these and other similar stories, we can look forward with greater insight to Lessing's quiet, restrained Susan Rawlings, who moves subconsciously toward a suicidal resolution, because we are familiar with the unheard cries of her literary predecessors.[17] Moreover, when we realise that Miss Havisham's character is a comment on the entire system within which she and the other characters operate, we see more clearly the world of *Great Expectations*.

While the cultural directives which influence Miss Havisham's behaviour make her a plausible character, the psychoanalytic concepts which underlie our understanding of her make the novel complex in suggestive ways. H. P. Sucksmith examines several sources which indicate that Dickens had a particular interest in the behaviour of recluses. In 1856 Dickens wrote to John Forster from Paris about an upper-class female recluse who had been murdered. What interested him were 'the odd facts of human behaviour it revealed' in terms of the reclusive woman herself, rather than the facts of the murder. Both her habit of living in the dark and the image of 'horses appearing to swim up to the haunches in the dead green sea of overgrown grass and weeds' fascinate him. Later that same spring, he wrote to Forster again about the horror of the death of an upper-class alcoholic woman who had purposely raised her daughter to be an alcoholic to spite her husband, a squire, from whom she was separated. And an article Dickens published in 1853 in *Household Words* describes the 'White Woman', who was dressed completely in white, in her wedding-dress, that is, and travelled frequently on Oxford Street. She went mad because a wealthy Quaker would not marry her. Sucksmith points out that Dickens stresses the facts rather than the effects in these cases, confirming his interest in the odd behaviour itself.[18]

Another source for understanding Dickens's attitude toward recluses may be found in the collection of *Christmas Stories*. The

Traveller ridicules the behaviour of Mr Mopes, the Hermit, in 'Tom Tiddler's Ground'. He scolds him for his desire to arouse curiosity by over-awing his visitors with the novelty of his filth, and insists that the only worthwhile way of life is to be 'up and doing'. 'All is vanity', the Traveller says of the hermit, arguing that the real proportions of Mopes are heightened because of 'a mist of home-brewed marvel and romance' which surrounds him.[19] The story of Mopes, based on a hermit who lived near Dickens, suggests Dickens's ability to perceive the psychological needs displayed in bizarre behaviour. When one insists that the world pay him unremitting attention, if not for admirable qualities, then for *some* reason he can devise, he discloses what we now call a narcissistic personality. Others may be fooled by the narcissist's behaviour, as the Mopes story indicates, and tend to romanticise and exaggerate his peculiar habits. Dickens includes some of the dynamics of Mopes's story in Miss Havisham's personality and in others' responses to her, but the irony and sympathy work together to make our responses to her complex.[20] Dickens included in his dramatisations of bizarre characters 'a mist of home-brewed marvel and romance' – and never more compellingly than when he asks us to view Miss Havisham at the scene of her dashed hopes, the putrefied wedding table.[21] Since narcissism demands repression of one's sense of lack and unmet desires, it is not surprising that the narcissist is not immediately recognised as such. In *Great Expectations* endless instances of repression counterbalance the dramatised neuroses, occurring in such clever narrative oppositions as Pip's descriptions of himself as at once 'ferocious and maudlin' or 'flaccid with admiration'. While repression often signals Pip's general feelings of guilt, repression and passion have worked together in the formation of Miss Havisham's personality. According to the model which John Kucich develops in *Repression in Victorian Fiction*, her inner life may have been unified by these forces. While Kucich generally understands repression and passion to be complementary qualities which lead to a positive inner development, he notes that the frightening passions of the villainous characters in Dickens's fiction are somehow related to the lack of passion in the heroes and heroines. Another common explanation of the consequences of repression concerns the loss of the necessary other which brings a shadow of despair. The strategy of the depressive – installing the lost loved one into the self in order to mitigate the loss – in fact incorporates the image of a partly hated one into the self. The process is further complicated by the other's rejection which now becomes self-rejection. Julia Kristeva amends this interpretation of the act of repression by suggesting that such a person considers himself as stricken by a fundamental lack, or congenital deficiency. In Miss Havisham's case, the sense of personal deficiency could have developed early. As the preferred child and centre of her father's attention, she may have suspected her own inadequacy as the object of another's continual favours. Both Kristeva's definition of narcissism and the one she amends may describe Miss Havisham. Her incorporation of her wedding clothes into a permanent part of herself suggests that she has installed the loved one in herself, while all aspects of her behaviour belie a violent self-hatred directed at the lost one who is now part of the self, as well as at the self, whose fundamental lack concerned the role in which society has placed her. When Estella accuses her of having a steady memory, we know her memory steadily creates her anguish and bitterness, and when Miss Havisham cries, 'Who am I, for God's sake, that I should be kind?' we know that she perceives herself as one who has not been a repository for acts of human kindness.

At the same time, Kucich's claims about the ways in which repressed material forms identity help to explain how Miss Havisham has repressed her desire to punish Compeyson for his rejection of her and has used this energy to create her self-image. Thus, she may see herself as powerful, the owner of Satis House and an authority over Estella. In each of these powerful roles, she represents the Victorian male figure rather than the female: she owns property and she possesses a female – and her own female addition to this is that she also gains power over a male, Pip. Elizabeth Wright's contention that the response of a repressed individual suggests the character of the repressive institution is particularly suggestive for our greater understanding of the world of *Great Expectations*, not the least of which concerns the illusory quality of power relationships. For despite Estella's practical dependence on her adoptive mother, she is forced into an uncomfortably powerful position which places her in the role of master to the alternately vicious and pathetic woman who pleads for her approval and acceptance. The reversibility of the slave–master relationship reveals itself continually through the novel, so that in one of the turns of the screw, when Estella turns on Miss Havisham with controlled but significant anger, we enjoy a release of our hostile feelings toward this manipulative witch-like figure through the expression of repressed rage of the female, Estella. And even though ultimately Estella represents the 'angel in the house' image for which Dickens is famous, the reversal of her character remains unconvincing in contrast to the representation of her as an abused and abusing female.

Narcissistic rage, which includes converting a passive experience into an active one, identification with the aggressor, and seeking revenge for past humiliations, becomes the modus operandi of Miss Havisham. In acting out the ambivalent passion for Compeyson which she has repressed through Estella, and thus against Pip, Miss Havisham converts her pitifully passive role in the fate of her betrothal into an active one, while her identification with the aggressor allows her endless repetitions of the painful wound. Dressed as herself, the bride, and acting as Compeyson, the aggressor, she incorporates into one person the potential for continual re-enactment, but her repetition never leads to a satisfying mastery. It is no wonder that Pip describes her as corpse-like – no character could be more desirous of death than Miss Havisham, for when her repetitions lead to mastery in the sense that she wounds Pip through Estella's marriage, she regrets her act, lights up in flames and moves steps closer to her death.

Not only does Miss Havisham function effectively in *Great Expectations*, but her character may serve to illuminate the causes for behaviour in less fully developed females in Dickens's novels.[22] An example from this novel, which addresses a question related to Miss Havisham's influence on Pip, concerns Mrs Joe. Pip suspects that his sister may misunderstand Miss Havisham, and he seeks to protect her by describing her as a large woman in black with a black coach. Not only does this description allude to more witch-like characteristics, but it in fact suggests that Pip may intuit that his sister, who at least is a raging woman, *will* understand Miss Havisham more than he cares for her to (lest he be deprived of future visits and favours from Miss Havisham):

> If a dread of not being understood be hidden in the breast of other young people to anything like the extent to which it used to be hidden in mine – which I consider probable, as I have no particular reason to suspect myself of having been a monstrosity – it is the key to my reservations. I felt convinced that if I described Miss Havisham's as my eyes had seen it, I should not be understood. Not only that, but I felt convinced that Miss Havisham too would not be understood; and although she was perfectly incomprehensible to me, I entertained an impression that there would be something coarse

and treacherous in my dragging her as she really was to say nothing of Miss Estella before the contemplation of Mrs Joe.[23]

The possibility that Mrs Joe may identify with and comprehend Miss Havisham in ways that Pip does not is also tied to his inability to perceive the reasons for his sister's acts against him (which we are left to explain only by conjecturing at various causes associated with female repression and class immobility, based on her sycophantic ways with more well-established relatives). But even more importantly, Mrs Joe shares with Miss Havisham and other females in Dickens's novels a particular place in history. The double messages Miss Havisham gives Estella – that nothing in the world is worth loving, but that Estella should love her – are unavoidable in terms of what we know about her world.

We have no reason to suspect that Miss Havisham understands her own misery as a consequence of more than having been jilted. The tragedy of her life is not that Compeyson failed to show up at the altar; it is not even that he and her step-brother had plotted against her – it is that she fails to understand the system that works against her. Rather than seeking whatever small, but personally significant, change she might effect, she seeks to revenge herself against society on its own terms. In other words, she acts on the belief that it is only through dehumanising and often brutal deceit and abuse that desire can be satisfied. Miss Havisham thus fails to offer a hope for a different future for the next generation. This is Dickens at his most pessimistic – the Dickens who reveals the vicious circularity of individual and social misery. The illusion that Miss Havisham holds onto sustains the dream that the role she intended to assume was one that could offer satisfaction. Dickens unmasks this illusion in various ways throughout the novel, but the world he depicts offers no alternative.

Once we are aware of the repressions which operate in the institutions and characters of *Great Expectations*, and once we recognise how we respond as readers to those familiar signs of repression, the full workings of the novel become even more impressive. For example, critics have discussed the role of Wemmick as a character who dramatises how one's public and private lives might be schizophrenically divided.[24] Wemmick provides an instructive example for Pip, who will need to bring into coherence his own drives, desires, and moral principles if he does not choose to live in a constant state of repression, but we could not fully comprehend

Wemmick without the example of Miss Havisham. Because she is emblematic of those forces which account for Wemmick's divided-self, Jagger's hauntingly controlled behaviour, Compeyson's valuation of others in terms of his own greed, and Joe's morality in living apart from the concerns of the capitalistic venturers of the novel, Miss Havisham has a pivotal role in *Great Expectations*. Not only does her existence bear a constant reminder of failed expectations, but it is a testimony to the necessity for and the effects of repression under a system which denies individuals full rights to self-development and undercuts principles of moral conduct with greedy self-interest. One critic has named this novel an instance of Dickens's very best writing because Pip is exposed along with the world around him.[25] Without the character of Miss Havisham, it seems doubtful that Dickens could have exposed the world around Pip and thus Pip as powerfully as he did.

From *Studies in the Novel*, 21 (1989), 400–12.

NOTES

[Linda Raphael's essay draws together many of the themes and methods of current Dickens criticism. Concentrating on the treatment of Miss Havisham, it is an example of how traditional character criticism can be transformed when linked to probing psychological analysis and to a feminist-structuralist critique of culture and literary intertextuality. Special attention is drawn to the passive role of women in the Victorian economy, whether as daughters, sisters, wives or spinsters, and to the psychological repressions and aggressive narcissism which could result from this. At the same time, the essay reflects the current critical interest in readers and historical distance (see Introduction pp. 27–33). Raphael frankly accepts that neither Miss Havisham herself nor the novel's first readers would have viewed her plight in the same way as a feminist structuralist does nowadays. But Raphael clearly also believes that a feminist structuralist cannot afford to be unaware of how Victorian reality seemed to those who had actually to live through it. She draws on a range of historical detail in order to establish this experiential counterbalance.

What Raphael is aiming at is an interpretative convergence of the two ever more widely different socio-cultural horizons. She signals this in her essay's title: 'A Re-vision of Miss Havisham: Her Expectations and Our Responses'. Raphael's strong historical sense will not allow her to fabricate a Dickens purely for her own purposes. But neither does she have the historical purist's urge to de-fuse the past by treating it like a configuration of fossils. Her Dickens is still Dickens. But also, he is still urgently relevant to the concerns of present-day readers.

Raphael's quotations are from *Great Expectations*, ed. Angus Calder, Penguin English Library (Harmondsworth, 1965). Ed.]

1. F. R. and Q. D. Leavis, *Dickens the Novelist* (New York, 1970), p. 277.

2. Ibid., pp. 281 and 289.

3. William Myers, 'The Radicalism of *Little Dorrit*', *Literature and Politics in the Nineteenth Century* (London, 1971), p. 79.

4. Michael Slater, *Dickens and Women* (London, 1983), p. 291.

5. Thomas Vargish, *The Providential Aesthetic in Victorian Fiction* (Charlottesville, Va., 1985), pp. 152–3.

6. Harvey Peter Sucksmith, *The Narrative Art of Charles Dickens: The Rhetoric of Sympathy and Irony in his Novels* (Oxford, 1970), p. 186.

7. Robert Alter provides an illuminating narrative analysis of betrothal scenes in *The Art of Biblical Narrative* (New York, 1981).

8. Frederic Jameson, *The Politic Unconscious: Narrative as a Socially Symbolic Act* (Ithaca, NY, 1981), p. 20.

9. Sandra Gilbert and Susan Gubar, *Madwoman in the Attic: The Woman Writer and the Nineteenth Century Literary Imagination* (New Haven, Conn., 1979), p. 73.

10. Leonore Davidoff and Catherine Hall, *Family Fortunes: Men and Women of the English Middle Class, 1780–1850* (London, 1987), p. 347.

11. The peculiar relationship between Bella Wilfer and her 'Pa' in *Our Mutual Friend* suggests an erotic tone to the father/daughter pairing which Davidoff and Hall indicate was sometimes the consequence of these sorts of arrangements. Although Bella's mother is living, she removes herself intellectually and emotionally from the doings of her husband and her daughter Bella. Charles Dickens, *Our Mutual Friend* (New York, Penguin, 1980).

12. Davidoff and Hall, *Family Fortunes*, p. 272.

13. Dickens subtly incorporates this aspect of the public/private split in chapter 49. Since Bella plays the role of parent to her father, her desire to relieve him of his job and place him as her husband's secretary further expresses the conflicted attitude toward the public world and the work done therein.

14. The discussion of Miss Havisham's background occurs in chapter 22.

15. Davidoff and Hall, *Family Fortunes*, describe the lifestyle of Robert Bretnall of Witham in the mid 1840s: he listed himself variously as a

miller or a landed gentleman proprietor since his income came in part from his trusteeship of a local brewery estate. He mixed with the elite of doctors, solicitors and large farmers in his town, attended the Anglican church, and dabbled in Whig politics. Yet his manners were crude, and he blended older forms of uncontrolled behaviour and new seriousness. In the words of the authors, 'Robert Bretnall was literate, wealthy and keen to adopt the outward trappings of gentility which meant some restraints on his conduct ... His social power stemmed from his ownership of property, farming activities, local business and charitable activity as trustee, witness or governor. Middle class women had no such power' (p. 398). The social and psychological dynamics of Bretnall's life describe in detail the background we might logically supply for Mr Havisham.

16. Sucksmith, *Narrative Art of Dickens*, p. 252.

17. Studies of Victorian women and of their fictional realisations have offered a wealth of information on feminist concerns about the nineteenth century. Following the work of Gilbert and Gubar in *Madwoman in the Attic* (1979), many other contributions have come from scholars with special interests in Victorian culture and fiction, including among others Steven Mintz, *A Prison of Expectations: The Family in Victorian Culture* (New York, 1983); Peter Gay, *The Bourgeois Experience: Victoria to Freud* (New York, 1984); Nina Auerbach, *Romantic Imprisonment: Women and Other Glorified Outcasts* (New York, 1985); Helena Michie, *The Flesh Made Word: Female Figures and Women's Bodies* (New York; 1987); Stephen Kerns, 'Explosive Intimacy: Psychodynamics of the Victorian Family', *The History of Childhood Quarterly* (1974), 437–61.

18. Sucksmith, *Narrative Art of Dickens*, pp. 177–88.

19. Charles Dickens, *Christmas Stories* (London, 1926), pp. 226–52.

20. For a discussion of the ways irony and sympathy interplay in Dickens, see Sucksmith, *Narrative Art of Dickens*, ch. 5.

21. Michael Slater's interpretation of Pip's response to Miss Havisham is congruent with the idea that Dickens has surrounded her existence with some romance: 'Pip sees Satis House as a fairy tale but misinterprets Miss Havisham, believing that she is aware of the evil of the enchantment she and her house lie under and that she is looking to him to release her from it' (*Dickens and Women*, p. 292).

22. Many Dickensian females' behaviour is suggestive in terms of its repressed qualities, particularly that of Mrs Wilfer in *Our Mutual Friend*, Mr. F's Aunt in *Little Dorrit*, or Mrs Jellyby in *Bleak House*.

23. Charles Dickens, *Great Expectations*, p. 95.

24. One of the early, and particularly insightful, discussions of Wemmick's role in dramatising the split between the public and private worlds occurs in Angus Calder's Introduction to the Penguin Edition.

25. Jenni Calder, *Women and Marriage in Victorian Fiction* (London, 1976), p. 96.

Further Reading

EDITIONS

Authoritative texts of Dickens's novels are being established in the Clarendon Edition (Oxford) of his works, and the Clarendon texts are being reproduced in the paperback World's Classics series (Oxford: Oxford University Press). The Clarendon Edition of *Great Expectations*, edited by Margaret Cardwell, appeared in 1993. Of the paperback editions available in late 1993, the Penguin English Library edition (Harmondsworth, 1965) is one of the most widely used. It includes an excellent introduction by Angus Calder, together with some notes and appendices, one of which reproduces the 'original' ending.

Other Dickens texts: *The Speeches of Charles Dickens*, ed. K. J. Fielding (Oxford: Clarendon Press, 1960); *The Letters of Charles Dickens* (The Pilgrim Edition), ed. Madeline House, Kathleen Tillotson and Graham Storey (Oxford: Clarendon Press, 1965 – [in progress]); *Dickens's Working Notes for his Novels*, ed. Harry Stone (Chicago: University of Chicago Press, 1987).

JOURNALS

The main Dickens journals are: *The Dickensian: A Magazine for Dickens Lovers* (1905–); *Dickens Studies: A Journal of Modern Research and Criticism* (1965–70); *Dickens Studies Newsletter* (1969–84); *Dickens Studies Annual* (1971–); and *Dickens Quarterly* (1984–).

BIBLIOGRAPHIES

General Dickens bibliographies are: Joseph Gold, *The Stature of Dickens: A Centenary Bibliography of Dickensian Criticism 1836–1975* (London: Macmillan, 1975); John J. Fenstermaker, *Charles Dickens, 1940–1975: An Analytical Subject Index to Periodical Criticism of the Novels and Christmas Books* (London: George Prior, 1979); Alan M. Cohn and K. K. Collins, *The Cumulated Dickens Checklist 1970–1979* (Troy: Whitston Publishing Company, 1982). *Dickens Quarterly* regularly includes a 'Dickens Checklist', and *Dickens Studies Annual* usually has a judicious survey of 'Recent Dickens Studies'.

There is also an invaluable descriptive bibliography of primary and secondary materials for *Great Expectations* up until 1983: George J. Worth, *Great Expectations: An Annotated Bibliography* (New York: Garland Publishing Company, 1986).

BIOGRAPHIES

Recent paperback biographies of Dickens are: Edgar Johnson, *Charles Dickens: His Tragedy and Triumph* (Harmondsworth: Penguin, 1986); Fred Kaplan, *Dickens: A Biography* (London: Sceptre, 1989); Peter Ackroyd, *Dickens* (London: Mandarin Paperbacks, 1991); Claire Tomalin, *The Invisible Woman: The Story of Nelly Ternan and Charles Dickens* (Harmondsworth: Penguin, 1991).

GENERAL CRITICISM OF DICKENS

There are numerous general studies of Dickens as a novelist. John Carey's *The Violent Effigy: A Study of Dickens's Imagination* (London: Faber, 1973) remains one of the most lively, and John Lucas's *Charles Dickens: The Major Novels* (Harmondsworth: Penguin, 1992) offers sensitive readings of six novels from *Dombey and Son* onwards. Two general studies which are in tune with literary theory of the 1980s are: Steven Connor, *Charles Dickens* (Oxford: Blackwell, 1985), from which essay 8 in the present volume is an extract, and Kate Flint, *Dickens* (Brighton: Harvester, 1986).

APPROACHES TO *GREAT EXPECTATIONS*

Far and away the best of the many student guides to *Great Expectations* is Anny Sadrin, *Great Expectations* (London: Unwin Hyman, 1988), from which essay 10 in the present volume is an extract. Genuinely original, well informed on textual and general history, and fully aware of secondary literature, Sadrin performs Freudian, structuralist, poststructuralist and intertextual analyses with effortless lucidity.

Among the traditional thematic approaches to *Great Expectations*, some of the most interesting are: Rowland McMaster, introduction to Macmillan College Classics edition of *Great Expectations* (Toronto: Macmillan, 1965), rep. in Rowland and Juliet McMaster, *The Novel from Sterne to James: Essays in the Relation of Literature to Life* (London: Macmillan, 1981), pp. 71–87; J. Hillis Miller, *Charles Dickens: The World of his Novels* (Cambridge, Mass.: Harvard University Press, 1958), pp. 249–78; Robert Barnard, 'Imagery and Theme in *Great Expectations*', *Dickens Studies Annual*, 1 (1970), 238–51; William F. Axton, '*Great Expectations* Yet Again', *Dickens Studies Annual*, 2 (1972), 279–93, 373–4; Barbara Hardy, *The Moral Art of Dickens* (London: Athlone Press, 1970), pp. 139–55; Sarah Gilead, 'Barmecide Feasts: Ritual, Narrative, and the Victorian Novel', *Dickens Studies Annual*, 17 (1988), 225–47, esp. 233–8; Elliot L. Gilbert, '"In Primal Sympathy": *Great Expectations* and the Secret of Life', *Dickens Studies Annual*, 11 (1983), 89–113; David Gervais, 'The Prose and Poetry of *Great Expectations*', *Dickens Studies Annual*, 13 (1984), 85–114.

Traditional studies of the novel's form and technique include: Thomas E. Connolly, 'Technique in *Great Expectations*', *Philological Quarterly*, 34 (1955), 48–55; John Hagan, 'Structural Patterns in Dickens's *Great Expectations*', *ELH: Journal of English Literary History*, 21 (1954), 54–66; Joseph A. Kestner, *The Spatiality of the Novel* (Detroit: Wayne State University Press, 1978), pp. 116–21.

The most useful starting-point for psychoanalytical approaches to literature is Elizabeth Wright, *Psychoanalytic Criticism: Theory and Practice* (London: Methuen, 1984), which presents a variety of frameworks including not only those of Freud and Jung but the poststructuralist model of Lacan. Among the Jungian approaches to Dickens and *Great Expectations* are: Edmund Wilson, 'Dickens: the Two Scrooges', in his *The Wound and the Bow* (Boston: Houghton Mifflin, 1941), pp. 1–104; Barbara Lecker, 'The Split Characters of Charles Dickens', *Studies in English Literature, 1500–1900*, 19 (1979), 689–704; Dorothy Van Ghent, 'The Dickens World: A View from Todgers's', *Sewanee Review*, 58 (1950), 419–38, incorporated into her *The English Novel: Form and Function* (New York: Reinhart, 1953), pp. 125–38; Roger D. Sell, 'Projection Characters in *David Copperfield*', *Studia Neophilologica*, 55 (1983), 19–30; Julian Moynaham, 'The Hero's Guilt: the Case of *Great Expectations*', *Essays in Criticism*, 10 (1960), 60–79; Brian Cheadle, 'Sentiment and Resentment in *Great Expectations*', *Dickens Studies Annual*, 20 (1991), 149–74. The Freudian interpretations include: Michal Peled Ginsburg, 'Dickens and the Uncanny: Repression and Displacement in *Great Expectations*', *Dickens Studies Annual*, 13 (1984), 115–24; Albert Hutter, 'Crime and Fantasy in *Great Expectations*', in Frederick Crews (ed.), *Psychoanalysis and the Literary Process* (Cambridge, Mass.: Winthrop, 1970), pp. 25–65; Curt Hartog, 'The Rape of Miss Havisham', *Studies in the Novel*, 14 (1982), 248–65; Ian Watt, 'Oral Dickens', *Dickens Studies Annual*, 3 (1974), 165–81, 240–2; Anny Sadrin, *Great Expectations* (London: Unwin Hyman, 1988), pp. 118–38.

An attractive general book on Dickens which pays attention to sociological considerations, richly illustrated with Victorian pictorial materials, is Angus Wilson, *The World of Charles Dickens* (London: Secker and Warburg, 1970). Of obvious general relevance to *Great Expectations* are: Philip Collins, *Dickens and Crime* (London: Macmillan, 1962); F. S. Schwarzback, *Dickens and the City* (London: Athlone Press, 1979); James M. Brown, *Dickens: Novelist in the Market-Place: A Sociological Reading* (London: Macmillan, 1982); and Grahame Smith, *Dickens, Money, and Society* (Berkeley: University of California Press, 1969). The sociological accounts of *Great Expectations* include: Humphrey House, 'G.B.S. on *Great Expectations*', *Dickensian*, 44 (1948), 63–70 and 183–6; George Orwell, 'Charles Dickens', in his *Inside the Whale* (London, 1940), pp. 9–85; Lionel Trilling, 'Manners, Morals, and the Novel', in his *The Liberal Imagination* (New York: Viking, 1950), pp. 205–22; Murray Baumgarten, 'Calligraphy and Code: Writing in *Great Expectations*', *Dickens Studies Annual*, 11 (1983), 61–72; and Q. D. Leavis, 'How we must read *Great Expectations*', in Q. D. and F. R. Leavis, *Dickens the Novelist* (London: Chatto & Windus, 1970), pp. 277–331.

Readable introductions to structuralist poetics and narratology are Jonathan Culler, *Structuralist Poetics: Structuralism, Linguistics and the Study of Literature* (London: Routledge & Kegan Paul, 1975) and Shlomith Rimmon-Kenan, *Narrative Fiction: Contemporary Poetics* (London: Methuen, 1983). Anny Sadrin's narratological analysis (in essay 10 in the present volume) can be supplemented by some remarks in Kate Flint (as above, pp. 48–51) and Moshe Ron, 'Autobiographical Narration and Formal Closure in *Great Expectations*', *Hebrew University Studies in Literature*, 5 (1977), 37–66. As for the ideological wing of structuralism, a lively introduction to Foucault is J. G. Merquior, *Foucault* (London: Fontana, 1985); Raymond Williams's *Marxism and Literature* (Oxford: Oxford University Press, 1977) is an illuminating and comprehensive account of its subject; and one of the many useful introductions to feminist criticism is Catherine Belsey and Jane Moore (eds), *The Feminist Reader: Essays in Gender and the Politics of Literary Criticism* (London: Macmillan, 1989). Ideological critiques of *Great Expectations* include: Pam Morris, *Dickens's Class Consciousness: A Marginal View* (London: Macmillan, 1991), esp. pp. 103–19; David Trotter, *Circulation: Defoe, Dickens and the Economies of the Novel* (London: Macmillan, 1988), esp. 124–36; Philip W. Martin, *Mad Women in Romantic Writing* (Brighton: Harvester, 1987) pp. 113–22; Richard Brickman, Susan MacDonald and Myra Stark, *Corrupt Relations: Dickens, Thackeray, Trollope, Collins and the Victorian Sexual System* (New York: Columbia University Press, 1982), pp. 59–110, esp. 68–75.

Katerina Clark and Michael Holquist, *Bakhtin* (Cambridge, Mass.: Harvard University Press, 1984) is an enthralling intellectual biography, and Bakhtinian studies of Dickens include: Roger Fowler, 'Polyphony and Problematic in *Hard Times*', in Robert Giddings (ed.), *The Changing World of Charles Dickens* (London: Vision Press, 1983), pp. 91–108; and Roger D. Sell, 'Dickens and the New Historicism: the Polyvocal Audience and Discourse of *Dombey and Son*', in Jeremy Hawthorn (ed.), *The Nineteenth-Century British Novel* (London: Arnold, 1986), pp. 62–79. A useful introduction to French and American deconstruction is Christopher Norris, *Deconstruction: Theory and Practice* (London: Methuen, 1982). A helpful short introduction to Lacan is Malcolm Bowie, 'Lacan', in John Sturrock (ed.), *Structuralism and Since: From Lévi Strauss to Derrida* (Oxford: Oxford University Press, 1979), pp. 116–53, but see also Elizabeth Wright (as above). One of the best deconstructive readings of *Great Expectations* is Christopher Morris, 'The Bad Faith of Pip's Bad Faith: Deconstructing *Great Expectations*', *ELH: Journal of English Literary History*, 54 (1987), 941–55.

A useful introduction to the earlier phase of research into reader activity is Robert C. Holub, *Reception Theory: A Critical Introduction* (London: Methuen, 1984). Susan R. Horton, *The Reader in the Dickens World: Style and Response* (London: Macmillan, 1981) brilliantly applies ideas put forward by Stanley Fish in his early work. For literary pragmatics see Roger D. Sell, *An Introduction to Literary Pragmatics* (forthcoming) and footnotes 51 and 58 to the Introduction. Other reader-oriented work includes: James A. Davies, *The Textual Life of Dickens's Characters* (London, 1989), which includes a discussion of *Great Expectations* (pp. 94–102); and John O. Jordan, 'The Medium of *Great Expectations*', *Dickens Studies Annual*, 11 (1983), 73–88. Two notable studies of Dickensian intertextuality, both of which deal with *Great Expectations* are: Harry Stone, *Dickens and the Invisible World: Fairy Tales, Fantasy and Novel-Making* (Bloomington: Indiana University Press, 1979), esp. pp. 298–339; and Jerome Meckier, *Hidden Rivalries in Victorian Fiction: Dickens, Realism, and Revaluation* (Lexington: University Press of Kentucky, 1987), esp. pp. 122–52. Two scholars who try to facilitate an interpretive convergence of horizons by means of historical detail are: Richard Witt, 'The Death of Miss Havisham', *Dickensian*, 80 (1984), 151–6; and Susan Shatto, 'Miss Havisham and Mr Mopes the Hermit: Dickens and the Mentally Ill', *Dickens Quarterly*, 2 (1985), 43–50, 79–84.

Notes on Contributors

Peter Brooks is Tripp Professor of Humanities, and Chairman of the Department of Comparative Literature, at Yale University. Recent publications include *Body Work* (Cambridge, Mass., 1993).

Steven Connor is Reader in Modern English Literature at Birkbeck College, University of London. Recent publications include: the New Casebook on *Waiting for Godot* and *Endgame* (1992); *Postmodernist Culture: An Introduction to Theories of the Contemporary* (Oxford, 1989); and *Theory and Cultural Value* (Oxford, 1992).

A. L. French is Reader in English at La Trobe University, Melbourne. He has written many articles for journals such as *Essays in Criticism*, *English Studies* and *Meridian*.

Lucy Frost teaches at La Trobe University. Her main interest is in Australian literature, and she has published *No Place for a Nervous Lady: Voices from the Australian Bush* (Harmondsworth, 1984) and *A Face in the Glass: The Journal and Life of Annie Baxter* (London, 1991).

Robin Gilmour teaches at Aberdeen University. He has edited Trollope's *The Warden* and *Barchester Towers* for the Penguin Classics series.

Eiichi Hara teaches at Tohoku University, Japan. Many of his publications are in Japanese, but he has written a number of articles in English on Dickens.

Thomas Loe teaches at State University of New York, Oswego. He has published a number of studies of the novella form, and also has articles on Charlotte Brontë and Jean Rhys.

James Phelan is Professor of English at Ohio State University. He edits *Narrative* and recent publications include *Beyond the Tenure Track* (Columbus, Ohio, 1991).

Linda Raphael teaches English at Georgetown University. She has published articles on Dickens and Henry James, and is at present working on narrative and scepticism.

Jack Rawlins teaches at California State University (Chico). Recent publications include *The Writer's Way* (Boston, 1987) and *Demon Prince: the Dissonant Worlds of Jack Vance* (San Bernadino. 1986).

Anny Sadrin teaches at the University of Burgundy. Among her publications are *L'être et l'avoir dans les romans de Charles Dickens* (Paris, 1985), and *Dickens ou le roman-théâtre* (Paris, 1992).

Jeremy Tambling teaches at the University of Hong Kong. His publications include *What is Literary Language?* (Milton Keynes, 1988) and *Confession: Sexuality, Sin and the Subject* (Manchester, 1990).

Index